MONTEREY PUBLIC LIBRARY
WITHDRAWN

P9-DTM-342

2005

9/05

190

READY-TO-USE
ACTIVITIES
THAT MAKE
MATH FUN!

George Watson

Illustrated by Alan Anthony

Hooked On Learning Library

JOSSEY-BASS
A Wiley Imprint
www.josseybass.com

J
510.712
WAT

Copyright © 2003 by John Wiley & Sons, Inc. All rights reserved.

Published by Jossey-Bass
A Wiley Imprint
989 Market Street, San Francisco, CA 94103-1741   www.josseybass.com

The materials that appear in this book (except those for which reprint permission must be obtained from the primary sources) may be freely reproduced for educational/training activities. There is no requirement to obtain special permission for such uses. We do, however, ask that the following statement appear on all reproductions:

Copyright © 2003 by John Wiley & Sons, Inc.

This free permission is limited to the reproduction of material for educational/training events. Systematic or large-scale reproduction or distribution (more than one hundred copies per year)—or inclusion of items in publications for sale—may be done only with prior written permission. Also, reproduction on computer disk or by any other electronic means requires prior written permission. Requests for permission should be addressed to the Permissions Department, John Wiley & Sons, Inc., 111 River Street, Hoboken, NJ 07030 (201) 748-6011, fax (201) 748-6008, e-mail: permcoordinator@wiley.com.

Jossey-Bass books and products are available through most bookstores. To contact Jossey-Bass directly, call our Customer Care Department within the U.S. at 800-956-7739, outside the U.S. at 317-572-3993 or fax 317-572-4002.

Jossey-Bass also publishes its books in a variety of electronic formats. Some content that appears in print may not be available in electronic books.

Library of Congress Cataloging-in-Publication Data

Watson, George, 1946–
    190 ready-to-use activities that make math fun! / George Watson ;
      illustrated by Alan Anthony.—1st ed.
        p. cm.—(Hooked on learning library)
    ISBN 0-7879-6585-5 (alk. paper)
    1. Mathematics--Study and teaching (Secondary)—Activity programs.
      I. Title: One hundred ninety ready-to-use activities that make math fun!.
      II. Title. III. Series.
QA11.2.W38 2003
510'.71'2—dc21   2002043357

Printed in the United States of America
FIRST EDITION
PB Printing
10 9 8 7 6 5 4 3

GEORGE WATSON

*Acknowledgments
and thanks
for your
professional support
in writing the
"Hooked on Learning" series.
I've truly "hooked" up
with the best crew.*

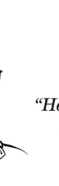

MARLENE TILFORD
Advisor

ALAN ANTHONY
Illustrator

ESTHER JOHNSON
Jiffy Steno Services

ACKNOWLEDGMENTS

Lyle Brenna	Deborah Rose	Lisa Barnett
Roger Haugen	Mary Mourlam	AnnMarie Woytowich

ABOUT THE AUTHOR

George Watson (B.A., University of Saskatchewan, Saskatoon, Saskatchewan, Canada) taught almost every subject including major academic subjects, special education, physical education, and art at the elementary and junior high levels during his teaching career. Mr. Watson recently retired after 28 years of service in the classroom and now dedicates his time to writing and to the building of a 1934 Ford street rod.

Mr. Watson is the author of *Teacher Smart: 125 Tested Techniques for Classroom Management and Control* and *The Classroom Discipline Problem Solver*, both published by The Center for Applied Research in Education.

Mr. Watson also conducts in-service programs for teachers, parent–teacher associations, and health organizations. Mr. Watson has also authored several short stories for magazines and a book on street rodding skills. He can be contacted at **geobravo396@hotmail.com**.

About the Hooked on Learning Library

The *Hooked on Learning Library* is a comprehensive, three-book series featuring teacher- and student-friendly activity sheets for the secondary classroom in the areas of English, Mathematics, and Science.

In writing these books, special effort was taken to understand students from a social, emotional, and cultural perspective. The results of that initiative is that the books are filled with highly-charged, attention-grabbing, and relevant activity sheets that not only cover the content, but also are fun to do.

An excellent educational resource, this series can be used to provide immediate skill reinforcement and to address skill attainment problems, or it can be used as an integral part of the long-term planning of English, Mathematics, and Science programs. *Hooked on Learning* not only fulfills the needs of the "at-risk" student, but it also satisfies the needs of the strong, independent, self-reliant learner.

The three books in the *Hooked on Learning Library* are:

- 190 Ready-to-Use Activities that Make English Fun!
- 190 Ready-to-Use Activities that Make Math Fun!
- 190 Ready-to-Use Activities that Make Science Fun!

All three books in the *Hooked on Learning Library* have unique areas called Quick Access Information pages. These pages target important information and skills to be learned or reinforced prior to commencing the worksheets. The Quick Access Information data may be on a full page or may be presented at the top of a related worksheet. We include flags to indicate the location of sites.

QUICK ACCESS information

ABOUT THIS BOOK

This math book of the *Hooked on Learning* series was a joy to write. I called upon many years of classroom experience and understanding to target how students think, comprehend, and react. I looked at what holds the interest of secondary students as well as how their popular culture functions. The result was this totally fresh approach that makes teaching and learning math concepts more enjoyable for you and your students.

The activities in *190 Ready-to-Use Activities that Make Math Fun!* are designed to be a natural complement to fundamental math skills instruction. At the same time, the activity sheets reach out and grasp students' interests through puzzles, riddles, and other intriguing presentations in a unique, high-interest, and "fun" style.

Throughout this book, as in all the books in this *Hooked on Learning* series, you will see strategically placed "Quick Access Information" flags. These flags are designed to make learning as successful as possible. They point to step-by-step explanations of the relevant concepts plus clear instructions for completing the page at hand. We found that students "just love" this feature because they can easily refer back to the flag as they complete the exercises on the page.

190 Ready-to-Use Activities that Make Math Fun! is an effective tool for students of all ability levels. There is something here for everyone—from the at-risk student to the high achiever. Here is an overview of the sections you'll find in this book:

- **Section 1, Essential Strategies for Whole Number Skills,** leads the way by presenting strong whole number skills exercises that have been specifically designed to motivate students and hold their interest. The "Rhyming Variety Page" is a wonderful example of this. We took an old English rhyme and made a successful whole number math skills page out of it—with a surprise bonus question at the end.

- **Section 2, Getting to the Point with Decimals,** presents decimals in a unique, high-interest format. The four-part "Move the Gears" activity is a fine example. Students must conceptualize moving gears in order to connect the necessary questions—a stimulating double challenge.

- **Section 3, Fractions in the Learning Process,** takes the often difficult areas of common fractions and makes them understandable through stimulating puzzles, charts, and "Quick Access Information" explanations. "Finding the Value of Names" is a good example here. Students are asked to add fractions through a name-game format.

- **Section 4, Understanding Percents for Skill Development,** looks at the many aspects of how percents are used in math. "Calculating Percent of Gain or Increase" is a jewel here. Through an interesting story page, students are able to hone their understanding of percents.

- **Section 5, Money Concepts for the Modern Classroom,** tackles the understanding that students must have of the real world of money. "The True Cost of an Item—Hours of Work Required" brings students to understand that money does not "grow on trees" and that for each item, there is a real-world cost of a certain number of work hours that they or someone else must put in to pay for that item.

- **Section 6, Geometry and Measurement—Facts and Insights,** presents these concepts in a unique and interesting way. Perimeter, for example, is learned by measuring the distance around the picture of a student's head and hat. This activity teaches the concept while being self-motivating.

- **Section 7, Charts and Graphs to Stimulate and Enrich,** presents the students with a very different approach to basic graph and chart formats. "A Cool Bar Graph" is a great example, whereby students study a graph and answer questions as to how "cool" are some people.

- **Section 8, Hooked on Ratio, Probability, and Averages,** looks at these concepts in an entertaining way. The "Introduction to Ratios" page, for example, asks students to create ratios by using pictures. The concept of ratios becomes easy to grasp by using a visual cue.

- **Section 9, Pre-Algebra and Early Algebra Skill Builders,** targets fundamental algebraic ideas and techniques, presenting them in easy-to-understand formats. Strong use of "Quick Access Information" flags makes this section a joy to complete.

Near the end of each section is a "Definition Puzzle" that checks students' understanding of the math terms and concepts covered in the section. Completing this page is an excellent way to reinforce the skills, along with being a genuinely fun thing to do!

Each section concludes with a "Skills Mastery" test or tests. These tests serve to reinforce and evaluate the learning that has taken place.

All in all, I know you will enjoy using this math book in the *Hooked on Learning* series. It will be a totally unique, fresh, and worthwhile addition to the ongoing dynamics of your classroom. It was a joy to write, and I know it will be a joy to use.

George Watson

CONTENTS

SECTION 2
GETTING TO THE POINT WITH DECIMALS 37

SECTION 3
FRACTIONS IN THE LEARNING PROCESS   65

SECTION 4
UNDERSTANDING PERCENT FOR SKILL DEVELOPMENT   95

SECTION 5
MONEY CONCEPTS FOR THE MODERN CLASSROOM   113

SECTION 6
GEOMETRY AND MEASUREMENT: FACTS AND INSIGHTS   139

SECTION 7
CHARTS AND GRAPHS TO STIMULATE AND ENRICH   165

SECTION 8
HOOKED ON RATIO, PROBABILITY, AND AVERAGE   179

SECTION 9
Pre-Algebra and Early Algebra Skill Builders   193

SECTION 1

ESSENTIAL STRATEGIES FOR WHOLE NUMBER SKILLS

1. The Math Completion Puzzle

★ Below are a series of addition problems. Do all of the problems and then use the process of elimination to place each in the answer box below. The answers in the box are partially completed.

1.	327	2.	440	3.	383	4.	454	5.	302	6.	232
	283		396		351		429		307		343
	+ 428		+ 427		+ 318		+ 265		+ 305		+ 248

7.	671	8.	949	9.	749	10.	711	11.	814	12.	792
	329		949		821		713		841		791
	+ 842		+ 999		+ 327		+ 744		+ 148		+ 777

13.	624	14.	791	15.	796	16.	371	17.	927	18.	837
	629		243		791		311		101		713
	+ 377		+ 811		+ 888		+ 349		+ 901		+ 211

Copyright © 2003 by John Wiley & Sons, Inc.

```
 927
 101
+901
 19__
```

ANSWER BOX   (not in order of problems)

__ 8 __ 3	10 __ __	__ __ 38
8 __ __	__ __ 61	1 __ __ 7
__ __ 45	12 __ __	__ __ 60
1 __ 3 __	2 __ 6 __	__ 0 __ 1
2 __ 9 __	1 __ __ 8	2 __ __ 5
19 __ __	18 __ __	__ __ 4

2. Adding Sweet 7's Through the Grid

★ Follow the trail of 7's from start to finish. Start at the 7 in the corner and add 7 to find the next sum each time to get to the finish. The sums of the increases in 7's are beside each other. For example, $7 + 7 = \underline{14}$, $7 + 14 = \underline{21}$, $7 + 21 = \underline{28}$, etc. Draw a line through 7, 14, 21, 28, etc.

Start

7	0	9	3	7	6	4	5	3	2	1	5	7	8	1	3	0	2	4	3
3	1	6	7	0	3	2	0	9	1	5	4	6	8	9	1	9	1	2	6
4	3	4	2	1	0	9	1	4	3	3	6	8	0	2	1	1	0	1	3
1	3	2	2	6	8	9	3	5	6	7	8	8	1	4	4	1	3	9	8
5	6	8	7	3	4	7	5	6	4	0	9	1	2	3	2	3	1	2	5
6	7	3	5	2	2	9	2	4	7	2	1	7	8	2	1	1	9	4	6
5	8	5	1	0	4	8	6	7	5	4	2	1	5	8	1	4	7	9	0
0	1	3	4	2	5	8	4	8	6	5	1	8	1	0	5	0	1	4	7
1	3	7	5	3	6	4	8	4	0	2	9	1	4	9	3	5	9	1	0
2	4	6	8	9	1	3	2	7	9	1	5	7	6	3	0	1	5	2	3
7	9	3	2	1	7	8	9	4	5	3	9	0	3	0	1	4	1	5	8
8	0	1	4	5	3	7	9	4	3	5	9	5	3	3	0	2	8	6	1
9	1	8	2	7	5	6	3	9	3	9	3	6	8	7	5	3	4	5	1

↑
Finish

Copyright © 2003 by John Wiley & Sons, Inc.

4

3. Adding Sweet 8's Through the Grid

★ Follow the trail of 8's from start to finish. Start at the 8 in the corner and add 8 to find the next sum each time to get to the finish. The sums of the increases in 8's are beside each other. For example, $8 + 8 = \underline{16}$, $8 + 16 = \underline{24}$, $8 + 24 = \underline{32}$, etc. Draw a line through 8, 16, 24, 32, etc.

Start

8	7	3	5	3	0	1	6	2	3	5	4	2	3	1	8	9	3	4	5
0	1	4	3	5	7	5	6	8	0	9	6	1	2	0	3	5	8	5	8
4	6	2	4	3	8	1	4	3	5	9	2	3	2	1	2	4	3	1	9
5	3	3	3	5	4	4	5	7	4	2	1	4	9	2	2	0	1	0	4
7	5	8	2	4	0	9	0	1	2	1	1	7	4	8	9	3	4	2	3
9	0	3	9	1	7	9	2	8	1	2	4	5	1	0	2	5	7	6	2
2	4	5	4	6	5	2	0	6	9	0	7	3	7	3	4	6	5	7	1
3	0	8	2	6	9	8	6	2	1	7	6	1	4	4	1	5	2	1	8
8	9	3	7	2	8	8	9	6	2	6	9	3	7	3	9	1	8	5	4
5	3	2	1	5	4	7	8	0	3	2	5	8	9	2	6	6	4	3	1
4	3	1	5	7	8	9	0	5	3	2	6	1	0	0	1	2	1	9	5
1	0	9	1	5	6	3	4	8	5	6	7	2	4	3	5	4	2	0	5
3	7	5	8	3	6	2	5	1	0	7	8	6	5	3	1	0	2	0	0

↑
Finish

Copyright © 2003 by John Wiley & Sons, Inc.

4. Addition Number Boxes

★ You must climb up through each number box starting at the bottom and add the correct numbers to get the total at the top of each box. You must always go up straight or diagonally. Draw a line through the numbers you use. The first one has been done for you.

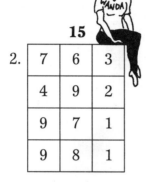

8

1.
2	3	4
4	2	7
7	1	1
4	1	2

15

2.
7	6	3
4	9	2
9	7	1
9	8	1

21

3.
2	1	9
4	2	8
5	3	7
7	1	7

16

4.
3	7	1
2	9	2
9	1	7
4	1	3

20

5.
2	4	6
2	9	3
8	8	2
7	9	1

9

6.
6	3	2
1	7	1
8	4	2
9	7	1

54

7.
5	10	11
14	6	12
3	18	9
17	7	8

40

8.
14	17	20
13	10	1
4	9	2
10	8	10

72

9.
19	21	16
22	17	18
14	13	25
16	14	9

Copyright © 2003 by John Wiley & Sons, Inc.

5. The Wonderful Addition Puzzle

★ Calculate the answers to the following addition problems. Locate each answer in the puzzle. Answers are vertical, horizontal, and diagonal.

1	8	6	3	4	7	8	9	2	0	7	8	4	3	8	5	2
6	3	1	5	2	8	4	3	2	5	2	6	8	9	1	7	4
1	0	7	0	4	6	7	9	5	0	2	1	6	4	8	0	6
3	4	1	0	5	0	3	2	1	7	4	0	1	1	3	0	3
2	4	8	8	2	6	7	9	1	4	7	3	2	7	1	3	2
1	0	9	8	9	5	1	3	5	8	8	9	4	1	5	6	2
8	2	5	1	0	9	1	8	7	9	0	2	3	8	0	2	3
1	3	6	9	2	4	8	0	1	9	0	7	3	1	1	4	5
7	9	1	4	4	5	7	9	3	9	3	6	1	2	5	6	8
3	5	6	9	1	3	2	1	5	1	6	2	0	9	5	4	3

1. 427	2. 641	3. 471	4. 853	5. 821
283	327	472	487	821
+ 340	+ 911	+ 321	+ 777	+ 821

6. 747	7. 829	8. 444	9. 645	10. 311
767	491	333	109	301
+ 737	+ 927	+ 222	+ 106	+ 101

11. 647	12. 774	13. 141	14. 747	15. 622
922	711	191	811	317
+ 811	+ 327	+ 229	+ 922	+ 924

16. 647	17. 311	18. 631	19. 632	20. 374
329	922	111	194	123
+ 841	+ 283	+ 209	+ 244	+ 321

Copyright © 2003 by John Wiley & Sons, Inc.

6. Subtraction Number Boxes

★ You must climb down through each number box starting at the top. Subtract the correct numbers to get the total at the bottom. You must start with a number from the top row and subtract only those other numbers that will give you the correct number at the bottom. Draw a line through the numbers you use. The first one has been done for you.

1.
11	17	20
2	3	8
4	2	1
9	8	7

4

2.
10	9	11
4	2	2
3	6	1
1	8	1

5

3.
4	17	20
3	7	2
2	1	9
1	1	2

7

4.
40	20	10
3	2	7
8	4	9
10	7	11

17

5.
20	19	18
1	4	9
2	7	1
3	2	9

6

6.
14	17	30
4	1	4
9	10	2
8	7	6

5

7.
60	20	19
4	10	2
11	1	9
8	21	9

18

8.
3	17	13
8	2	3
7	1	2
6	1	9

1

9.
14	13	15
7	8	4
3	1	7
9	2	1

4

Copyright © 2003 by John Wiley & Sons, Inc.

7. The Wonderful Subtraction Puzzle: Part One

★ Calculate the answers to the following subtraction problems. Locate each answer in the puzzle. Answers are vertical and horizontal only.

1. 927
    − 284

2. 647
    − 229

3. 884
    − 392

4. 779
    − 584

5. 642
    − 138

6. 841
    − 229

7. 975
    − 327

8. 982
    − 427

9. 847
    − 229

10. 672
     − 370

11. 891
     − 547

12. 837
     − 317

13. 427
     − 123

14. 849
     − 375

15. 982
     − 377

16. 477
     − 179

17. 892
     − 377

18. 884
     − 227

19. 984
     − 222

20. 834
     − 248

Copyright © 2003 by John Wiley & Sons, Inc.

9	5	7	6	8	4	3	1	2	4	9	0	2	4	3	7	9
4	3	3	0	4	5	7	6	4	8	0	9	1	9	5	5	5
6	7	8	0	4	1	9	4	1	8	5	6	6	1	0	0	2
7	9	1	5	3	7	8	3	6	6	0	1	5	4	4	3	0
1	2	3	5	8	6	4	5	6	4	9	2	7	8	6	5	2
4	6	9	9	3	2	8	6	0	5	8	4	2	3	4	4	9
9	5	1	0	0	1	9	1	5	9	1	0	4	0	5	7	6
6	7	5	3	1	2	9	8	9	1	3	1	3	2	0	4	5
4	5	1	9	0	1	2	3	8	5	3	4	6	7	3	5	9
5	1	5	4	3	1	0	9	5	6	3	5	1	9	0	7	8

8. The Wonderful Subtraction Puzzle: Part Two

★ Calculate the answers to the following subtraction problems. Locate each answer in the puzzle. Answers are vertical and horizontal only.

1. 6742 − 731	2. 3275 − 289	3. 6427 − 477	4. 6471 − 329
5. 3712 − 842	6. 6899 − 327	7. 4815 − 215	8. 6414 − 419
9. 4777 − 998	10. 1101 − 292	11. 3271 − 273	12. 4717 − 427
13. 6471 − 921	14. 4271 − 272	15. 7742 − 399	16. 4781 − 834
17. 8924 − 911	18. 4671 − 282	19. 4694 − 291	20. 6419 − 844

Copyright © 2003 by John Wiley & Sons, Inc.

9	5	2	2	5	4	3	1	2	4	9	0	2	4	3	5	9
4	3	3	9	9	9	7	6	4	8	3	9	1	9	5	5	5
6	7	8	8	5	1	6	5	7	2	5	6	6	1	0	5	2
7	9	1	6	0	1	1	3	6	4	5	1	4	2	9	0	0
1	2	3	5	8	6	4	5	3	6	9	8	0	9	6	5	2
4	6	9	9	3	2	2	8	7	0	8	4	2	9	4	4	9
7	3	4	3	8	9	9	1	7	0	1	0	4	8	0	1	3
6	7	5	9	1	2	9	5	9	9	5	5	7	5	0	4	5
4	5	1	4	4	0	3	3	8	5	3	4	6	7	3	5	9
5	1	5	7	3	1	0	9	5	6	3	5	1	9	0	7	8

Copyright © 2003 by John Wiley & Sons, Inc.

9. Being Careful in Math

★ We must be careful in math because the answers must be exact. Below is an exercise that may at first glance appear easy but can be a challenge. Answer the questions below the limerick. Be careful!

Arrogant, a boy was counting with dignity
These letters with skill and ability;
He thought he knew it all
But pride before a fall
He missed the "ty" in modesty.

1. What is the total number of r's? _____

2. What is the total number of s's? _____

3. What is the total number of a's and o's? _____

4. Subtract the number of l's from the number of t's.
_____

5. Multiply the number of m's times the number of k's.
_____

6. Add the number of g's to the number of u's and b's. _____

7. Subtract the number of c's from the number of h's. _____

8. Subtract the number of d's from the number of y's. _____

9. Add the number of w's to the total number of n's. _____

10. Subtract the total number of vowels (a, e, i, o, u) from the total number of letters in the limerick. _____

10. Math Connections

★ Calculate the problems below and put your answers in the individual boxes beside each problem. If an answer above another answer has one or more of the same numbers in it as the answer below, a line has been drawn from the box above to the box below that contains that same number. The first one has been done for you.

1. $672 \times 841 =$

5	6	5	1	5	2

2. $325 \times 725 =$

3. $692 \times 841 =$

4. $397 \times 455 =$

5. $283 \times 327 =$

6. $258 \times 369 =$

7. $987 \times 654 =$

8. $321 \times 357 =$

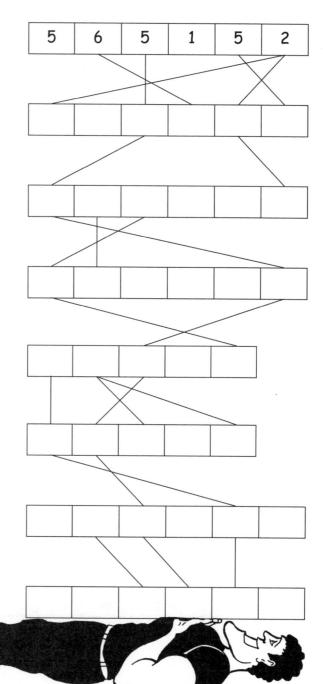

Copyright © 2003 by John Wiley & Sons, Inc.

NAME _____   DATE _____

11. The Wonderful Multiplication Puzzle

★ Locate each answer in the puzzle. Answers are vertical and horizontal only.

9	9	3	3	5	1	7	2	5	7	2	5	8	6	3	8	1	0	2	8
3	0	7	0	2	3	3	4	3	5	7	6	1	3	9	4	8	6	3	5
7	9	8	4	8	0	1	2	4	3	8	2	2	2	8	9	7	3	1	6
2	3	1	0	8	3	7	5	8	3	3	1	2	1	8	7	3	5	4	0
8	7	4	6	4	5	3	1	7	1	7	0	8	2	2	2	7	0	3	1
2	3	5	3	3	6	2	9	3	6	0	9	6	5	4	3	5	8	3	9
6	9	4	2	2	4	5	7	4	8	2	7	2	0	5	8	2	5	2	0
9	0	3	5	0	6	0	2	9	7	3	6	1	8	0	5	4	3	1	7
3	2	5	7	1	9	2	0	1	4	3	8	7	1	9	1	5	0	3	8
7	1	2	3	5	8	4	3	1	5	9	2	9	9	6	0	6	1	5	6
2	1	3	4	8	4	0	8	3	7	3	1	0	5	9	4	4	2	4	3
9	4	0	3	3	1	1	7	6	0	2	4	6	3	2	1	7	0	4	3
6	8	6	5	6	9	7	3	0	4	8	5	3	0	6	5	8	4	2	9

1. 327
    × 7

2. 283
    × 3

3. 427
    × 4

4. 318
    × 9

5. 350
    × 7

6. 170
    × 8

7. 440
    × 4

8. 428
    × 7

9. 429
    × 5

10. 454
     × 5

11. 402
     × 9

12. 396
     × 9

13. 351
     × 7

14. 240
     × 8

15. 360
     × 7

16. 340
     × 8

17. 426
     × 4

18. 307
     × 8

19. 305
     × 7

20. 302
     × 7

Copyright © 2003 by John Wiley & Sons, Inc.

12. Shady Division

★ Shade in all the squares in a set that can be divided evenly by the number on top of each set.

Divisible by 7

14	13	35	65	42	61
21	9	99	81	79	56
33	86	63	69	7	88
19	70	81	31	77	18
84	14	34	32	33	19
13	33	20	17	22	28

Divisible by 4

20	83	36	61	91	24
44	77	95	8	73	71
45	41	4	9	40	97
47	12	62	32	67	69
55	82	7	86	89	93
28	10	48	81	1	16

Divisible by 2

7	19	2	1	9	20
9	22	35	4	15	61
11	45	75	17	12	67
13	77	6	79	99	73
10	31	65	81	37	8
25	39	14	83	16	18

Divisible by 3

3	11	7	8	6	10
68	67	21	41	22	27
23	9	37	38	33	47
18	35	40	43	44	15
13	9	12	2	1	20
24	65	36	64	30	46

Divisible by 5

15	46	71	17	16	20
44	69	45	52	74	35
30	72	54	73	10	48
55	51	5	77	47	50
49	18	91	25	76	92
93	60	19	21	53	40

Divisible by 9

81	94	52	9	89	72
42	43	18	41	27	83
37	49	14	7	3	99
38	36	44	90	1	20
47	69	46	48	45	40
63	50	79	39	51	54

Divisible by 6

12	46	31	18	45	36
39	72	2	1	10	9
38	32	42	40	41	24
30	43	44	9	66	7
37	47	48	8	54	3
34	49	33	6	35	60

Divisible by 8

72	15	14	31	37	81
25	11	8	69	56	52
9	80	20	88	53	51
24	2	32	17	16	19
1	12	87	33	83	34
13	96	10	40	91	48

Divisible by 10

68	94	10	2	1	8
90	67	73	30	74	84
78	27	20	81	80	83
60	32	14	9	7	3
18	70	81	40	76	79
77	85	21	75	50	89

Copyright © 2003 by John Wiley & Sons, Inc.

Copyright © 2003 by John Wiley & Sons, Inc.

NAME _____   DATE _____

13. Logical Deductive Reasoning

★ In each division circle below is a number in the middle of the circle. Around the edge are numbers that may or may not divide into the center number evenly. Your task is to write YES if the number in the outer circle will divide *evenly* into the center number or NO if it will not divide evenly into the center number. The first one has been done for you.

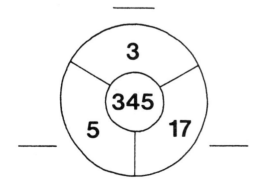

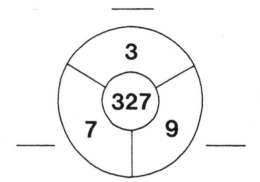

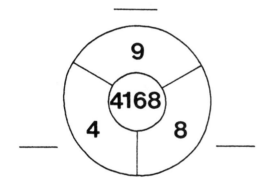

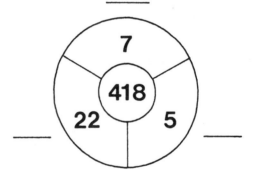

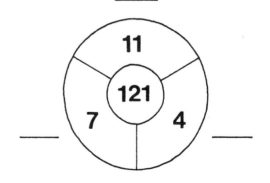

14. The Wonderful Division Puzzle: Part One

★ Calculate the answers to the following division problems. Locate each answer in the puzzle. Answers are vertical and horizontal only.

1. 2080 ÷ 5 =

2. 696 ÷ 3 =

3. 4212 ÷ 4 =

4. 3945 ÷ 5 =

5. 4131 ÷ 9 =

6. 1625 ÷ 5 =

7. 2064 ÷ 4 =

8. 735 ÷ 5 =

9. 3364 ÷ 4 =

10. 5922 ÷ 6 =

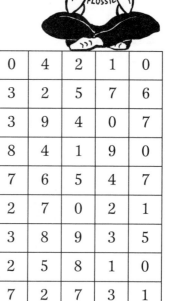

0	6	5	4	0	9	3	4	3	2	8	6	0	4	2	1	0
1	9	7	3	1	8	2	4	1	6	3	4	3	2	5	7	6
9	3	1	2	1	0	9	2	4	5	7	6	3	9	4	0	7
2	7	5	5	2	3	0	7	7	1	6	8	8	4	1	9	0
2	5	2	2	6	3	8	8	9	6	4	3	7	6	5	4	7
8	5	3	2	1	4	5	9	0	3	6	0	2	7	0	2	1
8	4	2	1	0	1	9	8	0	1	5	1	3	8	9	3	5
0	9	3	1	0	5	3	2	5	7	8	1	2	5	8	1	0
7	5	4	3	1	9	2	5	8	5	3	9	7	2	7	3	1
2	5	9	7	0	1	3	4	9	2	6	9	8	6	8	9	0

11. 4851 ÷ 7 =

12. 5886 ÷ 9 =

13. 2064 ÷ 8 =

14. 2735 ÷ 5 =

15. 954 ÷ 6 =

16. 3255 ÷ 7 =

17. 5301 ÷ 9 =

18. 2792 ÷ 4 =

19. 2615 ÷ 5 =

20. 4179 ÷ 7 =

Copyright © 2003 by John Wiley & Sons, Inc.

Copyright © 2003 by John Wiley & Sons, Inc.

NAME _____   DATE _____

15. The Wonderful Division Puzzle: Part Two

★ Calculate the answers to the following division problems. Locate each answer in the puzzle. Answers are vertical and horizontal only.

1. $390 \div 15 =$

2. $2400 \div 25 =$

3. $4485 \div 65 =$

4. $7921 \div 89 =$

5. $1120 \div 32 =$

6. $3132 \div 58 =$

7. $5586 \div 98 =$

8. $2704 \div 52 =$

9. $3367 \div 37 =$

10. $3782 \div 62 =$

0	3	0	1	8	7	3	0	2	1	5	0	8	9	0	4	0
2	0	1	7	8	5	3	8	4	0	8	9	4	8	1	7	1
9	1	3	5	0	2	2	3	6	9	0	0	3	0	2	6	2
0	6	0	0	2	4	6	7	0	6	0	0	7	7	0	5	5
9	0	1	2	8	9	3	6	5	0	0	3	3	4	5	1	0
6	2	0	1	3	5	7	0	3	1	5	0	7	2	0	0	3
0	1	2	4	0	6	0	2	0	9	4	9	0	5	2	4	0
2	3	1	0	9	0	2	0	6	0	0	0	9	0	7	6	9
0	1	0	5	4	6	4	0	1	3	4	3	1	3	2	0	1
0	9	1	2	5	3	0	0	7	2	1	4	5	0	0	2	1

11. $3968 \div 64 =$

12. $2754 \div 51 =$

13. $2256 \div 47 =$

14. $1886 \div 46 =$

15. $2058 \div 21 =$

16. $5049 \div 99 =$

17. $7744 \div 88 =$

18. $7007 \div 91 =$

19. $2585 \div 55 =$

20. $704 \div 22 =$

17

16. The Wonderful Division Puzzle: Part Three

★ Calculate the answers to the following division problems. Locate each answer in the puzzle. Answers are vertical and horizontal only.

1. $87843 \div 89 =$

2. $24128 \div 32 =$

3. $61815 \div 65 =$

4. $62784 \div 96 =$

5. $34986 \div 98 =$

6. $67326 \div 98 =$

7. $49416 \div 58 =$

8. $17018 \div 67 =$

9. $19902 \div 62 =$

10. $32860 \div 53 =$

5	3	5	0	1	2	4	6	9	7	8	2	5	9	5	6	8
5	7	2	1	0	1	7	5	8	3	4	0	0	9	0	1	4
5	0	3	2	2	1	4	3	7	6	0	7	1	0	5	2	4
8	7	7	8	5	7	6	9	1	0	9	2	3	5	4	7	2
9	5	6	5	4	3	7	4	3	2	1	2	7	9	3	4	6
1	4	5	2	0	9	3	7	4	6	0	3	9	5	1	1	2
3	2	2	1	5	6	6	3	7	8	5	4	2	0	0	8	0
3	2	7	8	1	0	8	5	0	5	4	0	6	5	3	9	3
2	8	9	1	3	6	8	7	5	0	7	8	8	4	2	1	0
3	3	5	4	8	2	3	1	2	8	3	7	0	1	8	4	1

11. $37845 \div 45 =$

12. $51965 \div 95 =$

13. $30691 \div 47 =$

14. $24087 \div 93 =$

15. $31080 \div 56 =$

16. $24581 \div 47 =$

17. $44764 \div 62 =$

18. $31228 \div 37 =$

19. $28449 \div 87 =$

20. $26036 \div 92 =$

Copyright © 2003 by John Wiley & Sons, Inc.

17. Multiplication and Division Crossnumber Puzzle

★ Answer the problems below and place the answers in the appropriate place in the puzzle.

Copyright © 2003 by John Wiley & Sons, Inc.

ACROSS

7. 5,893,137 ÷ 9
9. 432 ÷ 9
10. 4810 ÷ 5
11. 738 × 10
14. 10,450 ÷ 475
15. 9,024 ÷ 96
16. 3,195 ÷ 45
19. 1,558 ÷ 41
20. 123,409 × 8
22. 9,936,890 ÷ 10
23. 1,469,550 ÷ 3

DOWN

1. 427 × 21
2. 3 × 31
3. 42,120 ÷ 9
4. 19 × 5
5. 168 ÷ 7
6. 18,960 ÷ 5
8. 29,439 ÷ 9
12. 1,308 ÷ 4
13. 336 ÷ 4
17. 395 × 25
18. 1,947 × 2
21. 5 × 5

18. Rounding Off Whole Numbers

QUICK ACCESS
information

QUICK ACCESS INFORMATION ➜ When we round off numbers, we first look at what place value the question asks us to round off to; then we look at the digit immediately after that place to see if it is 5 or greater. If it is 5 or greater, we go to the next highest digit in the required space.

For example: Using the number 2,874 . . .

Round to	Result	Why
Nearest ten	2,870	The 4 after the 7 is not 5 or greater, so we do not change the 7 to 8.
Nearest hundred	2,900	The 7 after the 8 is 5 or greater, so we change the 8 to 9.
Nearest thousand	3,000	The 8 after the 2 is 5 or greater, so we change the 2 to 3.

★ Round these numbers to the nearest thousand, nearest hundred, and nearest ten.

Number	Nearest Thousand	Nearest Hundred	Nearest Ten
4,745			
4,586			
8,488			
6,715			
13,546			
2,732			
1,184			
2,272			
4,111			
9,477			
14,557			
15,139			

Copyright © 2003 by John Wiley & Sons, Inc.

19. Prime Number Gaps

QUICK ACCESS
information

QUICK ACCESS INFORMATION ➔   A prime number is a number (other than 1) that can be divided evenly only by 1 and the number itself. The prime numbers below 10 are 2, 3, 5, and 7.

★   Below the puzzle are a series of problems. Answer each one and find those answers in the puzzle. All the prime numbers below 10 have been removed. You must fill in the blank spaces with the correct prime numbers from the answers to the problems.

Copyright © 2003 by John Wiley & Sons, Inc.

8	1	6	4	1	6	4	9	8	6	9	1	0	1	4
0	6	1	6	1	○	8	4	6	8	4	0	9	8	1
9	6	9	0	6	4	8	0	1	9	○	8	4	6	0
9	9	1	8	6	9	○	○	○	6	○	0	1	4	8
0	1	6	8	4	9	0	1	9	4	6	4	6	0	○
1	○	4	○	1	9	○	6	8	9	1	6	○	8	1
8	4	6	1	8	9	8	4	1	8	4	1	○	1	9
4	8	4	6	○	9	1	○	0	1	1	0	○	9	○
8	6	0	1	8	0	9	4	1	○	0	9	4	8	0
8	○	8	○	6	4	1	8	6	1	9	8	8	1	9

1.	6552	2.	7289	3.	6947	4.	6414	5.	8229
	− 3276		− 372		− 222		− 3217		− 4317

6.	6972	7.	9799	8.	8419	9.	7514	10.	8714
	− 814		− 327		− 298		− 321		− 329

20. The Prime Number Division Chart

★ Complete the following chart to see if the numbers in the column on the left can be divided by the prime numbers to the right. (Two of the answers have been put in place to help you get started.)

Numbers	Can the number on the left be divided evenly by these prime numbers? (Yes or No)					
	2	**3**	**5**	**7**	**11**	**13**
26	YES					
56						
27						
33				NO		
44						
52						
30						
105						
42						
154						
143						
195						

Copyright © 2003 by John Wiley & Sons, Inc.

21. Composite Number Gaps

QUICK ACCESS information

QUICK ACCESS INFORMATION ➜ Composite numbers are the numbers that result from multiplying any number (other than 1) by another number. For example, 8 is a composite number because $2 \times 4 = 8$. The composite numbers below 10 are 4, 6, 8, and 9.

★ Below the puzzle are a series of problems. Answer each one and find those answers in the puzzle. All the composite numbers below 10 have been removed. You must fill in the blank spaces with the correct composite number from the answer to the problems.

◯	◯	5	1	1	◯	3	5	◯	5	3	7	◯	2	1
1	3	2	3	5	1	7	5	3	1	2	5	7	1	3
2	5	7	5	5	7	1	3	7	2	7	1	7	2	5
5	1	1	2	7	5	◯	◯	5	3	1	2	◯	3	5
◯	2	5	3	2	1	5	3	2	1	◯	5	7	5	3
3	1	3	7	5	2	3	3	5	2	◯	3	5	2	7
1	3	5	5	7	3	2	5	◯	5	3	5	3	◯	2
5	◯	◯	2	5	3	5	2	◯	2	5	3	1	◯	5
2	3	5	1	3	5	2	5	5	7	3	2	5	2	3
1	5	2	3	◯	◯	7	7	7	2	1	5	3	7	1

1.	7871	2.	6416	3.	5271	4.	3414	5.	7198
	− 322		− 931		− 497		− 922		− 347

6.	3294	7.	4822	8.	4270	9.	4835	10.	8147
	− 731		− 397		− 383		− 479		− 963

Copyright © 2003 by John Wiley & Sons, Inc.

22. Greatest Common Factor and Least Common Multiple

QUICK ACCESS information

QUICK ACCESS INFORMATION ➔ The greatest common factor (GCF) is the largest number that will divide evenly into two or more numbers. All composite numbers are the product of smaller prime numbers called prime factors. For example:

Do not use lone factors with GCF. Use only factors that are common to both numbers.

$$12 = 2 \mid 2 \mid 3$$
$$18 = 2 \mid \mid 3 \mid 3$$

$2 \times 3 = 6$ is GCF

OR

$12 = 2 \times 2 \times 3$
$18 = 2 \times 3 \times 3$

$2 \times 3 = 6$

The GCF is 6.

★ **A. Find the Greatest Common Factor for these numbers.**

1. 6 and 15
2. 18 and 30
3. 15 and 20

4. 15 and 25
5. 15 and 18
6. 18 and 24

QUICK ACCESS INFORMATION ➔ The Least Common Multiple (LCM) is the lowest number that can be divided evenly by two or more numbers. For example:

You must use lone factors with LCM.

$$9 = 3 \mid 3$$
$$6 = \mid 3 \mid 2$$

$3 \quad 3 \quad 2 = 18$ is LCM

OR

$9 = 3 \times 3$
$6 = 3 \times 2$

$3 \times 2 \times 3 = 18$

The LCM is 18.

★ **B. Find the Least Common Multiple of these numbers.**

1. 4 and 10
2. 4 and 15
3. 6 and 10

4. 15 and 25
5. 16 and 24
6. 12 and 15

Copyright © 2003 by John Wiley & Sons, Inc.

23. The Rhyming Variety Page

★ Calculate the following problems. Each answer corresponds with a word. When you obtain the word, place it in the rhyme that matches the problem number. The first one is done for you.

1. $327 + 721 =$

2. $283 - 265 =$

3. $47 \times 42 =$

4. $824 + 224 =$

5. $287 + 92 =$

6. $27 \times 8 =$

7. $48 + 9^2 =$

8. $262 \times 4 =$

9. $67 + 49 =$

10. $23 \times 23 =$

11. $379 - 81 =$

12. $387 + 321 =$

13. $427 - 408 =$

14. $43 \times 3 =$

15. $131 \times 8 =$

16. $475 \div 25 =$

17. $3^2 + 9 =$

18. $437 - 321 =$

19. $1320 + 654 =$

20. $118 \times 6 =$

<u>1048</u>	<u>18</u>	<u>1974</u>	<u>379</u>	<u>708</u>	<u>19</u>
seven	St. Ives	going	man	cats	Kits

<u>298</u>	<u>216</u>	<u>529</u>	<u>116</u>	<u>129</u>
many	met	wife	sacks	wives

As I was **going** to _____
       3   2

I _____ a _____ with _____ _____.
    6   5   1   7

Each _____ had _____ _____.
     10   4   9

Each sack had _____ _____.
          15   12

Each cat had _____ _____.
         8   13

_____, _____, _____, and _____.
  16   20   18   14

How _____ were _____ to _____?
     11   19   17

(Old English Rhyme)

Bonus Question: How many living things went to St. Ives? _____

Copyright © 2003 by John Wiley & Sons, Inc.

24. The Partially Completed Choice Puzzle

★ In the puzzle below, the question numbers on the side require answers to be placed from left to right (horizontally). Question numbers at the top require answers to be placed from top to bottom (vertically). It is your choice as to which questions to calculate. As the puzzle is partially completed, it may be a benefit to calculate a combination of vertical and horizontal answers.

HORIZONTAL

1. $\begin{array}{r} 3,146,298 \\ +\ \ \ 12,345 \end{array}$

2. $\begin{array}{r} 2,834 \\ \times\ 2,831 \end{array}$

3. $\begin{array}{r} 7,832,549 \\ -\ 1,279,984 \end{array}$

4. $\begin{array}{r} 14,134 \\ \times\ \ \ \ \ 327 \end{array}$

5. $\begin{array}{r} 7,271,349 \\ -\ \ \ 129,879 \end{array}$

6. $\begin{array}{r} 4,719,327 \\ +\ \ \ \ \ 92,983 \end{array}$

7. $\begin{array}{r} 92,729 \\ \times\ \ \ \ \ \ 23 \end{array}$

VERTICAL

8. $\begin{array}{r} 3,827,755 \\ +\ \ \ \ 36,987 \end{array}$

9. $\begin{array}{r} 150,883 \\ \times\ \ \ \ \ \ \ \ 7 \end{array}$

10. $\begin{array}{r} 5,399,671 \\ -\ \ \ 147,258 \end{array}$

11. $\begin{array}{r} 8,312,595 \\ +\ \ \ \ \ 8,527 \end{array}$

12. $\begin{array}{r} 288,497 \\ \times\ \ \ \ \ \ \ 21 \end{array}$

13. $\begin{array}{r} 4,239,729 \\ +\ \ \ 321,987 \end{array}$

14. $\begin{array}{r} 4,112,796 \\ -\ \ \ 654,789 \end{array}$

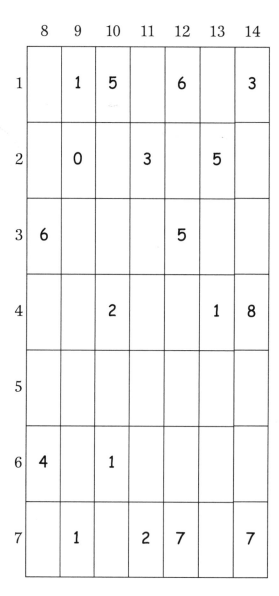

Copyright © 2003 by John Wiley & Sons, Inc.

NAME _____   DATE _____

25. The Number Match Game

★   Calculate the answers to the problems on the left and draw a line to the correct answer on the right.

Copyright © 2003 by John Wiley & Sons, Inc.

$784 \div 14$	5798
327×9	2943
$8113 - 475$	69
$479 + 8472$	757
$6762 \div 98$	55
283×9	6919
$9143 - 879$	89
$348 + 409$	8264
$3025 \div 55$	731
427×9	3447
$7841 - 922$	780
$351 + 429$	56
$6942 \div 78$	3999
440×9	7638
$4567 - 568$	8951
$302 + 429$	7395
$805 \div 23$	2547
383×9	3843
$6587 - 789$	3960
$6541 + 854$	35

26. Take Your Pick

★ Listed below are a series of double problems. You must pick or choose one from each pair to calculate. It does not matter which one you do for each pair because they will have the same answer. Find each answer in the grid on the right and draw a line through it.

1. $327 - 283$ OR $220 \div 5$

2. $426 + 340$ OR 383×2

3. $327 - 124$ OR $98 + 105$

4. 68×5 OR $961 - 621$

5. $987 - 99$ OR 8×111

6. $7371 \div 91$ OR 9×9

7. $374 \div 2$ OR $926 - 739$

8. $327 + 240$ OR 9×63

9. $789 - 231$ OR 62×9

10. $699 + 116$ OR 163×5

11. $521 + 96$ OR $986 - 369$

12. $484 - 256$ OR $535 - 307$

13. 58×6 OR 116×3

14. 149×5 OR $987 - 242$

15. $951 + 32$ OR $547 + 436$

0	9	7	6	4	3	1	1	9	8
8	2	4	3	4	5	7	0	1	2
8	0	9	1	4	1	0	2	4	7
8	6	1	7	5	9	7	5	2	4
0	7	9	3	2	3	4	0	0	5
2	6	7	5	7	0	8	3	4	5
0	1	2	0	3	3	5	5	1	9
2	7	2	9	8	3	6	6	2	0
2	8	5	4	2	1	5	7	2	1
8	5	7	6	6	5	2	3	0	9
9	1	0	6	7	0	2	3	4	8
2	5	9	5	5	8	0	1	3	5
4	3	0	2	9	1	8	3	8	6
8	0	1	8	7	0	1	7	1	5
3	6	9	1	2	1	5	2	4	3

Copyright © 2003 by John Wiley & Sons, Inc.

27. Vertical and Horizontal Calculations

★ Place the correct answers from the calculations in the appropriate boxes. Add up the digits in each box both horizontally and vertically, putting the totals at the end of each row. Calculate the total of the digits and put that answer in the grand total box.

A. $12{,}589 + 36{,}389$

B. $98{,}753 - 21{,}516$

C. $8{,}861 \times 4$

D. $182{,}583 \div 9$

E. $2{,}306{,}775 \div 25$

Place answers vertically

Horizontal Totals

A	B	C	D	E	

Vertical Totals

Grand Total

F. $87{,}657 + 327$

G. $83{,}785 - 6{,}548$

H. $35{,}507 - 963$

I. $87{,}874 - 852$

J. $4{,}093 \times 3$

Place answers horizontally

Horizontal Totals

F					
G					
H					
I					
J					

Vertical Totals

Grand Total

Copyright © 2003 by John Wiley & Sons, Inc.

28. The James Q. Dandy (Jim Dandy) Variety Puzzle

★ Answer the problems below, then search for the answers in the puzzle and draw a line through them.

1. $321 + 252 =$ _____
2. $1837 \times 4 =$ _____
3. $795 \div 5 =$ _____
4. $454 - 396 =$ _____
5. $4914 \div 9 =$ _____
6. $283 + 265 =$ _____
7. $327 + 398 =$ _____
8. $302 \div 2 + 351 =$ _____
9. $302 + 351 =$ _____
10. $292 + 260 + 289 =$ _____

11. $351 + 352 + 392 =$ _____
12. $400 \times 429 =$ _____
13. $2824 \div 8 =$ _____
14. $2718 \div 9 =$ _____
15. $426 + 360 + 320 =$ _____
16. $1477 \times 5 =$ _____
17. $340 + 426 - 324 =$ _____
18. $360 + 440 =$ _____
19. $440 - 319 =$ _____
20. $426 + 441 =$ _____

3	5	9	8	1	3	7	7	5	7	1	3	4	8	2	3	4	8	9	7
5	9	7	3	5	6	8	2	7	4	6	2	8	4	8	8	5	1	6	3
5	9	7	6	0	1	2	5	7	8	6	4	8	4	6	5	4	2	8	·5
5	8	0	3	1	0	9	5	3	1	9	2	3	5	3	9	5	8	3	6
1	5	9	6	3	4	2	9	7	0	2	1	5	8	4	0	1	3	8	6
2	6	4	3	1	6	9	2	0	9	0	5	8	5	1	5	6	3	8	7
0	3	8	3	8	1	8	0	5	1	9	3	8	9	5	6	2	3	7	1
7	7	1	7	2	6	3	9	5	1	5	6	1	8	5	9	5	1	2	0
5	9	1	4	5	8	6	7	9	7	5	2	8	9	6	1	4	3	1	7
8	5	6	1	4	0	1	3	8	3	2	8	3	1	2	4	5	4	6	0
8	9	6	2	3	5	5	8	1	2	3	5	1	3	5	9	9	0	8	2
5	0	3	6	5	3	2	4	6	8	1	0	9	0	1	7	1	6	0	0
0	2	3	1	5	7	2	6	8	3	1	2	5	9	5	9	6	1	2	1
1	3	8	1	7	4	1	5	3	6	9	8	5	4	4	1	3	5	9	2
2	2	4	0	2	6	6	4	1	5	4	3	6	8	9	7	5	6	6	8
8	6	8	6	3	2	0	7	3	1	0	5	9	7	3	4	8	8	9	0
5	0	2	8	8	5	6	1	9	3	3	8	3	8	6	5	6	4	4	0
9	5	7	6	5	2	1	3	8	9	8	1	3	3	5	6	4	1	1	3
8	9	6	2	5	4	8	8	6	4	4	2	8	5	7	2	1	0	6	4
0	5	4	8	3	4	5	9	4	3	0	2	9	6	3	4	7	3	8	5

Copyright © 2003 by John Wiley & Sons, Inc.

29. Math Puzzle Boxes

★ Do the calculations across and/or down in order to fill in the puzzle.

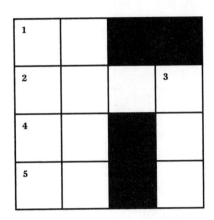

ACROSS

1. 4×4

2. $737 + 562$

4. $1564 \div 68$

5. $988 \div 19$

DOWN

3. $1558 - 621$

Copyright © 2003 by John Wiley & Sons, Inc.

ACROSS

1. 25×5

2. 64×32

3. $3523 + 856$

4. $580932 \div 652$

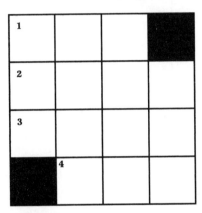

ACROSS

1. $428 \div 4$

3. 7×7

4. $5372 \div 68$

5. $989 - 695$

DOWN

2. $903 - 104$

3. $987 - 505$

The Long Box: Do the calculations below the box, then place the answer in the box. Add all answers to get a grand total.

$283 + 402$	$327 + 351$	$318 + 360$	$427 + 426$	$428 + 402$	$396 + 305$	**Grand Total**

30. Center Math Vocabulary

★ In the center of the puzzle below are math vocabulary words that need to be found in the surrounding puzzle. Words are forward, backward, and diagonal.

C	E	N	T	I	M	E	T	E	R	A	L	C	B	V	W	E	L	L	I	P	S	E	R	I	O	L	C
U	R	Y	T	P	L	F	Q	W	R	E	X	C	O	A	M	I	N	T	E	R	S	E	C	T	P	O	M
M	N	E	R	A	A	T	F	W	N	A	P	L	Y	M	U	L	A	S	E	U	N	E	V	Q	U	R	T
R	E	U	P	C	H	W	O	G	I	K	M	U	L	T	I	P	L	E	S	U	P	O	R	N	F	G	U
C	V	B	T	O	S	A	T	R	E	O	I	N	F	D	E	G	H	I	P	V	N	P	T	R	E	R	T
L	L	O	C	K	B	H	P	E	R	P	E	N	D	I	C	U	L	A	R	E	R	K	Y	U	M	C	Z
B	R	A	V	I	V	E	M	B	R	A	N	G	L	E	R	G	M	H	W	P	O	E	S	U	T	B	O

V	A	S	C	U	K	L	E		B	O	L	T	Y	B	M	F
T	N	A	V	I	S	T	W		E	D	U	T	I	T	A	L
I	T	N	B	I	G	W	O		L	N	M	I	L	O	P	R
P	G	K	U	N	J	O	T		O	B	M	K	D	E	R	S
M	H	I	L	I	G	H	L		N	S	T	T	H	G	I	R
R	N	R	T	N	I	O	P		G	O	T	N	J	I	N	J
T	M	W	I	P	O	N	J		I	N	B	M	E	X	T	R
I	K	T	Y	O	L	D	L		T	O	L	B	D	J	I	Y
V	L	E	R	M	I	C	O		U	M	O	N	E	Y	E	W
P	O	R	B	V	A	E	M		D	R	I	U	N	M	E	R
C	P	R	I	A	P	S	K		E	X	T	V	E	R	A	W
Q	L	D	E	R	E	L	P		B	E	R	U	S	A	E	M
U	E	P	E	G	L	K	I		P	E	R	T	I	C	M	L
U	C	J	M	I	K	R	E		L	D	U	M	B	R	E	T
I	M	E	B	U	P	L	S		C	T	I	D	E	W	B	R
O	N	O	I	T	A	R	S		J	O	H	V	N	S	T	R
T	P	G	U	L	P	A	W		I	V	B	M	I	U	R	Y
G	I	S	U	M	H	J	A		N	P	O	K	L	S	E	W

Center word list:

angle	measure
arithmetic	money
centimeter	multiples
count	numbers
degrees	obtuse
divide	pair
divisor	perpendicular
ellipse	plane
factor	point
intersect	power
latitude	ratio
length	right
logical	segment
longitude	sum
math	triangle

G	H	I	J	D	L	F	K	D	E	O	P	R	N	O	M	W	A	S	M	M	A	S	R	T	Y	O	W
P	O	W	E	R	W	E	E	G	H	I	V	U	M	B	E	N	A	L	P	B	A	T	N	R	O	V	R
P	R	T	Y	M	N	G	R	G	P	F	M	S	A	T	B	V	R	U	T	I	M	T	R	E	W	R	T
R	R	E	N	K	R	L	R	T	Y	B	B	T	W	Q	U	E	S	Y	O	L	U	B	H	A	S	T	R
E	T	T	I	E	M	V	N	A	E	S	T	E	L	E	L	G	N	A	I	R	T	N	B	G	H	E	L
Y	E	R	E	M	B	T	Y	R	E	R	G	K	H	I	L	P	O	N	W	E	T	V	C	R	E	L	P
N	O	S	T	R	E	M	S	B	C	F	M	A	R	I	T	H	M	E	T	I	C	N	E	T	I	R	B

Copyright © 2003 by John Wiley & Sons, Inc.

NAME _____   DATE _____

31. Definition Puzzle on Whole Number Terms

★ Place the answers to this puzzle in their correct locations across or down. A Choice Box has been provided.

Copyright © 2003 by John Wiley & Sons, Inc.

[Crossword grid with numbered cells: 15, 12, 5, 4, 2, 13, 7, 10, 9, 1, 8, 14, 3, 6, 11]

ACROSS

1. When you multiply two numbers
3. A product of prime numbers
6. An expression related to numbers
7. Rent paid on borrowed money
11. Not up and down, but sideways
12. All of something
13. Not wrong
15. What you do to get an answer

DOWN

2. A number with two factors: itself and 1
4. The answer in a division problem
5. A line up and down or north and south
8. To find something
9. When you divide two numbers
10. Common sense
14. The result when you calculate

CHOICE BOX

prime	composite	logical	horizontal	division
answer	numerical	quotient	complete	interest
multiplication	locate	vertical	correct	calculate

33

32. Skills Mastery Test—Whole Numbers: Part One

★ You will need extra (scratch) paper to calculate these test questions.
Answer the following problems in the space provided.

1. $14 + 14 =$

2. $741 + 748 =$

3. $927 + 784 =$

4. $327 - 149 =$

5. $672 - 298 =$

6. $454 - 350 =$

7. $737 \times 9 =$

8. $847 \times 19 =$

9. $928 \times 24 =$

10. $425 \div 5 =$

11. $510 \div 85 =$

12. $686 \div 7 =$

13. Start at the top and draw a line down to subtract only those numbers that will give you the number at the bottom.

7	9	14
8	4	13
3	2	7
2	9	1

7

14. Cross out all numbers divisible by 5.

5	21	95	25
11	10	36	92
64	19	7	200
60	65	70	20
15	75	84	18

15. $\begin{array}{r} 6714 \\ + 3271 \\ \hline \end{array}$

16. $\begin{array}{r} 6714 \\ - 3271 \\ \hline \end{array}$

17. $\begin{array}{r} 8452 \\ \times \ \ 52 \\ \hline \end{array}$

18. $\begin{array}{r} 4273 \\ \times \ 273 \\ \hline \end{array}$

19. $\begin{array}{r} 752 \\ 821 \\ + 947 \\ \hline \end{array}$

20. $\begin{array}{r} 7943 \\ \times \ \ 43 \\ \hline \end{array}$

21. $3\overline{)456}$

22. $9\overline{)702}$

23. $89\overline{)2047}$

24. $\begin{array}{r} 7772 \\ - 4449 \\ \hline \end{array}$

25. $\begin{array}{r} 47532 \\ - 9499 \\ \hline \end{array}$

Copyright © 2003 by John Wiley & Sons, Inc.

NAME _____   DATE _____

33. Skills Mastery Test—Whole Numbers: Part Two

★ **Find the Greatest Common Factor of these number pairs:**

1. 15 and 21   2. 10 and 25   3. 12 and 32

★ **Find the Least Common Multiple of these number pairs:**

4. 2 and 7   5. 8 and 12   6. 27 and 45

★ **Round off the numbers below to the place indicated:**

	Nearest Thousand	Nearest Hundred	Nearest Ten
7. 4,539			
8. 8,315			

★ **Answer these problems:**

9. How many vowels (a, e, i, o, u) are there in this question? _____

10. Subtract 231,769,483 from 913,427,891. _____

11. Shade all those numbers that are divisible by 12:

36	14	60	99
84	32	96	98
86	24	48	72
89	94	62	144

12. Circle the prime numbers in the following line of numbers:
    7,   11,   14,   19,   2,   3,   88,   17,   9,   5

13. Find the square root of the numbers below:

$\sqrt{9}$ $\sqrt{100}$ $\sqrt{81}$

Copyright © 2003 by John Wiley & Sons, Inc.

SECTION 2

GETTING TO THE POINT WITH DECIMALS

34. Adding Decimals

Copyright © 2003 by John Wiley & Sons, Inc.

QUICK ACCESS INFORMATION ➜ When adding decimal numbers, the decimal points must align in a column. For example, when we add 7.1, 3.23, and 4.441, we must line up the decimals in a column and add zeros where necessary.

7.1	with zeros added →	7.100
3.23		3.230
+ 4.441		+ 4.441
14.771		14.771

★ Look at each problem below that is written horizontally. Only part of it has been written vertically. You must complete the writing of each problem, then answer it correctly.

1. 72.1 + 32.7 + 8.1

```
     .1
   32.
 +  8.
```

6. 727.413 + 9.82 + 9.2

```
   72 .
      9.
 +    9.
```

2. 17.413 + 9.87 + 3.744

```
   17.41
    9.
 +  3.  4
```

7. 36.415 + 8.92 + 78.31

```
    3 .
       .9
 +  78.3
```

3. 82.171 + 92.11 + 81.10

```
    2.1
    9 .1
 +  1.1
```

8. 42.141 + 16.2 + 34.411

```
    4 .
    6.
 +    .4
```

4. 6.7 + 8.931 + 2.444

```
     .7
    .  1
 +  2.4
```

9. 67.79 + 22.413 + 0.784

```
    7.
     .
 +    .7
```

5. 73.415 + 2.941 + 7.8

```
   73.
    2.9
 +   .8
```

10. 37.25 + 48.8 + 92.99

```
    3 .
     .
 +    .
```

QUICK ACCESS
information

35. True or False Decimals

> **QUICK ACCESS INFORMATION** ➡ In order for numbers with decimals to be added or subtracted, the points or decimals must be aligned in a column.

★ Below are three problems with answers. Be careful, though! There may be something wrong with each problem. You must:

- Decide if each problem is written properly according to the Quick Access Information above. Circle YES or NO.
- Write it correctly in the space provided if it is not written properly.
- Figure out each problem to see if the answer is correct. Write the correct answer in the space provided.

1. 0.270 Is the problem written correctly? (YES or NO)

    0.830 If not, write it correctly here. ➡

  + 74.5 Is the answer correct? (YES or NO)
   ――――――

    987.5 If not, put the correct answer here. ➡

2. 132.5 Is the problem written correctly? (YES or NO)

    132.9 If not, write it correctly here. ➡

  + 175.4 Is the answer correct? (YES or NO)
   ――――――

    440.8 If not, put the correct answer here. ➡

3. 771.5 Is the problem written correctly? (YES or NO)

    67.01 If not, write it correctly here. ➡

  + 7.625 Is the answer correct? (YES or NO)
   ――――――

   846.135 If not, put the correct answer here. ➡

Copyright © 2003 by John Wiley & Sons, Inc.

YES NO

yes! oh no!

36. Move the Gears: Part One
(Addition of Decimals)

★ In your mind, move the gears around to make the spokes of one gear fit into the slots of the other. Create an addition problem wherever the gears connect. The first problem has been done for you.

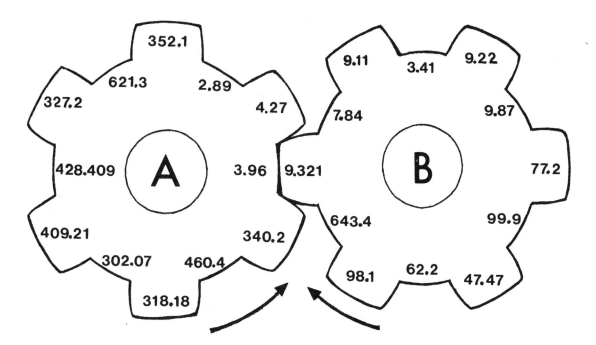

Copyright © 2003 by John Wiley & Sons, Inc.

1.   3.96
     + 9.321
      13.281

2. _____
   + _____
   _____

3. _____
   + _____
   _____

4. _____
   + _____
   _____

5. _____
   + _____
   _____

6. _____
   + _____
   _____

7. _____
   + _____
   _____

8. _____
   + _____
   _____

9. _____
   + _____
   _____

10. _____
    + _____
    _____

11. _____
    + _____
    _____

12. _____
    + _____
    _____

37. Subtracting Decimals

QUICK ACCESS INFORMATION ➜ When subtracting decimal numbers, the decimal points must all be aligned in a column. For example, if we subtract 7.142 from 9.91, we must line up the decimals and add zeros where necessary.

QUICK ACCESS information

$$
\begin{array}{r}
9.91 \\
-\ 7.142 \\
\hline
2.768
\end{array}
$$
with zeros added ➜
$$
\begin{array}{r}
9.910 \\
-\ 7.142 \\
\hline
2.768
\end{array}
$$

★   Look at the problem that is written horizontally. Only part of it has been written vertically. You must complete the writing of the problem, then answer it correctly.

1. $6.713 - 5.982$

$$
\begin{array}{r}
6.71 \\
-\ \ \ .98 \\
\hline
\end{array}
$$

6. $327.42 - 98.17$

$$
\begin{array}{r}
32\ \ \ .\ \ \ \ \\
-\ \ \ 8.1\ \ \\
\hline
\end{array}
$$

2. $8.341 - 2.99$

$$
\begin{array}{r}
8.34 \\
-\ \ \ .9 \\
\hline
\end{array}
$$

7. $427.135 - 327.153$

$$
\begin{array}{r}
4\ \ .\ \ 5 \\
-\ 3\ \ .1 \\
\hline
\end{array}
$$

3. $22.71 - 3.129$

$$
\begin{array}{r}
22.\ \ \ \ \ \\
-\ \ \ 3.1\ \ \\
\hline
\end{array}
$$

8. $648.71 - 72.457$

$$
\begin{array}{r}
8.\ \ \ \ \ \ \\
-\ 72.\ \ \ \ \ \\
\hline
\end{array}
$$

4. $14.44 - 8.219$

$$
\begin{array}{r}
4.\ \ \ \ \ \\
-\ \ \ 8.21\ \ \\
\hline
\end{array}
$$

9. $471.41 - 19.1919$

$$
\begin{array}{r}
4\ \ .4\ \ \ \ \ \\
-\ \ \ \ \ .\ \ \ \ \ \\
\hline
\end{array}
$$

5. $37.17 - 9.21$

$$
\begin{array}{r}
37.\ \ \ \ \\
-\ \ \ 9.2\ \ \\
\hline
\end{array}
$$

10. $19.49 - 3.773$

$$
\begin{array}{r}
.4\ \ \ \ \ \\
-\ \ \ \ .\ \ \ \ \ \\
\hline
\end{array}
$$

Copyright © 2003 by John Wiley & Sons, Inc.

NAME _____   DATE _____

38. Move the Gears: Part Two
(Subtraction of Decimals)

★ In your mind, move the gears around to make the spokes of one gear fit into the slots of the other. Create a subtraction problem wherever the gears connect. Subtract the numbers of A from the numbers of B. The first problem has been done for you.

Copyright © 2003 by John Wiley & Sons, Inc.

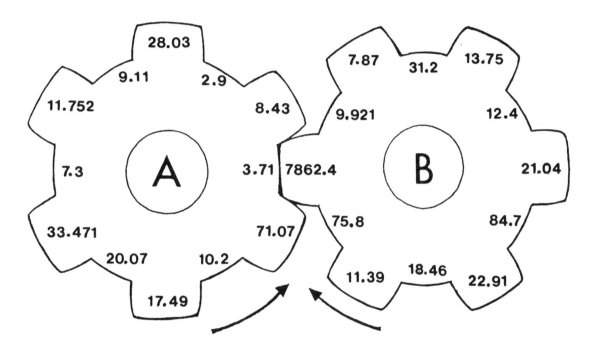

1. $\begin{array}{r} 7862.4 \\ -3.71 \\ \hline 7858.69 \end{array}$

2. _____ − _____ = _____

3. _____ − _____ = _____

4. _____ − _____ = _____

5. _____ − _____ = _____

6. _____ − _____ = _____

7. _____ − _____ = _____

8. _____ − _____ = _____

9. _____ − _____ = _____

10. _____ − _____ = _____

11. _____ − _____ = _____

12. _____ − _____ = _____

39. Multiplying Decimals

Copyright © 2003 by John Wiley & Sons, Inc.

> **QUICK ACCESS**
> **information**

QUICK ACCESS INFORMATION ➜ When we multiply decimals, we must count the number of digits that occur to the right of the decimal in each number being multiplied. The answer must have the same total number of digits after the decimal.

For example: Number of digits

$$
\begin{array}{r}
2.27 \rightarrow 2 \\
\times\ 4.73 \rightarrow 2 \\
\hline
681 \\
1589 \\
908 \\
\hline
10.7371 \rightarrow 4
\end{array}
$$

There are a total of 4 spaces in the problem, so we must count back from the extreme right side 4 spaces and put our decimal point there.

★   **Answer these problems. The answers can be found in the Choice Box.**

1.	2.	3.	4.	5.
32.7	4.27	77.7	778	36.11
× 2.2	× 3.6	× 9.9	× 9.4	× 0.28

6. $379.42 \times 92 =$ _____   7. $827.31 \times 47 =$ _____   8. $92.31 \times 0.98 =$ _____

9.	10.	11.	12.	13.
671.37	747.21	72.31	9.74	6.38
× 6.3	× 2.8	× 4.2	× 0.89	× 0.37

14. $7.31 \times 0.92 =$ _____   15. $84.3 \times 0.91 =$ _____

CHOICE BOX   (If you can't find your answers here, you must recalculate.)

71.94	8.6686	769.23	76.713	2.3606
2092.188	6.7252	34906.64	303.702	90.4638
10.1108	4229.631	38883.57	7313.2	15.372

40. Move the Gears: Part Three
(Multiplication of Decimals)

★ In your mind, move the gears around to make the spokes of one gear fit into the slots of the other. Create a multiplication problem wherever the gears connect. The first problem has been done for you.

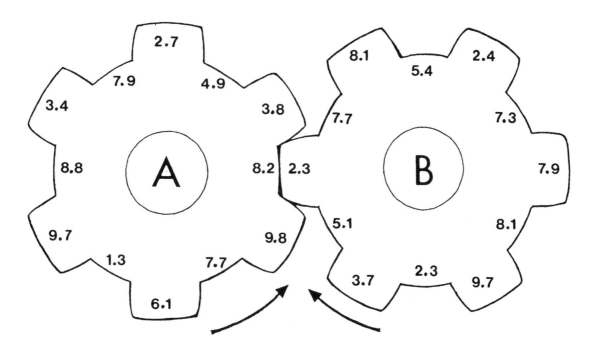

1.   8.2
     × 2.3
       18.86

2. _____
    ×_____
    _____

3. _____
    ×_____
    _____

4. _____
    ×_____
    _____

5. _____
    ×_____
    _____

6. _____
    ×_____
    _____

7. _____
    ×_____
    _____

8. _____
    ×_____
    _____

9. _____
    ×_____
    _____

10. _____
    ×_____
    _____

11. _____
    ×_____
    _____

12. _____
    ×_____
    _____

Copyright © 2003 by John Wiley & Sons, Inc.

41. Double-Up Decimals

★   Answer each multiplication problem below, then use the answers to answer the "Double-Up Problems."

MULTIPLICATION OF DECIMALS:

1. $107.8 \times 4 =$ _____

2. $43.8 \times 92 =$ _____

3. $7.7 \times 7 =$ _____

4. $64.31 \times 5 =$ _____

5. $854.2 \times 9 =$ _____

6. $67.7 \times 2 =$ _____

7. $97.13 \times 8 =$ _____

8. $365.11 \times 8 =$ _____

9. $74.7 \times 22 =$ _____

10. $747.3 \times 19 =$ _____

11. $247.14 \times 4 =$ _____

12. $819.12 \times 74 =$ _____

DOUBLE-UP PROBLEMS:

1. Add the answer of problem 3 to the answer of problem 12.   _____

2. Subtract the answer of problem 11 from the answer of problem 10.   _____

3. Add the answers of problems 5, 6, and 10.   _____

4. Subtract the answer of problem 4 from the answer of problem 5.   _____

5. Divide the answer for problem 1 by the answer for problem 3.   _____

6. Add the answer of problem 5 to the answer of problem 2.   _____

7. Subtract the answer of problem 9 from the answer of problem 8.   _____

8. Add the answer of problem 11 to the answer of problem 1.   _____

Copyright © 2003 by John Wiley & Sons, Inc.

 x 2 =

42. Dividing Decimals

QUICK ACCESS information

QUICK ACCESS INFORMATION ➜ (1) In order to divide decimals, we must be careful to not have any decimals in the number we are dividing with. In the example $0.42)\overline{3.192}$, the 0.42 must be changed to 42 and the decimal point in 3.192 must be moved to the right the same number of spaces (in this case, 2), so it becomes 319.2. If there is no room to the right, then a zero is added. Now we can divide $42)\overline{319.2}$; the answer is 7.6. (2) We must also make sure our decimal point is placed directly above where it is in the problem, for example:

$$42)\overline{319.2} \quad 7.6$$

★ Rewrite and answer these problems. You'll find the answers in the Choice Box. The first one has been started for you.

PROBLEM	REWRITE	PROBLEM	REWRITE
1. $0.42)\overline{323.4}$	$42)\overline{32340}$	6. $7.4)\overline{3.774}$	
2. $0.37)\overline{129.5}$		7. $0.7)\overline{49.49}$	
3. $0.47)\overline{3.525}$		8. $0.8)\overline{.776}$	
4. $0.87)\overline{.8613}$		9. $0.8)\overline{.704}$	
5. $4.3)\overline{382.7}$		10. $0.5)\overline{.175}$	

CHOICE BOX (If you do not find your answers here, you must recalculate.)

350	0.97	0.88	0.51	770
70.7	7.5	0.35	89	0.99

Copyright © 2003 by John Wiley & Sons, Inc.

43. Move the Gears: Part Four
(Division of Decimals)

★ In your mind, move the gears around to make the spokes of one gear fit into the slots of the other. Create a division problem wherever the gears connect. Divide the numbers of A by the numbers of B. The first problem has been done for you.

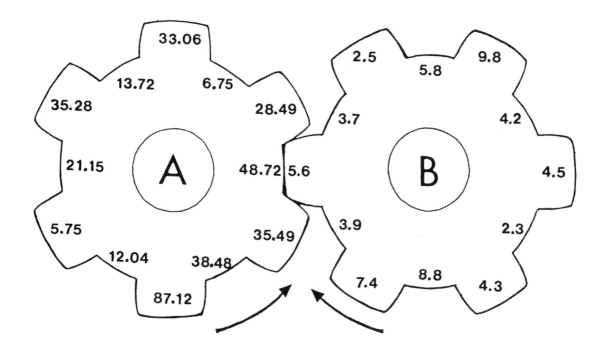

1. 48.72 ÷ 5.6 = 8.7

2. _____ ÷ _____ = _____

3. _____ ÷ _____ = _____

4. _____ ÷ _____ = _____

5. _____ ÷ _____ = _____

6. _____ ÷ _____ = _____

7. _____ ÷ _____ = _____

8. _____ ÷ _____ = _____

9. _____ ÷ _____ = _____

10. _____ ÷ _____ = _____

11. _____ ÷ _____ = _____

12. _____ ÷ _____ = _____

Copyright © 2003 by John Wiley & Sons, Inc.

Copyright © 2003 by John Wiley & Sons, Inc.

NAME _____   DATE _____

44. Rounding Off and Comparing Decimal Numbers

★ Round off these decimals to the nearest place indicated. For example, 9.754 (tenth) would be rounded off to 9.8.

ROUND OFF TO THE NEAREST PLACE INDICATED		COMPARE USING > OR < OR =		
1. 3.479 (tenth)	_____	3.479	◯	3.477
2. 2.952 (hundredth)	_____	2.952	◯	2.4
3. 8.911 (tenth)	_____	8.911	◯	17.13
4. 14.37 (tenth)	_____	14.37	◯	14.37000
5. 122.03 (tenth)	_____	122.03	◯	122.30
6. 127.741 (hundredth)	_____	127.741	◯	127.751
7. 409.3487 (thousandth)	_____	409.348	◯	409.426
8. 1272.4 (one)	_____	127.42	◯	1272.4
9. 747.3 (ten)	_____	747.300	◯	747.3
10. 327.283 (tenth)	_____	327.283	◯	427.428

GOSH, ORG, THERE'S GOT TO BE A BETTER WAY TO ROUND OFF!

Bonus Question: What is technically wrong with this picture? _____

_____

45. Expressing Decimals as Fractions: Part One

★   Change the following decimals to fractions or mixed numbers and simplify.

★   **Bonus Question:** Place the answers with the star into the puzzle to make the sum or total match the answers of 34 and 61.

1.   7.1   _____ ★

2.   8.27   _____

3.   9.5   _____ ★

4.   9.25   _____ ★

5.   7.3   _____ ★

6.   9.2   _____ ★

7.   7.75   _____ ★

8.   0.40   _____

9.   3.75   _____ ★

10. 4.5   _____ ★

11. .90   _____

12. 27.4   _____ ★

13. 0.20   _____

14. 7.9   _____

15. 8.92   _____

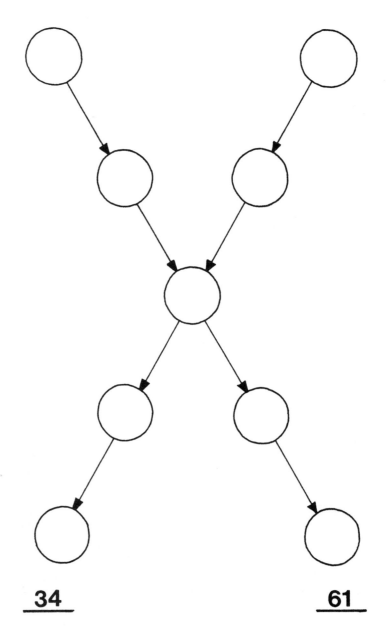

Copyright © 2003 by John Wiley & Sons, Inc.

46. Expressing Decimals as Fractions: Part Two

★ **A. Complete the following. Express all fractions in the simplest form.**

1. $7.3\overline{3} = \underline{\hspace{0.5cm}}\frac{1}{3}$

2. $7.31 = 7\frac{}{100}$

3. $7.5 = 7\frac{}{2}$

4. $7.25 = 7\frac{1}{}$

5. $7.6\overline{6} = \underline{\hspace{0.5cm}}\frac{2}{3}$

6. $3.9 = 3\frac{9}{}$

7. $8.02 = \underline{\hspace{0.5cm}}\frac{1}{}$

8. $4.5 = 4\frac{1}{}$

9. $7.125 = 7\frac{1}{}$

10. $3.6 = 3\frac{3}{}$

★ **B. Match the decimals on the left to their fractions on the right.**

1. 0.75

2. 1.5

3. $2.3\overline{3}$

4. 0.6

5. 0.12

6. 0.40

7. 0.15

8. 3.59

9. 9.1

10. 4.05

$4\frac{1}{20}$

$1\frac{1}{2}$

$\frac{3}{5}$

$\frac{2}{5}$

$\frac{3}{25}$

$\frac{3}{20}$

$\frac{3}{4}$

$3\frac{59}{100}$

$2\frac{1}{3}$

$9\frac{1}{10}$

Copyright © 2003 by John Wiley & Sons, Inc.

47. Humans vs. Aliens: Metric Comparison/Conversion

★ Read the following facts about humans and aliens, then answer the questions below.

Facts about Average-Sized Humans	Facts about Average-Sized Aliens
Average weight male: 68.1 kg (kilograms)	Average weight male: 51.7 kg
Average weight female: 56.2 kg	Average weight female: 41.1 kg
Skin weight: 17 kg	Skin weight: 7 kg
Walking speed: 5 km/h (kilometers per hour)	Walking speed: 18 km/h
Weight of spaceship: 20,520 kg	Speed of spaceship: 50,204 km/h

1 kg (kilogram) = 2.2 lbs. (pounds)   0.454 kg (kilograms) = 1 lb. (pound)

1 km (kilometer) = 0.62 miles   1 mile = 1.61 km

1. How many pounds does the human female weigh? _____

2. How many pounds does the alien female weigh? _____

3. How many pounds does the human male weigh? _____

4. How many pounds does the alien male weigh? _____

5. Which "being" is the heaviest? _____ How many pounds heavier is it than the next heaviest "being"? _____

6. Which "being" is the lightest? _____ How many pounds lighter is it than the next lightest "being"? _____

7. The alien spaceship can be smaller and lighter than the human's spaceship by 20%. What is the weight of the alien spaceship? _____ kg _____ lbs.

8. How many miles per hour can the alien walk? _____

9. How many miles per hour can the human walk? _____

10. How fast does the alien ship travel in miles per hour (mph)? _____

11. How many more pounds does an average-sized human's skin weigh than the average alien's skin? _____

Copyright © 2003 by John Wiley & Sons, Inc.

48. The Great Overlapping Math Puzzle

★ In this puzzle, you must calculate the first problem under Set A (2251×25). The last two numbers of the answer for each problem in Set A are the first two numbers of the answer to the problem in Set B. Similarly, the last two numbers of Set B are the first two numbers to the answer in Set C. (The answer for A-1 is 56,275. This means that the answer for B-1 starts with 75.) Write the overlapping answers in the grid at the bottom.

	Set A	Set B	Set C
1.	$2251 \times 25 =$	$5057 \times 15 =$	$4652 \times 12 =$
2.	$241 \times 214 =$	$2323.25 \times 32 =$	$2794.25 \times 16 =$
3.	$1304 \times 53 =$	$1047 \times 12 =$	$3218.45 \times 20 =$
4.	$657 \times 48 =$	$2276.5 \times 16 =$	$1245.9 \times 20 =$
5.	$654 \times 35 =$	$3613 \times 25 =$	$1612.75 \times 16 =$
6.	$589 \times 65 =$	$5669 \times 15 =$	$1431.56 \times 25 =$
7.	$897 \times 51 =$	$1478 \times 32 =$	$4031 \times 24 =$
8.	$258 \times 98 =$	$5298.25 \times 16 =$	$3614.2 \times 20 =$

Copyright © 2003 by John Wiley & Sons, Inc.

	Set A			Set B				Set C		
1.	5	6	2	7	5					
2.										
3.										
4.										
5.										
6.										
7.										
8.										

I LIKE IT WHEN EVERYTHING OVERLAPS.

49. Four-Function Crossnumber Choice Puzzle

★ Study the "across" and "down" sets of problems below. Either set alone will complete the puzzle. Choose one set to calculate the answers.

ACROSS

1. 327×2
4. $369 + 102$
7. $18391 \div 53$
8. $555 - 333$
9. $10942 - 2320$
11. $18925 \div 5$
12. 10.25×24
14. $1564 \div 17$
15. $99999 - 51560$
17. $541 + 291$
18. $84523 - 10274$
20. $22 + 17 + 98 + 200 + 10$
21. 16×51.5
23. $10924 - 2026$
25. $7650 - 258$
28. 44.875×16
29. $119 + 789$
30. 24.5×12
31. $952 - 149$

DOWN

1. 159.5×4
2. $4914 \div 9$
3. $9632 - 4910$
4. $6159 - 5732$
5. 182×4
6. 25×5
10. 30.5×8
11. $8554 \div 26$
13. $327 + 283 + 428 + 67809$
14. 5828×16
16. 16×27
18. $73304 \div 98$
19. $1000 - 73$
20. $2147 + 1837$
22. 1099.5×4
23. 218×4
24. $89 + 98 + 632$
26. 30×30
27. $698 - 415$

THE GREAT SYMBOL SACK

Copyright © 2003 by John Wiley & Sons, Inc.

50. Cruising Route 66 with Math

★ You are in your totally awesome and hyper cool 1961 red-and-white Corvette traveling Route 66 looking for some action. Well, here it is. You must fill up with gas every 66 miles. Follow the route that calculates to 66 at each gas station. Use the number 66 to start you off from each gas station. Do the calculations in the order they occur. Draw a line through Route 66 to complete the maze.

Start at Flagstaff, Arizona

55	-	5	+	16	=	GAS	×	3	-	8	+	4
-		3			÷			7.4				=
5		÷			16.5			+				GAS
+	9	-	7	÷	3	+	7	-	2	-	17	+
4		+			14			÷				8.7
=		2			-			3				=
GAS	-	7	+	8	÷	8	+	26	+	30	=	GAS
-		17			÷			9				÷
13.2		-			2			÷				11
+	7	-	17	+	GAS	=	10	+	2	×	22	+
2		+			GAS			=				17
4		3			+			GAS				-
GAS	×	8	÷	2	+	23	=	GAS	+	79	-	45
-		9			-			8				-
14		÷			8			-				34
+	7	÷	74	+	2	-	9	+	14	÷	2	=

66

End at St. Louis, Missouri

Bonus Question: A 1961 Corvette could be purchased for $3,420.00 in 1961. Today that same Corvette in used condition sells for up to $64,980.00! How many more times the original price is the price today? _____

Copyright © 2003 by John Wiley & Sons, Inc.

51. Pirate Math

★ Pirates, or buccaneers, are people of intrigue. Let's find out more about them. First, read these facts. Then answer the questions below and on worksheet 52.

IMPORTANT PIRATE FACTS:

A. The female pirate Anne Bonny, in 1720, had a ship *The Contessa* that weighed 4.749 tons when empty. It was 57.32 feet long by 21.31 feet wide.

B. The male pirate Edward Teach, known as Blackbeard, had a ship *The Sea Bandit* that weighed 4.629 tons and was 53.37 feet long by 21.30 feet wide.

C. One statute mile across land is 5,280 feet.

D. One nautical mile across water (called a knot) is 6,076.1033 feet.

E. The Spanish Main, where pirates traveled, was the mainland coast of South America. That coastline is 3,948.27 nautical miles (knots) long.

F. 1 doubloon = 4 Spanish Pistoles = $15.71 U.S. dollars.

G. 1 piece of eight = 8 Spanish Reals = $1.14 U.S. dollars.

H. 1 ton = 2,000 pounds.

PIRATE QUESTIONS:

1. Blackbeard bought a rowboat for 12.71 pieces of eight. How much is this in U.S. dollars? _____

2. Anne Bonny loaded 4,028 doubloons into her boat. Each doubloon weighed 0.42 lbs. How much money did she have in U.S. dollars? _____ What was the weight of the doubloons? _____ What was the new weight of her ship? _____

3. How many pieces of eight does it take to equal the value of a doubloon in U.S. dollars? _____

4. Blackbeard went up and down the Spanish Main five times. How many nautical miles (knots) did he travel? _____

5. Blackbeard buried 7,847 doubloons near Ooracoke Inlet in North Carolina that has not been found to this day. What is the value of this buried treasure in U.S. dollars? _____

6. How many feet longer is a nautical mile than a statute mile? _____

7. How many feet longer is *The Contessa* than *The Sea Bandit*? _____ How many feet wider? _____

Copyright © 2003 by John Wiley & Sons, Inc.

52. More Pirate Math

PIRATE QUESTIONS:

8. Which is worth more in U.S. dollars: 5 doubloons or 79 pieces of eight? _____

9. What is the value in U.S. dollars of one Spanish Real? _____

10. What is the value in U.S. dollars of one Spanish Pistole? _____

11. Blackbeard's crew of 21 rough sailors on average weighed 151 pounds. What was the weight of his ship with the crew on board? _____

12. *The Contessa* would travel at 7 knots per hour. How many hours would it take her to travel 322.14 nautical miles? _____

13. In 1719, passengers from the new world of South America would travel on the ship with gold chain wrapped around their bodies. If the gold weighed the same as 127 doubloons and each doubloon was 0.42 pounds, what was the total weight of the gold the person was wearing? _____

14. Take the answer from question 13 and add it to the weight of a 210.32-pound man. What is the total weight of the person with the gold? _____ Would this person have a slight problem if the ship began to sink? _____

Copyright © 2003 by John Wiley & Sons, Inc.

Contessa

53. Decimal Stew: Tenths Place

★   **Answer the following problems.**

1. Add 3.2 to 7.6, then subtract 1.4:   _____

2. Add 3.9 to 8.2 and 7.4:   _____

3. Add 8.4 to 9.9 and 3.2:   _____

4. Subtract 7.2 from 19.7, then add 32.1:   _____

5. Divide 4.2 by 2.1, then add 7.1:   _____

6. Divide 20.4 by 0.4, then subtract 2.1:   _____

7. Multiply 3.2 by 2.1, then add 0.4:   _____

8. Multiply 2.2 by 7.1, then add 4.4:   _____

9. Add 4.7 to 3.6 and 1.1:   _____

10. Add 2.3 to 3.1, then subtract 1.1:   _____

11. Subtract 3.1 from 7.7, then add 4.1:   _____

12. Add 3.4 to 9.1 and 3.7:   _____

13. Add 9.9 to 7.4 and 9.1:   _____

14. Multiply 7.9 by 0.2, then subtract 0.7:   _____

15. Add 27.2 to 9.4 and 1.9:   _____

Copyright © 2003 by John Wiley & Sons, Inc.

54. Decimal Stew: Hundredths Place

★ **Answer the following problems.**

1. Add 27.23 to 9.31, then subtract 2.79: _____

2. Add 2.47 to 9.32 and 9.33: _____

3. Multiply 3.27 by 4, then add 17.76: _____

4. Divide 34.95 by 6.99, then add 1.11: _____

5. Divide 399.96 by 0.99, then add 4.01: _____

6. Add 7.22 to 3.27 and 4.27: _____

7. Subtract 4.54 from 9.01, then add 7.11: _____

8. Subtract 4.41 from 13.41, then add 0.75: _____

9. Add 6.27 to 4.54 and 3.96: _____

10. Subtract 3.07 from 4.27, then add 3.18: _____

11. Divide 0.56 by 0.14, then add 27.11: _____

12. Divide 6.23 by 0.89, then add 283.07: _____

13. Multiply 2.22 by 3.33, then add 4.44: _____

14. Subtract 2.22 from 11.11, then add 7.78: _____

15. Add 7.22 to 3.27 and 4.27: _____

Copyright © 2003 by John Wiley & Sons, Inc.

55. Decimal Stew: Thousandths Place

★ **Answer the following problems.**

1. Add 3.721 to 9.372 and 1.371: _____

2. Subtract 3.971 from 12.333, then add 1.272: _____

3. Multiply .327 by 1.764, then add 1.641: _____

4. Divide 15.705 by 1.745, then add 2.211: _____

5. Multiply 3.271 by 2.132, then subtract 1.411: _____

6. Add 1.141 to 9.714, and add 1.727: _____

7. Subtract 3.214 from 92.271, then add 7.631: _____

8. Divide 44.440 by 5.555, then add 17.034: _____

9. Add 6.274 to 327.701 and 8.209: _____

10. Add 7.241 to 7.907 and 79.234: _____

11. Subtract 77.943 from 98.927, then add 7.149: _____

12. Subtract 847.231 from 9732.114, then add 29.444: _____

13. Divide 35.552 by 4.444, then add 247.551: _____

14. Multiply .901 by 3.171, then add 427.282: _____

15. Add 572.249 to .914, then subtract 67.237: _____

Copyright © 2003 by John Wiley & Sons, Inc.

56. The Velocity Page

QUICK ACCESS INFORMATION ➡ When we want to calculate velocity or the speed of a car, we must use the formula *velocity (speed) equals the distance divided by the time* or $V = \frac{d}{t}$. For example, you drove your Classic 1962 Jaguar XKE coupe to boarding school. The distance was 165 miles and it took you 3 hours to arrive at your dorm. We calculate the velocity or speed to be:

$$V = \frac{d}{t} = \frac{165}{3} = 55 \text{ miles per hour}$$

★ **Answer these velocity questions.**

1. Your Uncle Al drove his 1967 Corvette (427, 4-speed) from Boise to the family gathering at your place. It took him 3 hours and Boise is 180 miles away. What was his average speed? _____ mph

2. Your Aunt Wanda bought a new Viper (V10, 6-speed). She also lives 180 miles away at Boise, but it took her only 2.5 hours to get to your home. On average, how fast did she travel? _____ mph

3. Your cousin Bob loves cars, so he bought a Lamborgini Convertible (V12, 5-speed). He lives 360 miles from you. What would his average speed need to be if he has only 4.5 hours to get to your place? _____ mph

4. Mike (Bob's brother) feels differently about cars. He bought a 1962 Chevrolet Nova (4-cylinder automatic). He thinks it is a wonderful machine, but it took him 6 hours to cover the 240 miles to your place. What was his average speed? _____ mph

5. Your sister and her husband drove their classic 1970 Hemi Cuda (4-speed) to the gathering from North Battleford in the province of Saskatchewan in Canada. It took them 38 hours of driving time to cover the 2,736 miles. What was their average speed? _____ mph

Copyright © 2003 by John Wiley & Sons, Inc.

57. Definition Puzzle on Decimals

★ Place the answers to this puzzle in their correct locations across or down. A Choice Box has been provided.

ACROSS

1. The name of the 3rd place to the right of the decimal
4. The name of the 2nd place to the right of the decimal
5. The way of doing something, like a math problem
7. The name of the 4th place to the left of a decimal
8. The place a thing or number is
12. An empty spot
13. Round working parts inside a machine
14. The name of the 1st place to the left of a decimal

DOWN

2. When you judge between two things
3. A process used when exact numbers are not needed
6. The name of the 1st place to the right of the decimal
9. The name of the 3rd place to the left of the decimal
10. The Canadian and European system of measurement
11. A thing that represents something else
15. The name of the 2nd place to the left of a decimal

CHOICE BOX

comparing	procedure	thousands	ones	tenths
metric	space	hundreds	thousandths	symbol
location	rounding	tens	hundredths	gears

Copyright © 2003 by John Wiley & Sons, Inc.

58. Skills Mastery Test—Decimals: Part One

★ **Rewrite these problems correctly, then calculate the answer:**

1.   3.25
     0.629
   + 47.3

2.   773.29
   − 49.979

★ **Round off 52.594 to the places requested:**

3. nearest hundredth place = _____   4. nearest tenths place = _____

★ **Subtract the following decimal problems:**

5.   327.4
   − 37.9

6.   73.29
   − 2.49

7.   647.31
   − 524.99

8. 727.49 − 656.32 = _____

9. 621.04 − 294.195 = _____

★ **Add the following decimal problems:**

10. 747.3 + 732.91 + 327.33 = _____

11. 6.98 + 7.32 + 7.77 = _____

12.   37.50
       7.84
    + 9.11

13.   327.42
       29.91
    + 31.77

14.   32.4711
       2.9872
    + 8.9147

★ **Use > or < or = to compare these numbers:**

15. 3.477 ◯ 3.478

16. 2.792 ◯ 2792

17. 81.1 ◯ .911

18. The average female space alien weighs 41.1 kg. The average male space alien weighs 57.1 kg. What is the difference in their weight? _____

19. The alien space saucer (made by UFO Inc.) travels at 47.894 km per second. The human spacecraft (made by NASA) travels at 39.826 km per second. How much faster is the alien machine? _____

20. Blackbeard the pirate ate 2.47 chickens for breakfast, 3.27 for lunch, and 5.39 for supper. What was his total for the day? _____

Copyright © 2003 by John Wiley & Sons, Inc.

59. Skills Mastery Test—Decimals: Part Two

★ Answer these multiplication problems:

1.	3.27	2.	4.27	3.	31.8	4.	440	5.	28.3
	× 7		× 3		× 0.5		× .37		× 8.3

6. $4.26 \times 21 =$ _____

7. $4.28 \times 34 =$ _____

★ Change the following decimal numbers to fractions or mixed numbers. Make sure the fractions are reduced to lowest form.

8. 8.22 = _____ 10. 0.75 = _____ 12. 3.14 = _____ 14. 0.5 = _____

9. 9.5 = _____ 11. 0.8 = _____ 13. 7.25 = _____ 15. 0.1 = _____

★ Answer these problems and questions:

16. Anne Bonny, the female pirate, had three Jolly Roger flags on her ship *The Contessa*. Each flag weighed 7.84 pounds. What was the total weight of the three Jolly Roger flags? _____

17. Add 3.7 to 7.4, then subtract 1.8: _____

18. Divide 49 by 5, then subtract 9.7: _____

19. Subtract 3.1 from 8.8, then add 6.2: _____

20. Multiply 8.9 by .2, then subtract .7: _____

21. Anne Bonny had 13.56 tons of jewels and other booty that she shared with the pirates Mary Read and Captain Kidd. How much did each pirate get? _____

22. You can buy a "Descriptive List of Treasure Maps and Charts in the Library of Congress" for a small fee. If the fee is $3.52 (not the correct amount) from the U.S. Government Printing Office in Washington, D.C., and 7,842 students who see this question send for it, how much money will go to the U.S. Government because of this question? _____

23. Add 572.04 to 0.919, then subtract 68.96: _____

24. Subtract 78.471 from 82.489, then subtract 0.4: _____

25. Add 67.42 to 92.894, then subtract 1.876: _____

Copyright © 2003 by John Wiley & Sons, Inc.

SECTION 3

FRACTIONS IN THE LEARNING PROCESS

Copyright © 2003 by John Wiley & Sons, Inc.

60. The Eight-Piece Fraction Puzzle: Part One

★ Each letter takes the combined value of the fractions in the overlapping figures. Add the value of the figures for each letter. See the example to help get you started.

Example: $\frac{3}{4} + \frac{1}{2} = \frac{3}{4} + \frac{2}{4} = \frac{5}{4} = 1\frac{1}{4}$

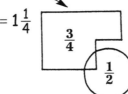

A. _____ + _____ =

B. _____ + _____ =

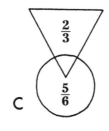

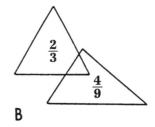

C. _____ + _____ =

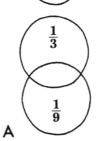

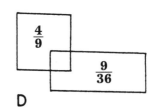

D. _____ + _____ =

E. _____ + _____ =

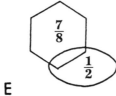

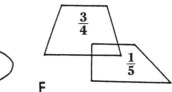

F. _____ + _____ =

G. _____ + _____ =

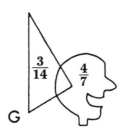

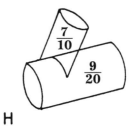

H. _____ + _____ =

61. The Eight-Piece Fraction Puzzle: Part Two

★ Each letter takes the combined value of the mixed numbers in the
  overlapping figures. Add the value of the figures for each letter. See the
  example to help get you started.

Example: $1\frac{1}{2} + 2\frac{1}{6} = 1\frac{3}{6} + 2\frac{1}{6} = 3\frac{4}{6} = 3\frac{2}{3}$

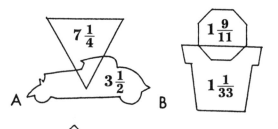

A. _____ + _____ =

B. _____ + _____ =

C. _____ + _____ =

D. _____ + _____ =

E. _____ + _____ =

F. _____ + _____ =

G. _____ + _____ =

H. _____ + _____ =

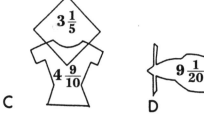

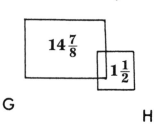

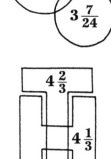

Copyright © 2003 by John Wiley & Sons, Inc.

68

62. Finding the Value Of Names: Part One

★ Study the Choice Box below. Each set of letters has a fraction beside it. Those fractions are the value of + letters. Each name below is made up of two sets of letters. Add the value of both sets of letters to get the total value of the persons name. The first one is done for you.

CHOICE BOX

Ak	$\frac{3}{4}$	Ty	$\frac{1}{9}$	Be	$\frac{4}{17}$	Anna	$\frac{1}{7}$
Ja	$\frac{1}{8}$	Jo	$\frac{3}{18}$	Ny	$\frac{5}{12}$	Lly	$\frac{1}{16}$
Mo	$\frac{3}{8}$	To	$\frac{1}{3}$	Ira	$\frac{1}{2}$	Rie	$\frac{5}{5}$
Bo	$\frac{2}{3}$	Di	$\frac{3}{14}$	Bby	$\frac{2}{3}$	Ia	$\frac{3}{4}$
Son	$\frac{1}{2}$	Bre	$\frac{9}{28}$	Hanne	$\frac{4}{9}$	Lene	$\frac{2}{5}$
Mar	$\frac{3}{15}$	Kar	$\frac{7}{20}$	Tty	$\frac{1}{34}$	ler	$\frac{3}{18}$

1. Akira $\frac{3}{4}$ + $\frac{1}{2}$ = $1\frac{1}{4}$ 11. Tony   _____ + _____ = _____

2. Sonia   _____ + _____ = _____   12. Breanna   _____ + _____ = _____

3. Jason   _____ + _____ = _____   13. Marlene   _____ + _____ = _____

4. Tyler   _____ + _____ = _____   14. Karrie   _____ + _____ = _____

5. Betty   _____ + _____ = _____   15. Karia   _____ + _____ = _____

6. Molly   _____ + _____ = _____   16. Jarie   _____ + _____ = _____

7. Bobby   _____ + _____ = _____   17. Jony   _____ + _____ = _____

8. Johanne   _____ + _____ = _____   18. Annarie   _____ + _____ = _____

9. Moira   _____ + _____ = _____   19. Beson   _____ + _____ = _____

10. Dianna   _____ + _____ = _____   20. Joanna   _____ + _____ = _____

Copyright © 2003 by John Wiley & Sons, Inc.

63. Finding the Value of Names: Part Two

★ Study the Choice Box below. Each set of letters has a mixed number (whole number and a fraction) beside it. Those mixed numbers are the value of the letters. Each name below is made up to 2 sets of letters. Add the value of both sets of letters to get the total value of the person's name.

CHOICE BOX

son	$19\frac{1}{10}$	Br	$1\frac{3}{4}$	mer	$11\frac{5}{16}$	her	$9\frac{1}{6}$
Earn	$7\frac{4}{9}$	vinn	$2\frac{3}{8}$	Ara	$3\frac{1}{2}$	Floss	$4\frac{1}{16}$
ee	$2\frac{1}{4}$	Ho	$22\frac{3}{8}$	stine	$7\frac{1}{4}$	Jack	$2\frac{1}{5}$
Add	$2\frac{1}{2}$	Chri	$5\frac{1}{8}$	Jo	$3\frac{5}{14}$	Jay	$17\frac{2}{7}$
Tam	$3\frac{1}{4}$	Est	$3\frac{1}{3}$	Mabel	$2\frac{1}{7}$	ian	$22\frac{7}{8}$
Harri	$11\frac{9}{20}$	lene	$1\frac{1}{14}$	ie	$2\frac{7}{8}$	sta	$3\frac{1}{8}$

1. Bradd $1\frac{3}{4}$ + $2\frac{1}{2}$ = $4\frac{1}{4}$ 11. Jaylene   ____ + ____ = ____

2. Tamara   ____ + ____ = ____   12. Tamie   ____ + ____ = ____

3. Flossie   ____ + ____ = ____   13. Brian   ____ + ____ = ____

4. Jolene   ____ + ____ = ____   14. Christine   ____ + ____ = ____

5. Mabellene   ____ + ____ = ____   15. Homer   ____ + ____ = ____

6. Jackson   ____ + ____ = ____   16. Vinnson   ____ + ____ = ____

7. Christa   ____ + ____ = ____   17. Addie   ____ + ____ = ____

8. Esther   ____ + ____ = ____   18. Mervinn   ____ + ____ = ____

9. Vinnie   ____ + ____ = ____   19. Harrison   ____ + ____ = ____

10. Bree   ____ + ____ = ____   20. Earnest   ____ + ____ = ____

Copyright © 2003 by John Wiley & Sons, Inc.

64. Cool Name Fractions

★ Add the fractions below. Remember, they must have the same denominator in order to be added. Each problem is named after a person with one of the world's coolest names. The names are needed for the bonus questions below.

Flipper Twerpski	$\frac{2}{3} + \frac{1}{3} + \frac{2}{3} =$	Molly Golly	$\frac{1}{15} + \frac{1}{5} + \frac{1}{6} =$
Candy Barr	$\frac{1}{2} + \frac{1}{2} + \frac{1}{2} =$	Kimmel Yaggy	$\frac{1}{3} + \frac{1}{2} + \frac{1}{4} =$
Billy Bopper	$\frac{1}{2} + \frac{3}{4} + \frac{1}{2} =$	King Buckingham	$\frac{1}{2} + 1\frac{1}{2} + 1\frac{1}{2} =$
Vinny Kool	$\frac{2}{3} + \frac{1}{3} + \frac{1}{6} =$	Lovespace Joy	$7\frac{1}{4} + 8\frac{3}{4} + \frac{1}{2} =$
Agulik Eskimo	$\frac{7}{8} + \frac{3}{8} + \frac{1}{8} =$	Joan Joan Jones	$2\frac{1}{2} + 2\frac{1}{3} + 4\frac{1}{4} =$
Sunbeam Love	$\frac{4}{5} + \frac{2}{5} + \frac{1}{10} =$	Buck Shynkaruk	$2\frac{1}{14} + 3\frac{1}{7} + 9\frac{9}{14} =$
Butch Kelvington	$\frac{4}{5} + \frac{3}{8} + \frac{3}{8} =$	Horizon Sunshine	$7\frac{5}{6} + 1\frac{3}{8} + 1\frac{1}{2} =$
Jimmy Dandy	$\frac{1}{2} + \frac{2}{3} + \frac{2}{3} =$		

BONUS QUESTIONS

1. Join the total of Flipper Twerpski to the total of Joan Joan Jones: _____

2. Add the total of Butch Kelvington to the total of Lovespace Joy: _____

3. Combine the answer of Sunbeam Love to the total of Kimmel Yaggy: _____

4. Join the total of Molly Golly to the total of Jimmy Dandy: _____

5. Combine the total of Billy Bopper to the total of Vinny Kool: _____

Copyright © 2003 by John Wiley & Sons, Inc.

65. Subtraction with Common Denominators: Part One

QUICK ACCESS
information

QUICK ACCESS INFORMATION ➜ To subtract unlike fractions with different denominators, first change them to like fractions using the lowest common denominator. For example:

$$\frac{4}{5} - \frac{1}{15} = \frac{12}{15} - \frac{1}{15} = \frac{11}{15}$$

★ **Answer the following problems.**

1. $\frac{4}{5} - \frac{1}{15} =$

2. $\frac{2}{3} - \frac{1}{3} =$

3. $\frac{3}{4} - \frac{1}{4} =$

4. $\frac{3}{4} - \frac{1}{8} =$

5. $\frac{4}{5} - \frac{1}{10} =$

6. $\frac{3}{4} - \frac{5}{8} =$

7. $\frac{1}{3} - \frac{1}{6} =$

8. $\frac{7}{8} - \frac{3}{4} =$

9. $1\frac{1}{2} - \frac{1}{4} =$

10. $2\frac{3}{4} - \frac{3}{8} =$

11. $1\frac{7}{10} - \frac{2}{5} =$

12. $3\frac{6}{7} - \frac{1}{14} =$

13. $2\frac{9}{11} - \frac{3}{22} =$

14. $3\frac{4}{5} - \frac{11}{15} =$

15. $7\frac{19}{20} - \frac{1}{4} =$

Copyright © 2003 by John Wiley & Sons, Inc.

Copyright © 2003 by John Wiley & Sons, Inc.

66. Subtraction with Common Denominators: Part Two

QUICK ACCESS information

QUICK ACCESS INFORMATION ➡ If the fraction you are subtracting is larger than the fraction you are subtracting from in a mixed number, you must regroup before you can subtract. For example: $4\frac{1}{2} - \frac{3}{4}$.

Regroup the $4\frac{1}{2} = 4\frac{2}{4} = 4 + \frac{2}{4} = 3 + 1 + \frac{2}{4} = 3 + \frac{4}{4} + \frac{2}{4} = 3\frac{6}{4}$;

now subtract the $\frac{3}{4} = 3\frac{6}{4} - \frac{3}{4} = 3\frac{3}{4}$.

★   **Answer the following problems.**

1. $2\frac{1}{2} - \frac{3}{4} =$

2. $7\frac{1}{8} - \frac{3}{4} =$

3. $2\frac{1}{9} - \frac{7}{18} =$

4. $7\frac{2}{5} - \frac{7}{10} =$

5. $2\frac{1}{3} - \frac{5}{6} =$

6. $3\frac{1}{3} - \frac{4}{9} =$

7. $2\frac{1}{7} - \frac{8}{14} =$

8. $9\frac{1}{4} - \frac{7}{8} =$

9. $2\frac{1}{5} - \frac{3}{15} =$

10. $1\frac{1}{3} - \frac{7}{12} =$

67. Subtraction with Common Denominators: Part Three

QUICK ACCESS INFORMATION ➜   To subtract mixed numbers, first find the lowest common denominator (if necessary) and subtract the fractions, then subtract the whole number. For example:

$$4\frac{1}{2} - 2\frac{1}{3} = 4\frac{3}{6} - 2\frac{2}{6} = 2\frac{1}{6}$$

★   Answer the following problems.

1. $3\frac{1}{2} - \frac{7}{9} =$

2. $2\frac{1}{4} - \frac{4}{5} =$

3. $2\frac{1}{3} - \frac{6}{7} =$

4. $2\frac{1}{2} - \frac{5}{7} =$

5. $3\frac{1}{9} - \frac{4}{5} =$

6. $2\frac{1}{4} - \frac{6}{7} =$

7. $3\frac{1}{3} - 1\frac{4}{11} =$

8. $2\frac{1}{3} - 1\frac{5}{8} =$

9. $3\frac{1}{12} - 2\frac{5}{4} =$

10. $7\frac{1}{7} - \frac{1}{2} =$

Copyright © 2003 by John Wiley & Sons, Inc.

68. Addition, Subtraction, and Substitution Using Fractions

★ Letters have been substituted for the numbers. You must rewrite each problem, substituting the correct number for each letter. An example has been given to help you get started.

Example: $P + Q + M = \frac{1}{15} + \frac{2}{5} + \frac{1}{10} = \frac{17}{30}$

1. $X + R + R =$

2. $P + Q - M =$

3. $B + X + X =$

4. $G + B + Y =$

5. $Y + R + X =$

6. $M + Q - P =$

7. $R + X - Y =$

8. $M + P + P =$

9. $X - B - Y =$

10. $Y + B + R =$

All P's are worth $\frac{1}{15}$.

All Q's are worth $\frac{2}{5}$.

All M's are worth $\frac{1}{10}$.

All G's are worth $\frac{5}{8}$.

All B's are worth $\frac{3}{8}$.

All X's are worth $\frac{7}{8}$.

All Y's are worth $\frac{1}{4}$.

All R's are worth $\frac{1}{2}$.

Copyright © 2003 by John Wiley & Sons, Inc.

69. Boxing Up the Multiplication of Fractions

QUICK ACCESS INFORMATION ➜ (1) When multiplying fractions, it is only a matter of multiplying straight across:

$$\frac{1}{3} \times \frac{2}{5} = \frac{1 \times 2}{3 \times 5} = \frac{2}{15}$$

(2) When multiplying a fraction ($\frac{1}{4}$) times a whole number (7), you must place the whole number over 1, then multiply straight across:

$$\frac{1}{4} \times 7 = \frac{1}{4} \times \frac{7}{1} = \frac{7}{4} = 1\frac{3}{4}$$

Copyright © 2003 by John Wiley & Sons, Inc.

★ Multiply these using the same number indicated in the box. (The first one is done for you.)

$\frac{1}{2}$			$\frac{1}{5}$		
	$\times \frac{1}{4} = \frac{1}{8}$ (1)			$\times \frac{2}{3} =$ ____ (4)	
	$\times \frac{1}{3} =$ ____ (2)			$\times \frac{7}{8} =$ ____ (5)	
	$\times \frac{1}{5} =$ ____ (3)			$\times \frac{4}{5} =$ ____ (6)	

$\frac{2}{3}$			$\frac{1}{4}$		
	$\times 2$ ____ (7)			$\times \frac{7}{8} =$ ____ (10)	
	$\times 3$ ____ (8)			$\times \frac{4}{5} =$ ____ (11)	
	$\times 4$ ____ (9)			$\times \frac{7}{10} =$ ____ (12)	

$\frac{3}{4}$			$\frac{4}{5}$		
	$\times 7$ ____ (13)			$\times \frac{1}{5} =$ ____ (16)	
	$\times \frac{2}{3} =$ ____ (14)			$\times \frac{1}{9} =$ ____ (17)	
	$\times \frac{9}{10} =$ ____ (15)			$\times 15$ ____ (18)	

NAME _____ DATE _____

70. Interesting Name Math

Some place names in the United States are downright interesting and unusual. We have assigned the place names with a mixed number.

Ali Chuk, Arizona	$1\frac{1}{2}$
Chicken, Alaska	$7\frac{1}{3}$
Atascadero, California	$3\frac{1}{4}$
Burnt Corn, Alabama	$7\frac{1}{4}$
Pawcatuck, Connecticut	$2\frac{1}{2}$

Bone Gap, Illinois	$2\frac{1}{3}$
Bippers, Indiana	$1\frac{1}{4}$
Cooks Hammock, Florida	$3\frac{1}{3}$
Pray, Montana	$9\frac{1}{2}$
Winnemucca, Nevada	$4\frac{1}{2}$

★ **Multiply (answer in lowest term) using the assigned place names.**

1. Pray × Bone Gap _____

2. Burnt Corn × Chicken _____

3. Ali Chuk × Bippers _____

4. Atascadero × Cooks Hammock _____

5. Pawcatuck × Winnemucca _____

6. Winnemucca × Pray _____

7. Bone Gap × Burnt Corn _____

8. Atascadero × Bippers _____

9. Chicken × Pray _____

10. Ali Chuk × Bone Gap _____

Copyright © 2003 by John Wiley & Sons, Inc.

71. Bubble-Bath Math

When multiplying mixed numbers, first change the mixed number to an improper fraction and then multiply. Example:

$$2\frac{1}{2} \times 1\frac{1}{4} = \frac{5}{2} \times \frac{5}{4} = \frac{25}{8} = 3\frac{1}{8}$$

★ Multiply the mixed number in the larger center bubble with each of the mixed numbers, regular fractions, or whole numbers in the smaller bubbles.

1. _____
2. _____
3. _____
4. _____
5. _____
6. _____
7. _____
8. _____
9. _____
10. _____

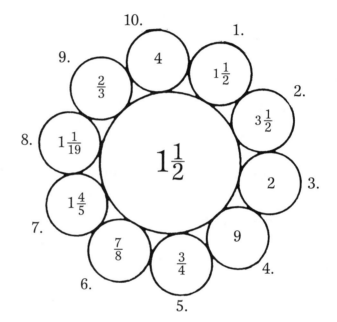

11. _____
12. _____
13. _____
14. _____
15. _____
16. _____
17. _____
18. _____
19. _____
20. _____

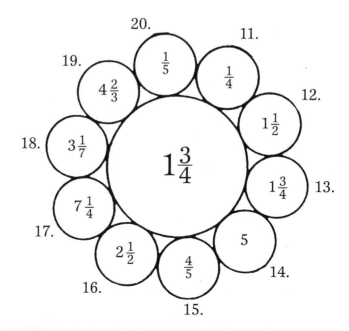

Copyright © 2003 by John Wiley & Sons, Inc.

72. The Zippy Way to Equivalent Fractions

QUICK ACCESS
information

<table>
<tr><td>QUICK ACCESS INFORMATION → Fractions that represent the same number are called equivalent fractions.</td></tr>
</table>

Here is the zippy or quick way to obtain equivalent fractions: Multiply the top (numerator) and the bottom (denominator) of the fraction by the same number. Our examples will use the numbers 4 and 5.

	the fraction	the equivalent fraction		the fraction	the equivalent fraction
	$\frac{2}{3}$ multiplied by $\frac{4}{4}$	$=$ $\frac{8}{12}$		$\frac{3}{4}$ multiplied by $\frac{5}{5}$	$=$ $\frac{8}{12}$

★   Complete the chart below.

Fraction	Number Multiplied By	Equivalent Fraction
$\frac{1}{2}$	$\frac{5}{5}$	
$\frac{3}{4}$	$\frac{7}{7}$	
$\frac{7}{8}$	$\frac{9}{9}$	
$\frac{7}{11}$	$\frac{11}{11}$	
$\frac{4}{5}$	$\frac{4}{4}$	
$\frac{1}{3}$	$\frac{3}{3}$	
$\frac{2}{9}$	$\frac{6}{6}$	
$\frac{3}{5}$	$\frac{2}{2}$	
$\frac{5}{6}$	$\frac{9}{9}$	
$\frac{3}{8}$	$\frac{8}{8}$	

Copyright © 2003 by John Wiley & Sons, Inc.

73. Division of Fractions: Part One

QUICK ACCESS INFORMATION ➜ To divide fractions, multiply the first fraction by the reciprocal of the second fraction. For example:

$$\frac{3}{4} \div \frac{1}{2} = \frac{3}{4} \times \frac{2}{1} = \frac{6}{4} = 1\frac{2}{4} = 1\frac{1}{2}$$

★ Each answer corresponds to a letter. Put the letters in the order of the problems to spell one of the most important things to a teenager. Answer in simplest form.

1. $\frac{1}{7} \div \frac{1}{8} =$ (I)   3

2. $\frac{3}{4} \div \frac{1}{4} =$ (O) $1\frac{3}{7}$

3. $\frac{2}{3} \div \frac{1}{8} =$ (V) $1\frac{1}{7}$

4. $\frac{7}{8} \div \frac{1}{4} =$ (E) $1\frac{1}{3}$

5. $\frac{5}{7} \div \frac{1}{2} =$ (D) $5\frac{1}{3}$

6. $\frac{2}{3} \div \frac{7}{8} =$ (A) $1\frac{7}{8}$

7. $\frac{3}{8} \div \frac{1}{5} =$ (M) $2\frac{6}{7}$

8. $\frac{4}{7} \div \frac{1}{5} =$ (G) $\frac{16}{21}$

9. $\frac{2}{9} \div \frac{1}{6} =$ (S) $3\frac{1}{5}$

10. $\frac{4}{5} \div \frac{1}{4} =$ (E) $3\frac{1}{2}$

One of the most important things to a teenager:

___ ___ ___ ___ ___   ___ ___ ___ ___ ___
 1   2   3   4   5   6   7   8   9   10

Copyright © 2003 by John Wiley & Sons, Inc.

NAME _____ DATE _____

74. Division of Fractions: Part Two

QUICK ACCESS
information

QUICK ACCESS INFORMATION ➡ To divide mixed numbers, first write the mixed numbers as improper fractions. For example: $1\frac{1}{2} \div 1\frac{1}{4} = \frac{3}{2} \div \frac{5}{4}$ (Improper Fractions). Then multiply by the reciprocal:

$$\frac{3}{2} \times \frac{4}{5} = \frac{12}{10} = 1\frac{2}{10} = 1\frac{1}{5}$$

★ **Each answer corresponds to a letter. Put the letters in the order of the problems to spell the most exciting thing for a student to own. Answer in simplest form.**

1. $1\frac{1}{2} \div 1\frac{1}{3} =$ (T) $1\frac{4}{9}$

2. $2\frac{1}{2} \div 1\frac{1}{2} =$ (O) $\frac{44}{65}$

3. $3\frac{1}{4} \div 2\frac{1}{4} =$ (L) $1\frac{11}{17}$

4. $2\frac{1}{5} \div 3\frac{1}{4} =$ (E) $\frac{5}{8}$

5. $4\frac{3}{4} \div 1\frac{3}{8} =$ (B) $\frac{1}{2}$

6. $3\frac{1}{3} \div 2\frac{1}{2} =$ (U) $1\frac{2}{3}$

7. $1\frac{1}{4} \div 2\frac{1}{2} =$ (A) $1\frac{1}{8}$

8. $2\frac{1}{5} \div 1\frac{3}{4} =$ (O) $1\frac{1}{3}$

9. $3\frac{1}{2} \div 2\frac{1}{8} =$ (I) $1\frac{9}{35}$

10. $3\frac{1}{4} \div 5\frac{1}{5} =$ (M) $3\frac{5}{11}$

The most exciting thing to own:

___ ___ ___ ___ ___ ___ ___ ___ ___ ___
1   2   3   4   5   6   7   8   9   10

Copyright © 2003 by John Wiley & Sons, Inc.

75. Dividing Whole Numbers and Mixed Numbers By Fractions

★ Complete the following problems.

1. $9 \div \frac{1}{3}$

6. $11 \div \frac{5}{6}$

5. $7 \div \frac{6}{7}$

Divide Whole Numbers by Fractions

2. $8 \div \frac{3}{4}$

3. $32 \div \frac{4}{9}$

4. $27 \div \frac{5}{7}$

7. $1\frac{1}{2} \div \frac{2}{3}$

12. $1\frac{1}{4} \div \frac{1}{2}$

11. $1\frac{7}{8} \div \frac{2}{3}$

Divide Mixed Numbers by Fractions

8. $4\frac{1}{2} \div \frac{1}{7}$

9. $3\frac{1}{3} \div \frac{1}{3}$

10. $5\frac{1}{4} \div \frac{1}{4}$

1. _____

2. _____

3. _____

4. _____

5. _____

6. _____

7. _____

8. _____

9. _____

10. _____

11. _____

12. _____

Copyright © 2003 by John Wiley & Sons, Inc.

76. Fraction Squares

★ Here are four sets of connected squares containing fractions. Above each set are instruction telling you whether to add, subtract, multiply, or divide. Place answers in the simplest form on the appropriate lines below each set. The first answer in simplest form on the appropriate lines below each set. The first answer is in place to get you started.

Copyright © 2003 by John Wiley & Sons, Inc.

SET 1:
Add top fractions
to bottom fractions.

SET 2:
Subtract bottom fractions
from top fractions.

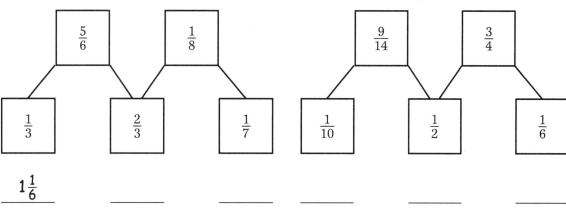

$1\frac{1}{6}$ _____   _____   _____   _____

_____   _____

SET 3:
Multiply bottom fractions
by top fractions.

SET 4:
Divide top fractions
by bottom fractions.

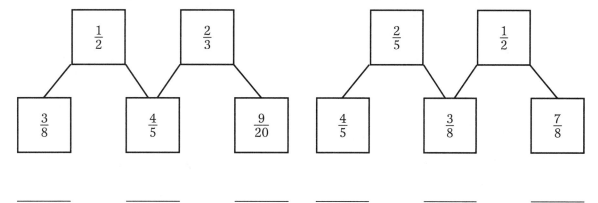

_____   _____   _____   _____

_____   _____   _____   _____

77. Fractions Are A Breeze

★ **Calculate each fraction problem below. Read the wind speed information before starting.**

Wind Speed Information from Meteorologists

A breeze is said to be any wind from 4 to 31 miles per hour (mph).

A gale is any wind from 32 to 63 mph.

A storm is any wind from 64 to 75 mph.

A hurricane is any wind 76 mph and higher.

1. Add $\frac{1}{2}$ of the lowest wind speed of a gale to the lowest wind speed of a hurricane _____ mph

2. $\frac{1}{3}$ of the highest wind speed of a storm is _____ mph.

3. $\frac{1}{8}$ of the lowest wind speed of a gale is _____ mph.

4. Add $\frac{1}{4}$ of the lowest wind speed of a gale to the lowest wind speed of a breeze. _____ mph.

5. What fraction is the lowest wind speed of a gale to the lowest wind speed of a storm? _____

6. What fraction is the highest wind speed of a breeze to the highest wind speed of a storm? _____

7. Subtract the lowest wind speed of a breeze from $\frac{1}{4}$ of the lowest wind speed of a hurricane. _____ mph

8. What fraction is the lowest wind speed of a breeze to the lowest wind speed of a hurricane? _____

9. What fraction is the highest speed of a gale to the highest speed of a storm? _____

10. What is the weather called when the wind is $\frac{1}{4}$ of the lowest wind speed of a storm? _____

Copyright © 2003 by John Wiley & Sons, Inc.

78. Life Span Math Questions: Part One
(Expressing Decimal and Fraction Equivalents)

★ **Each year has 12 months. Often it is necessary to express that year as a fraction or a decimal. Answer the following questions, then fill in the "Same As" column. The first one is completed for you.**

Copyright © 2003 by John Wiley & Sons, Inc.

	Number of Months	Same As
1. How many months is 0.25 of a year?	3	$\frac{1}{4}$ of a year
2. How many months is 0.5 of a year?		
3. How many months is 0.75 of a year?		
4. How many months is $\frac{1}{2}$ of a year?		
5. How many months is $\frac{1}{4}$ of a year?		
6. How many months is $\frac{1}{3}$ of a year?		
7. How many months is 2.0 years?		
8. How many months is 2.5 years?		
9. How many months is 2.75 years?		
10. How many months is $\frac{2}{3}$ of a year?		
11. How many months is 3.25 years?		
12. How many months is 3.75 years?		
13. How many months is 2.25 years?		
14. How many months is 4.5 years?		
15. How many months is $17\frac{1}{2}$ years?		
16. How many months is $21\frac{3}{4}$ years?		

79. Life Span Math Questions: Part Two
(Expressing Fractions as Decimals and Decimals as Fractions)

The following are the ages of some of the world's most wonderful people.

Kathy	50.5 years
Karrie	22.25 years
Alan	$50\frac{3}{4}$ years
Kevin	13.25 years
Marlene	$47.3\overline{3}$ years

Eugene	$48\frac{2}{3}$ years
Wanda	47.5 years
Christa	26.75 years
Tony	22.25 years
Carol	$49.3\overline{3}$ years

Mr. Carpenter	82.25 years
Mike	18.75 years
Jim	$24\frac{1}{2}$ years
Clifford	$47\frac{1}{3}$ years
Emil	48.75 years

★ **Using the information above and the data from worksheet 78, answer the following questions. (Be careful—some answers are in months and some are in years.)**

1. How many months older is Carol than Eugene? _____

2. How old is Kevin in months? _____

3. What is the total in months of Karrie's and Tony's ages? _____

4. How many months older is Christa than Kevin? _____

5. How many years older is Wanda than Mike? _____

6. How many years older is Emil than Jim? _____

7. What is the total in months of Karrie's age and Kathy's age? _____

8. What is the total in months of Carol's age, Eugene's age, and Jim's age? _____

9. How many years younger is Christa than Alan? _____

10. Who is older, Marlene or Clifford? _____

Copyright © 2003 by John Wiley & Sons, Inc.

Copyright © 2003 by John Wiley & Sons, Inc.

NAME _____   DATE _____

80. Expressing Fractions as Decimals: Part One

★ **A. Complete the following.**

1. $\frac{3}{4} = 0.\underline{\hspace{1cm}}5$

2. $\frac{1}{4} = 0.2\underline{\hspace{1cm}}$

3. $7\frac{1}{2} = 7.\underline{\hspace{1cm}}$

4. $2\frac{4}{5} = 2.\underline{\hspace{1cm}}$

5. $\frac{1}{20} = 0.0\underline{\hspace{1cm}}$

6. $\frac{3}{8} = 0.3\underline{\hspace{1cm}}\ \underline{\hspace{1cm}}$

7. $\frac{9}{10} = 0.\underline{\hspace{1cm}}$

8. $\frac{4}{9} = 0.4\underline{\hspace{1cm}}4\overline{4}$

9. $\frac{1}{10} = 0.\underline{\hspace{1cm}}$

10. $\frac{5}{8} = 0.\underline{\hspace{1cm}}2\underline{\hspace{1cm}}$

★ **B. Match the fractions to their decimal equivalents.**

$1\frac{1}{3}$	9.16
$7\frac{1}{5}$	2.6
$\frac{1}{2}$	0.7
$\frac{103}{1000}$	$1.33\overline{3}$
$9\frac{4}{25}$	0.32
$\frac{8}{25}$	0.5
$2\frac{3}{5}$	7.2
$\frac{7}{10}$	0.103

81. Expressing Fractions as Decimals: Part Two

★ Change the following fractions to decimals.

★ **Bonus Question:** Place the answers with the star ★ into the puzzle to make the sum or total match the answers of 32 and 23.

1. $3\frac{1}{10}$ _____ ★

2. $4\frac{1}{4}$ _____ ★

3. $\frac{1}{3}$ _____

4. $4\frac{1}{5}$ _____ ★

5. $3\frac{1}{4}$ _____

6. $2\frac{1}{8}$ _____

7. $2\frac{3}{4}$ _____ ★

8. $2\frac{9}{10}$ _____ ★

9. $7\frac{3}{5}$ _____

10. $14\frac{1}{10}$ _____ ★

11. $3\frac{1}{2}$ _____ ★

12. $2\frac{2}{5}$ _____

13. $7\frac{3}{10}$ _____ ★

14. $8\frac{7}{10}$ _____ ★

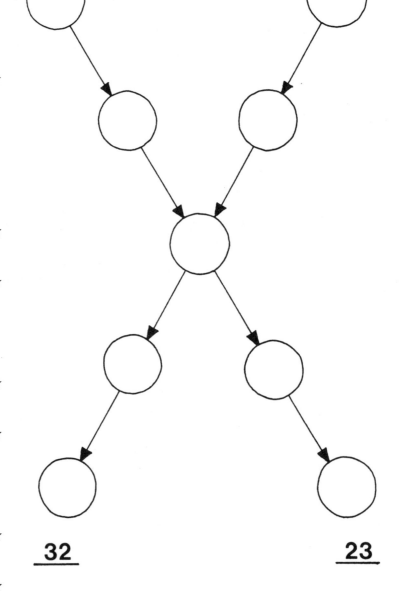

32   **23**

Copyright © 2003 by John Wiley & Sons, Inc.

82. The Fraction Name Game

★ **Bighampton Butler Jones is concerned about his name. He thinks it weighs too much. Let's take a look at it and see for ourselves. Answer the questions below his name.**

BIGHAMPTON BUTLER JONES

24lb. 9lb. 12lb. 16lb. 4lb. 14lb. 11lb. 22lb. 3lb. 5lb.   24lb. 4lb. 22lb. 15lb. 2lb. 5lb.   30lb. 3lb. 5lb. 2lb. 10lb.

1. What is the total weight of his name? _____

2. Use the weight of the "I" as the numerator (top) and the weight of one of the "B"s for a denominator (bottom). What fraction does this make? _____
   In simplest form: _____

3. Use the weight of the "G" for a numerator and the weight of one of the "B"s for the denominator. What fraction does this make? _____
   In simplest form: _____

4. Use the weight of an "N" for a numerator and the weight of an "S" for a denominator. What fraction does this make? _____
   In simplest form: _____

5. Use the weight of the "P" for the numerator and the combined weight of both the "T"s for the denominator. What fraction does this make? _____
   In simplest form: _____

6. Add the weight of the "M" to the weight of the "A" for a numerator and add the weight of the "L" to the weight of both the "B"s for a denominator. What fraction does this make? _____ In simplest form: _____

7. Use the weight of the "R" as the numerator and use the weight of the "N" subtracted from the weight of the "L" as the denominator. What fraction does this make? _____ In simplest form: _____

8. Combine the weight of the two "B"s and add it to the weight of the "J" as the numerator and use the total weight of his name as the denominator. What fraction does this make? _____ In simplest form: _____

Copyright © 2003 by John Wiley & Sons, Inc.

83. Symplifying Fractions

QUICK ACCESS
information

QUICK ACCESS INFORMATION ➜ To simplify a fraction, we must find the single largest number that will go evenly into both the top (called the numerator) and the bottom (called the denominator) of the fraction. For example, to simplify $\frac{2}{8}$ we can divide both the top and the bottom by 2. Therefore, $\frac{2}{8}$ is simplified as $\frac{1}{4}$. $\frac{2 \div 2}{8 \div 2} = \frac{1}{4}$. Since both the numerator and denominator of $\frac{1}{4}$ are "smaller" than the numerator and denominator of $\frac{2}{8}$, $\frac{1}{4}$ is called a "reduced" fraction.

★ Below are a few friends of mine who need to go on a diet in order to play volleyball. Put the amount they need to lose over their body weight and reduce this fraction. The first one is done for you.

Name	Body Weight (in Pounds)	Pounds Needed to Lose	Fraction	"Reduced" Fraction
Flipper Twerpski	200 lbs.	50 lbs.	$\frac{50}{200}$	$\frac{1}{4}$
Akira Tsutsumi	350 lbs.	200 lbs.		
Kimmel Florentine	168 lbs.	18 lbs.		
Molly Sousa	132 lbs.	22 lbs.		
Bighampton Butler Jones	260 lbs.	65 lbs.		
Wonder Skyblue Jones	148 lbs.	30 lbs.		
Marylou Pettigrew	225 lbs.	75 lbs.		
Clyde Manning	98 lbs.	2 lbs.		
Horizon Sunshine	286 lbs.	98 lbs.		
Moira Moonbeam	175 lbs.	3 lbs.		

Copyright © 2003 by John Wiley & Sons, Inc.

84. Definition Puzzle on Fraction Terms

★ Place the answers to this puzzle in their correct locations across or down. A Choice Box has been provided.

Copyright © 2003 by John Wiley & Sons, Inc.

ACROSS

1. In $\frac{1}{2}$, the 2 is this
5. $\frac{3}{4}$ is this type of fraction
6. The top most amount
10. The name of a whole number and a fraction
12. When one fraction is not like another, they are like this
14. Opposite of under

DOWN

2. When two or more things or numbers are equal
3. In $\frac{7}{8}$, the 7 is this
4. $\frac{11}{4}$ is this type of fraction
7. Not all of something
8. Plain or ordinary
9. Another name for a simplified fraction
11. The bottom or least amount
13. Grouped numbers
15. All of something

CHOICE BOX

denominator	over	numerator	lowest	mixed
proper	part	unlike	common	improper
equivalent	whole	highest	reduced	sets

85. Skills Mastery Test—Fractions: Part One

★ **Add the following fractions:**

1. $\frac{1}{2} + \frac{1}{2} =$

2. $\frac{1}{4} + \frac{1}{4} =$

3. $\frac{3}{4} + \frac{3}{4} =$

4. $\frac{3}{4} + \frac{1}{8} =$

5. $\frac{7}{8} + \frac{5}{6} =$

6. $\frac{4}{5} + \frac{1}{9} =$

★ **Add these mixed numbers:**

7. $2\frac{1}{2} + 3\frac{1}{2} =$

8. $2\frac{1}{8} + 3\frac{5}{8} =$

9. $2\frac{1}{8} + 1\frac{3}{4} =$

10. $7\frac{1}{7} + 2\frac{5}{14} =$

11. $14\frac{1}{5} + 3\frac{7}{10} =$

12. $9\frac{2}{3} + 1\frac{1}{6} =$

★ **Subtract these fractions:**

13. $\frac{3}{4} - \frac{1}{4} =$

14. $\frac{4}{5} - \frac{2}{5} =$

15. $\frac{3}{14} - \frac{1}{7} =$

16. $\frac{5}{9} - \frac{1}{18} =$

17. $\frac{1}{2} - \frac{1}{8} =$

18. $\frac{61}{64} - \frac{5}{8} =$

★ **Subtract these mixed numbers:**

19. $3\frac{1}{2} - 1\frac{1}{2} =$

20. $9\frac{1}{4} - 2\frac{3}{4} =$

21. $7\frac{1}{7} - 6\frac{1}{7} =$

22. $3\frac{3}{8} - 1\frac{1}{2} =$

23. $2\frac{1}{2} - 1\frac{1}{4} =$

24. $3\frac{7}{11} - 1\frac{4}{11} =$

★ **Add the following:**

25. $1\frac{1}{2} + 7\frac{3}{4} + 1\frac{3}{8} + 4\frac{1}{16} + 2\frac{7}{8} =$

Copyright © 2003 by John Wiley & Sons, Inc.

86. Skills Mastery Test—Fractions: Part Two

★ **Express these fractions in simplest:**

1. $\frac{5}{15} =$

2. $\frac{15}{24} =$

3. $\frac{22}{132} =$

4. $\frac{200}{300} =$

★ **Multiply these fractions:**

5. $\frac{2}{3} \times \frac{1}{4} =$

6. $\frac{7}{8} \times \frac{1}{2} =$

7. $3\frac{1}{2} \times \frac{1}{4} =$

8. $4\frac{1}{4} \times 1\frac{1}{2} =$

★ **Divide the following fractions:**

9. $\frac{1}{4} \div \frac{1}{8} =$

10. $\frac{3}{4} \div \frac{1}{4} =$

11. $3\frac{2}{3} \div \frac{7}{9} =$

12. $1\frac{4}{5} \div 1\frac{2}{3} =$

★ **Express these fractions as decimals:**

13. $\frac{1}{2} =$

14. $\frac{2}{5} =$

15. $2\frac{1}{4} =$

16. $7\frac{1}{5}$

★ **Solve these:**

17. $\frac{1}{2}$ of 42 =

18. $\frac{2}{3}$ of 66 =

19. $\frac{1}{5}$ of 20 =

20. $\frac{3}{4}$ of 40 =

★ **Answer these:**

21. x + y =

22. B   A =

23. x   A =

24. x + B =

25. x + A + y =

$x = \frac{1}{2}$

$y = \frac{1}{3}$

$A = \frac{4}{5}$

$B = \frac{1}{7}$

Copyright © 2003 by John Wiley & Sons, Inc.

SECTION 4

UNDERSTANDING PERCENT FOR SKILL DEVELOPMENT

87. Percent Basics
(Fractions to % and % to Decimals)

QUICK ACCESS
information

QUICK ACCESS INFORMATION ➜ The word "percent" means hundredths. We use the symbol % or % to indicate percent. Here are three examples of how to change a fraction to a decimal and then to a percent.

$$\frac{17}{100} = 0.17 \text{ or } 17\%$$

$$\frac{11}{25} = \frac{44}{100} = 0.4\,4 = 44\%$$

$$\frac{124}{100} = 1.24 = 124\%$$

Copyright © 2003 by John Wiley & Sons, Inc.

★ A letter appears under some answers. On the lines at the bottom of the page, put the letters that match the answer in order to spell the most important things to teenagers.

★ A. Change these fractions to a percent.

1. $\frac{23}{100}$ = ____ **N**   2. $\frac{37}{100}$ = ____ **T**   3. $\frac{99}{100}$ = ____ **E**   4. $\frac{12}{50}$ = ____   5. $\frac{117}{100}$ = ____ **E**

6. $\frac{24}{25}$ = ____   7. $\frac{11}{100}$ = ____ **H**   8. $\frac{29}{100}$ = ____   9. $\frac{17}{50}$ = ____ **I**   10. $\frac{32}{100}$ = ____

★ B. To change a percent to a decimal, change the percent to a fraction over 100, then to a decimal. For example: 24% = $\frac{24}{100}$ = 0.24. Change these percents to decimals.

1. 12% = ____ **R**   2. 49% = ____   3. 7% = ____   4. 98% = ____ **S**   5. 64% = ____

6. 37% = ____ **F**   7. 90% = ____ **I**   8. 14% = ____   9. 99% = ____ **R**   10. 142% = ____ **D**

The most important things to teenagers:

___ ___ ___ ___ ___   ___ ___ ___ ___ ___ ___ ___
37% 11% 117% 0.90 0.99   0.37 0.12 34% 99% 23% 1.42 0.98

88. Understanding Values Less than 1%

QUICK ACCESS
information

> **QUICK ACCESS INFORMATION** ➜ Some percentages are less than 1%.
> This means you usually have a very small amount of something. Remember, if
> 1% is written 0.01 as a decimal, then 0.1% would be written 0.001; 0.01% would
> be written 0.0001; 0.001% would be written 0.00001; and so on.

★ **A.** Follow the pattern to learn where the decimal point goes in the following
questions.

1. 0.3%	_____	5. 0.009%	_____	9. 0.7%	_____
2. 0.03%	_____	6. 0.09%	_____	10. 0.00007%	_____
3. 0.4%	_____	7. 0.9%	_____	11. 0.007%	_____
4. 0.04%	_____	8. 0.5%	_____	12. 0.07%	_____

★ **B.** Follow the pattern to learn what the percent is for each of these decimal
numbers.

1. 0.009	_____ %	5. 0.0092	_____ %	9. 0.00808	_____ %
2. 0.0009	_____ %	6. 0.00842	_____ %	10. 0.000004	_____ %
3. 0.00009	_____ %	7. 0.00037	_____ %	11. 0.00123	_____ %
4. 0.005	_____ %	8. 0.0073	_____ %	12. 0.000029	_____ %

★ **C.** Shade in 53% of the blocks.

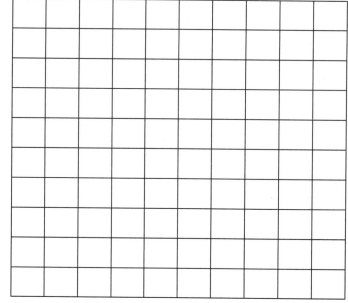

Copyright © 2003 by John Wiley & Sons, Inc.

Copyright © 2003 by John Wiley & Sons, Inc.

89. Fraction, Decimal, and Percent Equivalents

There are three basic ways to display and therefore compare numbers. They are:
(1) As a fraction: $\frac{1}{4}$; (2) As a decimal: 0.25; and (3) As a percent: 25%.

★ **Complete this chart of fractions, decimals, and percentages to find their equivalents.**

Fraction	Decimal	Percent	Fraction	Decimal	Percent
$\frac{1}{2}$			$\frac{1}{4}$		
	0.75			$0.16\bar{6}$	
		$12\frac{1}{2}\%$		0.1	
$\frac{1}{3}$			$\frac{5}{8}$		
	0.2				30%
		70%		$0.83\bar{3}$	
		60%	$\frac{4}{5}$		

90. Greater Than 100%

QUICK ACCESS
information

QUICK ACCESS INFORMATION ➡ When we convert a decimal number to a percent, we move the decimal point two places to the right.

For example: 2.45 = 245%. In this normal case, the decimal point is not used after the 5. Notice that the 2 is to the left of the decimal point in 2.45.

★ **Change these decimal numbers to percentages. Then match the answers to the written form on the right.**

1.25 = _____ %   Three hundred seventy-two percent

2.26 = _____ %   Six hundred ninety-eight percent

3.72 = _____ %   Seven hundred ninety-one percent

4.59 = _____ %   One hundred ninety percent

5.46 = _____ %   Three hundred seventy percent

6.98 = _____ %   Eight thousand seven hundred eleven percent

1.03 = _____ %   Five hundred forty-six percent

7.91 = _____ %   Three thousand four hundred thirty-four percent

1.9   = _____ %   Two hundred percent

3.7   = _____ %   Four thousand seven hundred percent

34.34 = _____ %   One hundred three percent

92.01 = _____ %   One hundred twenty-five percent

87.11 = _____ %   Two hundred twenty-six percent

2.00 = _____ %   Four hundred fifty-nine percent

47.00 = _____ %   Nine thousand two hundred one percent

Copyright © 2003 by John Wiley & Sons, Inc.

91. Percent Stew

★ Here is a great variety of numbers that need to be turned into percents. Choose the answers from the Choice Box below. Some answers are used more than once; some are not used at all.

1. $\frac{9}{10} =$ _____

2. $1.43 =$ _____

3. $\frac{1}{2} =$ _____

4. $0.75 =$ _____

5. $0.275 =$ _____

6. $\frac{3}{4} =$ _____

7. $0.755 =$ _____

8. $\frac{11}{4} =$ _____

9. $3\frac{1}{4} =$ _____

10. $2\frac{1}{2} =$ _____

11. $2\frac{3}{100} =$ _____

12. $\frac{61}{51} =$ _____

13. $\frac{9}{5} =$ _____

14. $7.00 =$ _____

15. $2.57 =$ _____

16. $\frac{1}{100} =$ _____

17. $\frac{37}{10} =$ _____

18. $9.0 =$ _____

19. $\frac{87}{100} =$ _____

20. $\frac{7}{2} =$ _____

21. $\frac{28}{25} =$ _____

22. $3.5 =$ _____

23. $\frac{7}{7} =$ _____

24. $2.17 =$ _____

CHOICE BOX

90%	180%	350%	275%	900%	75%
122%	236%	370%	$27\frac{1}{2}$%	207%	$75\frac{1}{2}$%
100%	700%	112%	257%	333%	143%
74%	50%	87%	203%	471%	217%
19.5%	1%	71%	325%	18%	250%

Copyright © 2003 by John Wiley & Sons, Inc.

92. Relating Percent To Diagrams

★   Study the diagrams below. A certain percentage has been separated from
what the value of the figure was. Using the percentages given, calculate the
amount separated from the value of each figure and the amount left over.

1.

Was
4,000

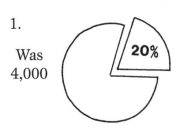

_____
Separated

_____
Left

2.

Was
9,000

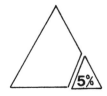

_____
Separated

_____
Left

3.

Was
3,050

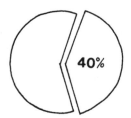

_____
Separated

_____
Left

4.

Was
5,440

_____
Separated

_____
Left

5.

Was
1,720

_____
Separated

_____
Left

6.

Was
375

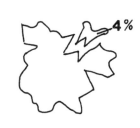

_____
Separated

_____
Left

7.

Was
180

_____
Separated

_____
Left

8.

Was
2,400

_____
Separated

_____
Left

9.

Was
890

_____
Separated

_____
Left

10.

Was
28,000

_____
Separated

_____
Left

Copyright © 2003 by John Wiley & Sons, Inc.

93. Presidential Percentages

★ Each U.S. President's name in the Choice Box has a number beside it. Your task is to calculate the answers and place the president's name in the puzzle that corresponds with the problem number and the number beside the president's name.

Copyright © 2003 by John Wiley & Sons, Inc.

ACROSS

1. 35% of 798
3. 14% of 654
6. 75% of 720
9. 25% of 125
10. 75% of 860
13. 80% of 204
15. 24% of 175
16. 12.5% of 96
17. 145% of 327

DOWN

1. 225% of 454
2. 87.5% of 900
4. 5% of 24
5. 10% of 720
7. 647% of 94
8. 60% of 81
11. 20% of 67
12. 84% of 84
14. 89% of 45

CHOICE BOX (Place last names only in the puzzle.)

Millard <u>Fillmore</u>, 40.05	Harry S <u>Truman</u>, 91.56	Abraham <u>Lincoln</u>, 48.6
Herbert C. <u>Hoover</u>, 540	Gerald <u>Ford</u>, 31.25	William H. <u>Taft</u>, 163.2
James <u>Madison</u>, 12	Rutherford B. <u>Hayes</u>, 13.4	John <u>Tyler</u>, 279.3
Franklin <u>Pierce</u>, 474.15	James <u>Buchanan</u>, 645	Woodrow <u>Wilson</u>, 72
John <u>Adams</u>, 70.56	James <u>Monroe</u>, 42	Martin <u>Van Buren</u>, 608.18
Zachary <u>Taylor</u>, 1012.5	Franklin D. <u>Roosevelt</u>, 1.2	Theodore <u>Roosevelt</u>, 787.5

94. Percent of A Hot Rod By Weight

★ Below is a 1932 Ford 3-window coupe (The Li'l Deuce Coupe). We have taken it apart and weighed the major pieces. The total weight of the car must be calculated first; then the percentages by weight of the pieces of the hot rod can be calculated.

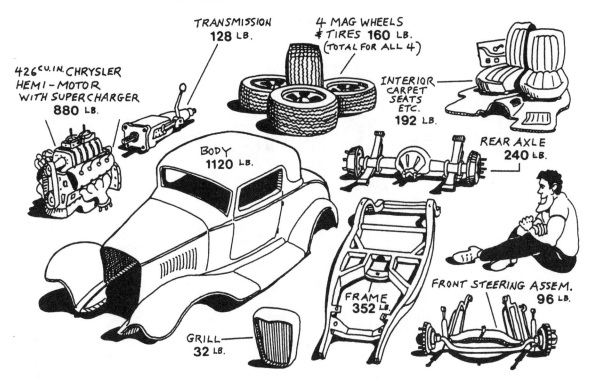

Copyright © 2003 by John Wiley & Sons, Inc.

1. What is the total weight of the hot rod? _____ lbs.

2. What percent of the total weight is the frame? _____ %

3. What percent of the total weight are the mag wheels and tires? _____ %

4. What percent of the total weight is the weight of the fram, the tires and the transmission? _____ %

5. What percent of the car weight is the motor weight? _____ %

6. What percent of the total weight is the body? _____ %

7. What percent of the total weight is the interior and the grill? _____ %

8. What percent of the total weight is the transmission? _____ %

9. What percent of the total weight is the rear axle? _____ %

10. What percent of the total weight is the front steering assembly? _____ %

95. Geo Math

★ Many of the place names in Alaska are derived from the rich Inuit language in the area. In order to print the names of the places on the map, you must calculate the math problems on the map itself and also calculate the map problems beside the place names. The answers on the map will match the correct place name answers.

Copyright © 2003 by John Wiley & Sons, Inc.

Map problems:
(7 x 9)
(40 + 47)
(100 − 40.5625)
(300% + 325%)
(3 x 25)
(126 x 350)
(7 x 343)
(3 x 8)
(331 + .38)
(20 x 115)
(5871+55138)
(3.15 x 5)
(777 − 444)
(999 + 33)
(133 x 18)

1. Anchorage (92 × 25)

2. Quinhagak (247 × 247)

3. Unalakleet (49 × 49)

4. Kotzebue (110 − 35)

5. Kobuk (62 + 25)

6. Alakanuk (42% of 789)

7. Fairbanks (63 × 700)

8. Takotna (753 − 729)

9. Ketchikan (16 × 149.625)

10. Bettles (Change 6.25 to a %)

11. Kivalina (125% of 47.55)

12. Yakataga (654 − 638.25)

13. Anaktuvuk Pass (50 + 13)

14. Skagway (456 − 123)

15. Juneau (1909 − 877)

96. Monster Math

Raw Monster Facts				
Name	**Length or Height**	**Weight**	**Speed on Land**	**Speed in Water**
Bigfoot (Sasquatch)	10 ft. (height)	730 lbs.	8 mph	3 mph
The Loch Ness Monster	37 ft. (length)	7150 lbs.	0 mph	74 mph
Abominable Snowman (Yeti)	8 ft. (height)	520 lbs.	9 mph	4 mph
Ogopogo (Serpent)	24 ft. (length)	2860 lbs.	0 mph	40 mph

1. What percent of Ogopogo's speed in water is the Abominable Snowman's speed in water? _____

2. How much <u>taller</u> by percent is Bigfoot than the Abominable Snowman? _____

3. How much <u>heavier</u> by percent is the Loch Ness Monster than Ogopogo? _____

4. Five members of a Bigfoot family (including women and children) weigh 20% of what the Loch Ness Monster weighs. What is the weight of the Bigfoot family? _____

5. The Abominable Snowman's wife weighs 25% less than her husband. What is her weight? _____

6. How much <u>faster</u> (water and land) by percent is the Abominable Snowman than Bigfoot? By Water: _____ By Land: _____

7. 20.7% of Ogopogo's speed on land is _____.

8. 22% of the Loch Ness Monster's weight is body fat. How many pounds is this? _____

Copyright © 2003 by John Wiley & Sons, Inc.

97. Calculating Percent of Gain or Increase

★ **Round your answers to the nearest whole number.**

1. Once upon a time, Fox tried to get some grapes by jumping. He couldn't reach the grapes that contained a total of 92 calories. On the last jump, he landed on a picnic table and ate the food on the table, consuming 748 calories. **How many more calories did he consume than were in the grapes?** _____ **Percent of increase in calories is** _____.

2. A Fairy Princess kissed a frog but nothing happened. She in fact had to kiss 64 frogs and 12 toads before one turned into a Prince Charming. Now, kissing toads and frogs is yucky. Her sister, the Tooth Fairy, had to kiss 73 frogs and 17 toads for a Prince Charming to appear for her. **How many more amphibians (frogs and toads) did the Tooth Fairy kiss than her sister?** _____ **What percent of increase in amphibian kissing occurred with the Tooth Fairy?** _____

3. Little Miss Muffet sat on a tuffet eating her curds and whey. Her supply of this product, however, was down to 12 pounds. A new shipment came in and she now has 69 pounds of curds and whey. **What was the amount of the shipment?** _____ **What was the percent of increase?** _____

4. Humpty Dumpty sat on a wall for 38 hours trying to figure out why his parents would call a kid Humpty in the first place, especially with a last name like Dumpty. "Perhaps it's because they were eggheads," he chortled. Anyway, after sitting there for a total of 89 hours he decided to get cracking. Suddenly all the king's horses and all the king's men shook the ground, making the wall vibrate—and the rest is history. **How many more hours did Humpty sit on the wall after the first 38?** _____ **What was the percent of increase in hours?** _____ **(No scrambled answers, please!)**

5. Androcles the Christian was scheduled to be fed to the lions in the Roman Colosseum, but no lions could be found. "Ship him to Detroit," the crowd shouted, but that was the wrong type of lion. Finally, a lion was found after 67 days. When Androcles was thrown in, the lion only licked his face because Androcles had pulled a thorn from his paw 6 months before. No other lions were found, so Androcles was released after 322 days in captivity. **What is the number of days Androcles stayed in captivity after the lion was found?** _____ **What was the percent of increase in days before release?** _____

Copyright © 2003 by John Wiley & Sons, Inc.

98. Calculating Percent of Loss or Decrease

★   **Round your answers to the nearest whole number.**

1. Rapunzel's hair was 35 feet long, but she used the wrong shampoo one day and now it is 25 feet. It was a bad hair day.

   Number of feet lost: _____

   Percent of loss: _____

2. A certain mouse called Hickory Dickory Dock ran up a clock at 195 mph; however, she was hit by the swinging pendulum (no permanent damage), but it slowed her to 86 mph.

   Number of mph lost: _____

   Percent of loss: _____

3. Three serious Billy Goats Gruff were doing their bridge thing when a company called Troll Inc. sued them for damages and loss of reputation. The goats had 420 bales of hay and were left with 110 bales after the court action.

   Number of bales lost: _____

   Percent of loss: _____

4. Three blind mice were in dispute with a farmer's wife and had their tails cut off. Normally with their tails on, each mouse was 7 inches long. Without their tails, they were 5 inches long.

   Total number of inches lost: _____

   Percent of mouse length lost: _____

5. Once upon a time a princess tried to rest on several mattresses, but got very little sleep because some joker had put a single pea under the bottom mattress. Because she was so sensitive and delicate, it affected her emotionally. Anyway, out of 48 hours of possible sleep in 6 nights, she only got a total of 8 hours.

   Number of hours of lost sleep: _____

   Percent of hours of lost sleep: _____

6. A really uptight character named Rumplestiltskin would not tell 43 people his name. This was rough because he was the landlord of their apartment complex. Seven dwarfs from this group did, however, pick it up from some old fairy tale on the Internet. The rest couldn't pay their rent because they didn't know to whom to make their checks.

   Number of people unable to pay rent: _____

   Percent of people unable to pay rent: _____

Copyright © 2003 by John Wiley & Sons, Inc.

Copyright © 2003 by John Wiley & Sons, Inc.

99. Understanding Percent from the Decimal Place

QUICK ACCESS INFORMATION ➔ When you are changing a decimal to a percent, you must see that the hundredths place in the decimal number is the key to success in understanding. *For example:* In 0.34, the 4 is in the hundredths place, so we write 34%.

Look at this chart to see how numbers fit into a pattern:

0.34	34%	0.034	3.4%
1.34	134%	0.0034	0.34%
71.34	7134%	0.003	0.3%

★ Study the patterns above and write the following decimal numbers as a percent. Then place the correct question number beside the written answers on the right.

1. 0.03 = _____%   _____ zero point three percent

2. 0.008 = _____%   _____ one point nine percent

3. 0.09 = _____%   _____ zero point eight percent

4. 0.009 = _____%   _____ six point three percent

5. 0.003 = _____%   _____ zero point three four percent

6. 0.11 = _____%   _____ eight point four three percent

7. 0.019 = _____%   _____ one point three seven percent

8. 0.063 = _____%   _____ zero point one percent

9. 0.0072 = _____%   _____ two point seven four percent

10. 0.0034 = _____%   _____ zero point zero one percent

11. 0.0843 = _____%   _____ zero point seven two percent

12. 0.0137 = _____%   _____ eleven percent

13. 0.001 = _____%   _____ three percent

14. 0.0001 = _____%   _____ zero point nine percent

15. 0.0274 = _____%   _____ nine percent

100. Definition Puzzle on Percent

★ Place the answers to this puzzle in their correct locations across or down. (A Choice Box has been provided.)

ACROSS

1. To figure out a math question
4. This means to multiply
7. A regular repeat of something
8. To reduce from one thing to another calculation
10. To change something to be something
11. To contrast

DOWN

2. What something is worth
3. Not wrong
5. The most important place in percent
6. If you have this, you have done your math correctly
9. 100 of this is all there is
12. An open area
13. To join similar things
14. A dot
15. The farthest down

CHOICE BOX

value	compare	convert	match	hundredth
percent	pattern	calculate	lowest	point
decrease	space	correct	of	success

Copyright © 2003 by John Wiley & Sons, Inc.

101. Skills Mastery Test—Percentage

★ **Complete the following questions:**

1. 20% of 98 = _____   2. 50% of 98 = _____   3. 35% of 98 = _____

4. 125% of 98 = _____   5. 165% of 98 = _____   6. 200% of 98 = _____

★ **Change these fractions to a percentage:**

7. $\frac{41}{100}$ = _____   8. $\frac{64}{100}$ = _____   9. $\frac{4}{5}$ = _____   10. $\frac{1}{10}$ = _____

11. $\frac{11}{5}$ = _____   12. $4\frac{1}{4}$ = _____   13. $\frac{7}{4}$ = _____   14. $2\frac{1}{2}$ = _____

★ **Change these decimals to percentages:**

15. 0.01 = _____   16. 0.42 = _____   17. 1.37 = _____

18. 0.0003 = _____   19. 3.19 = _____

★ **Change these written forms to numerical (number) forms:**

20. three percent = _____   21. seven and one-half percent = _____

★ **Complete the following chart:**

22.

Fraction	Decimal	Percent
$\frac{3}{4}$		
	0.2	

Copyright © 2003 by John Wiley & Sons, Inc.

SECTION 5

MONEY CONCEPTS FOR THE MODERN CLASSROOM

102. The Monthly Budget

★ You are finally living on your own in a totally cool apartment. Let's calculate your budget or cost of living for one month.

★ Your net income or your disposable income is $1,930.00 per month.

★ Some costs are fixed and have been put in place on your budget sheet. (These can't be avoided.) Some costs change with the circumstances of each month, like the cost of clothes. Some costs are unnecessary.

★ Distribute your $1,930.00 into the Budget Chart below. Place what is left over in savings.

Budget Chart

New Skateboard or Snowboard	Power Gas/Lights	Party Supplies	Laundry Fees	Club Registration
$_____	$200.00	$_____	$17.00	$_____
Cell Phone	Rent/Mortgage	Car Payment	Automobile Fuel/Oil	Automobile Repair
$_____	$575.00	$140.00	$_____	$75.00
Union Dues	Toiletries/ Haircuts	Eat at Joe's Fast Food Emporium	Cable or Satellite Fees	Internet Fees
$32.00	$_____	$_____	$37.00	$21.00
Water Bill	Repair Broken TV Set	Candy/ Junk Food	Parking Fees	Ordering Pizza
$50.00	$_____	$_____	$12.00	$_____
Movie Rentals	Payment on Engagement Ring Loan	Clothes	Telephone Bill	Groceries
$_____	$75.00	$_____	$_____	$_____

TOTAL $_____

Balance or amount left over is Savings $_____

Copyright © 2003 by John Wiley & Sons, Inc.

103. Better Buying Power—Division of Money

★ Underline the better buy. How much did you save on each unit? The first one has been done for you.

1. 3 yds. for $150.00 **OR** 6 yds. for $270.00   <u>$5.00 saved on each yard</u>

2. 5 lbs. for $115.00 **OR** 10 lbs. for $350.00   _____

3. 6 ft. for $150.00 **OR** 18 ft. for $432.00   _____

4. 4 ft. for $29.00 **OR** 8 ft. for $57.92   _____

5. 3 yds. for $2.94 **OR** 10 yds. for $31.20   _____

6. 5 lbs. for $35.00 **OR** 7 lbs. for $43.75   _____

7. 8 ft. for $40.00 **OR** 13 ft. for $68.25   _____

8. 8 yds. for $24.00 **OR** 2 yds. for $5.50   _____

9. 42 yds. for $37.80 **OR** 88 yds. for $78.32   _____

10. 5 oz. for $10.75 **OR** 12 oz. for $25.20   _____

11. 4 lbs. for $2.00 **OR** 17 lbs. for $8.33   _____

12. 6 ft. for $2.40 **OR** 19 ft. for $7.79   _____

13. 15 yds. for $7.20 **OR** 2 yds. for $1.00   _____

14. 12 oz. for $17.88 **OR** 15 oz. for $22.80   _____

15. 30 yds. for $4,950.00 **OR** 2 yds. for $340.00   _____

16. 16 ft. for $54.40 **OR** 10 ft. for $35.00   _____

17. 7 lbs. for $364.00 **OR** 17 lbs. for $918.00   _____

18. 10 oz. for $1.00 **OR** 361 oz. for $397.10   _____

19. 36 lbs. for $9.00 **OR** 11 lbs. for $2.42   _____

20. 1 ft. for $2.00 **OR** 827 ft. for $537.55   _____

Copyright © 2003 by John Wiley & Sons, Inc.

104. The True Cost of an Item—Hours of Work Required

★ You work for the John Henry Chocolate Bar Company. You make $7.00 per hour. After deductions, your net income or disposable income is $5.40 for every hour worked. Below is a list of items. Calculate how many hours it takes for you to work at the plant in Billings, Montana to pay for each item.

1. Inline skates: $113.40   _____ hours of work

2. Snowboard: $156.60   _____ hours of work

3. Party with friends: $70.20   _____ hours of work

4. A good pizza: $21.60   _____ hours of work

5. DVD Player: $172.80   _____ hours of work

6. High-quality sneakers or runners: $124.20   _____ hours of work

7. CD Player: $135.00   _____ hours of work

8. Name-brand blue jeans: $118.80   _____ hours of work

9. Engagement ring: $864.00   _____ hours of work

10. Vacation to warm resort: $8,375.40   _____ hours of work

11. A new car: $24,996.60   _____ hours of work

Copyright © 2003 by John Wiley & Sons, Inc.

105. Wages, Deductions, and Taxes

★ Bighampton Butler Jones has had three jobs in the last two years. Each job paid a different amount and had different deductions. Calculate his monthly net or disposable income after deductions for each job.

A. At the Car Wash
Hours of work in one week: <u>40</u>
Wages or salary per hour: <u>$6.75</u>

Deductions:
Income tax: <u>$13.84</u> per week
Social Security: <u>$17.55</u> per week
Health: <u>$47.00</u> per month

Based on a 4-Week Month
Hours per month: _____
Gross Income per month: _____

Income tax per month: _____
Social Security per month: _____
Health per month: _____
Net Income or Disposable
   Income After
   Deductions: ===============

B. At the Tire Shop
Hours of work in one week: <u>44</u>
Wages or salary per hour: <u>$6.95</u>

Deductions:
Income tax: <u>$17.47</u> per week
Social Security: <u>$19.88</u> per week

Based on a 4-Week Month
Hours per month: _____
Gross Income per month: _____

Income tax per month: _____
Social Security per month: _____
Net Income or Disposable
   Income After
   Deductions: ===============

C. At the Zoo
Regular hours of work in one
   week: <u>40</u>
Overtime hours per week: <u>17</u>
Wages or salary per hour for first
   40 hours a week $8.00 and $1\frac{1}{2}$
   times $8.00 for every hour
   after 40 hours per week

Deductions:
Income tax: <u>$48.46</u> per week
Social Security: <u>$34.06</u> per week

Based on a 4-Week Month
Regular hours per month: _____

Overtime hours per month: _____
Gross Income per month: _____

Income tax per month: _____
Social Security per month: _____
Net Income or Disposable
   Income After
   Deductions: ===============

Copyright © 2003 by John Wiley & Sons, Inc.

NAME _____ DATE _____

106. Money Stew (+, –): Part One

★ **A. Calculate the problems below.** <u>This is your money</u> in 15 different bank accounts!

1. $2.98 + $4.25 + $1.95 = _____

2. $4.27 + $3.27 + $4.54 = _____

3. $4.54 + $3.96 − $4.26 = _____

4. $3.60 + $3.40 + $3.18 = _____

5. $2.83 + $3.27 − $3.05 = _____

6. $3.40 − $1.92 − $0.22 = _____

7. $3.50 + $4.27 − $3.96 = _____

8. $4.02 + $3.83 − $3.60 = _____

9. $17.04 − $2.22 − $2.29 = _____

10. $3.17 + $2.42 − $1.19 = _____

11. $16.44 − $9.17 + $14.22 = _____

12. $3.71 + $2.49 − $1.22 = _____

13. $18.47 − $14.33 − $1.01 = _____

14. $18.92 + $42.76 + $86.97 = _____

15. $24.49 + $92.78 − $37.43 = _____

★ **B. Your friends at school are in serious need of your money. You are a nice person, so:**

1. You send Judy $2.75 from bank account 4. How much is left in bank account 4? _____

2. You give Jason $3.17 from bank account 2. How much is left in bank account 2? _____

3. You give Trevor $17.47 from bank account 14 in order to enter a bubble-gum blowing contest. How much is left in bank account 14? _____

4. You treat everyone to lunch from bank account 15. It costs you $79.84. How much do you have left in bank account 15? _____

5. See if you can complete this old worldly wise statement:

   A _____ and his _____ are soon _____.

Copyright © 2003 by John Wiley & Sons, Inc.

107. Money Stew (+, −, ×, ÷): Part Two

★ **A. Calculate the problems below. <u>This is your money</u> in 15 different bank accounts!**

1. $9.99 ÷ 3 + $14.77 =   _____

2. $372.20 + $984.30 + $227.94 =   _____

3. $3.94 ÷ 2 + $37.40 =   _____

4. $3.27 × 9 + $4.32 =   _____

5. $8.92 × 4 + $17.00 =   _____

6. $7.39 × 5 − $8.42 =   _____

7. $8.97 ÷ 3 + $6.21 =   _____

8. $7.77 × 5 + $42.00 =   _____

9. $3.27 − $2.99 + $17.42 =   _____

10. $2.19 × 7 − $12.00 =   _____

11. $11.11 × 8 − $61.00 =   _____

12. $33.47 × 2 − $17.22 =   _____

13. $22.47 ÷ 7 + $3.21 =   _____

14. $14.33 − $9.77 + $12.18 =   _____

15. $20.92 ÷ 4 + $10.46 =   _____

★ **B. Your friends are once again in serious need of your money. You have learned some lessons, so:**

1. You lend Molly $242.00 from bank account 2, but charge her interest of $7.77. How much will be in bank account 2 when she pays you back? _____

2. You give Katlyn $4.94 from bank account 3. You tell her she must pay back $5.42. How much will be in bank account 3 when she pays you back? _____

3. You invest $10.00 from bank account 8 in Dale's "hair-brained scheme" to make bubble gum from rubber boots. How much money does bank account 8 have now? _____

4. You buy a horse from your friend Mike for $1.98 from bank account 14. For that kind of money, it's not much of a horse, but being a shrewd businessperson you sell it for $427.32. How much does this add to your bank account 14? _____ (Be careful!)

5. See if you can complete this old worldly wise statement:
   A penny _____ is a penny _____.

Copyright © 2003 by John Wiley & Sons, Inc.

108. The Real Cost of Borrowing

QUICK ACCESS information

QUICK ACCESS INFORMATION → The problem with borrowing money is that it must be paid back with interest over a certain period of time. Here are some definitions you should know:

Principal—The amount of money you borrow.

Simple Interest—The rent or cost of borrowing someone else's money. This must be added to the principal as the loan is paid back.

Interest Rate—The extra amount in a percent that you must pay back. It is often calculated yearly.

Down Payment—The amount of money or ready cash you can afford to give as part payment.

Period of the Loan (Time)—The length of time in which a person has to pay back the loan. Payments on a loan are usually made once a month; however, other payment periods can be arranged with the lender.

★ You have a job and you want to borrow money to buy the coolest car in existence. Calculate the amount of simple interest you must pay for each of the following loans. Remember to add the amount of interest to the principal to get the amount to be repaid.

Cost of the Car	Down Payment	Principal or Amount Borrowed	Simple Interest Rate Per Year	Period of the Loan	Amount of Interest	Total Amount to Be Repaid	Total Cost of Your Cool Car
$900	$100	$800	7%	1 year	$56	$856	$956
$1,000	$300		6%	1 year			
$1,400	$300		9%	2 years			
$2,000	$400		10%	3 years			
$12,000	$700		$5\frac{1}{2}$%	1 year			
$12,000	$200		$7\frac{1}{2}$%	$1\frac{1}{2}$ years			

Copyright © 2003 by John Wiley & Sons, Inc.

109. The Cost of a Tiger

A tiger falls into the category of an "exotic pet." This means that there may be laws in your area prohibiting ownership. Now let's consider what it would cost you to keep a tiger in your backyard.

Raw Tiger Cost Data

Cost of the tiger: $14,079.40

Cost of fencing, bars, and cement floor for cage: $3,492.79

Food (raw beef, chicken, lamb, etc.): $63.94 per day

Motion detectors, security lights, and other devices to keep others out: $2,419.72

Cost of cleaning the cage: $74.38 per week

Cost of grooming (labor, oils, tiger shampoo, etc.): $14.92 per month

Monthly health inspections by professional veterinarian: $279.19 per month

---

★ **Answer these questions.**

1. How much does it cost to feed your tiger for a month (September)? _____

2. How much does it cost to clean the cage for a month (4 weeks)? _____

3. What is the cost of the tiger itself plus the cage? _____

4. What are the veterinarian charges for a year? _____

5. Your tiger needs special grooming for a show this month. Add $272.47 to the cost of this month's regular grooming costs. _____

6. Your tiger had kittens. You sold all seven for the regular tiger price. How much did you make? _____

7. What is the cost of cleaning the cage and grooming for one month? _____

8. What is the cost of the veterinarian fees plus the food for the month of September? _____

9. What is the cost of the security plus the cost of the cage? _____

10. Do you think it is worthwhile owning a tiger? _____

Copyright © 2003 by John Wiley & Sons, Inc.

Copyright © 2003 by John Wiley & Sons, Inc.

NAME _____   DATE _____

110. The Cost of a Dump Truck

★ Your task is to write the cost of each item in the appropriate spot. Remember that for some items, like tires, the price of only one is given and you would need five tires (including the spare), so you need to multiply the tire cost by five. Remember the rule for adding or subtracting decimals: Keep all decimals in a row from top to bottom.

COST OF RUBBER PARTS

Hoses _____

Tires _____

Spacers & body mounts _____

COST OF METAL PARTS

Truck body _____

Truck box _____

Frame _____

Bumpers _____

COST OF ENGINE AND DRIVE TRAIN

Engine _____

Transmission _____

Rear axle _____

COST OF INTERIOR PARTS

Seats _____

Dash gauges, knobs, etc. _____

Mats, rug, etc. _____

COST OF FLUIDS

Oil _____

Antifreeze _____

Transmission fluid _____

COST OF MISC. ITEMS

Electrical _____

Glass _____

Fuel _____

TOTAL COST OF DUMP TRUCK: _____

P.S. Watch out for dump trucks.

111. Comparing the U.S. Dollar to Other Currencies

★ In other countries the same object for sale may have a vastly different price due to a variety of factors. One of those factors is the value of money itself. Let's calculate the cost of various items in the chart. Using the U.S. Dollar as $1.00, all other money or currencies are compared to it.

United States Dollar $ = $1.00 One U.S. Dollar
Canadian Dollar $ = $1.61 to equal One U.S. Dollar
United Kingdom Pound £   = £.82 to equal One U.S. Dollar
Euro Dollar (European Countries) €   = €1.15 to equal One U.S. Dollar

★ Complete the chart below. Round the answers to the nearest hundredth.

Item	U.S. Price	Canadian Price	United Kingdom (British) Price	European Countries (Euro) Price
Football	$22.95	$36.95	£18.82	€26.39
CD	$15.95			
Makeup	$37.50			
Dress	$72.98			
Pen	$0.79			
Haircut	$24.95			
Gallon of Gas	$1.25			
Sneakers	$84.32			
Watch	$14.95			
Rock Concert Tickets	$40.00			

Copyright © 2003 by John Wiley & Sons, Inc.

112. Making Change

★ Everyone must become skillful in the use of money. This worksheet will sharpen your skills in making change. Complete the following chart. The first one is done for you.

Item	Cost of Item	Amount given in payment	$50	$20	$10	$5	$1	25¢	10¢	5¢	1¢	Total Change Received
Dress	$98.20	$100.00					1	3		1		$1.80
Football	$32.98	$50.00										
Video game	$14.20	$20.00										
Video game magazine	$4.99	$5.00										
Calculator	$14.62	$50.00										
Stapler	$3.95	$5.00										
Fast-food burger	$4.21	$10.00										
Entrance to zoo	$4.00	$20.00										
Pen	$2.49	$10.00										
Trail ride on horse	$179.40	$200.00										
CD	$12.49	$20.00										
Makeup	$17.37	$50.00										
Airplane ride	$50.52	$100.00										
Popcorn	$0.39	$100.00										
Lollipop	$0.29	$50.00										

Copyright © 2003 by John Wiley & Sons, Inc.

113. The Good Ol' Days, 1934

Before 1935, when Social Security came into existence, wages were low but costs were not high either. The following is the cost of living of Bighampton Butler Jones's grandfather who was 24 years old in 1934.

★ **Each statement gives a wage earned or the cost of an item. By multiplying or dividing, calculate the amount received, spent, or needed.**

1. Bighampton's grandfather earned 24¢ per hour on the railroad and worked 12 hours a day. What were his wages per day? _____ Per week (6 days)? _____ Per month (24 days or 4 weeks)? _____

2. The cost of a loaf of bread was 7¢. A family of five consumed 10 loaves a week. What was the cost of bread per week? _____

3. A new 1934 car cost $989.04. How many hours did Bighampton's grandfather need to work at 24¢ per hour to pay for the car? _____

4. Shoes were $1.25 a pair. What was the cost of shoes for a family of five? _____

5. Rent for their apartment was $21.00 per month. What was the total cost of rent for a year? _____

6. A lady's dress cost $1.29 if she sewed it herself. Bighampton's grandmother got a new dress every two years for 12 years. What was the total cost of the dresses? _____

7. Bighampton's father needed a new shirt in 1934. It cost $1.08. How long did Bighampton's grandfather have to work at 24¢ per hour to pay for it? _____

8. Each meal cost 8¢ ($0.08) for each person in the family. What was the cost of feeding Bighampton Butler Jones's father, grandfather, grandmother, Aunt Kathy, and Uncle Eugene for one week? They ate three meals a day except on Sunday when they didn't have to work so hard. On that day they each ate two meals. _____

Copyright © 2003 by John Wiley & Sons, Inc.

114. The More Recent Good Ol' Days, 1955

★ In 1955, Elvis Presley was the latest singing sensation and life in America was prosperous and booming. Children born between 1945 and 1955 were called "Post-War Baby Boomers." Let's see what it cost to live in those days.

1. Bighampton's father worked at the aircraft plant for 10 hours a day, five days a week. He earned $1.24 per hour. What were his wages per day? _____

2. Soda was now 10¢ a bottle, up 5¢ from what it was before the war. How much was a case of 60 bottles? _____ How much did you get back for the case of empty bottles at 2¢ each? _____

3. Cost of a quart of milk was $.12. A family of seven consumed 13 quarts a week. What was the cost of milk for the family for one week? _____

4. A new 1955 Chevy Bel Air 2-door hardtop was $2,100.56. How many hours did Bighampton's father need to work at $1.24 per hour to pay for the car? _____

5. Chocolate candy bars were 7¢ each. How much was a case of 24? _____

6. Rent for an apartment was $98.00 per month. What was the total cost of rent for a year? _____

7. Bighampton's brother needed a new bike in order to deliver papers. His father had to work 30 hours to pay for it. What was the cost of the bike if his father made $1.24 per hour? _____

8. There were no video games, so the family bought a black-and-white TV for $50.04 with tax. What would the monthly payments be for this TV over one year (assuming no interest)? _____

Copyright © 2003 by John Wiley & Sons, Inc.

115. Adding Money

The secret to adding money correctly is to keep the decimal points all in a column as you add.

★ **Perform these calculations:**

Ted	$0.75	**Molly**	$8.14	**Kathy**	$47.11	**Christa**	$64.44
	1.25		2.13		42.32		81.91
	+ 0.23		+ 3.19		+ 87.19		+ 92.43

John

$327.24 + $19.28 = _____

Al

$671.12 + $989.14 = _____

Wanda

$327.47 + $82.18 = _____

Bill

$641.99 + $22.62 = _____

Tony	$327.42	**Karrie**	$671.34	**Esther**	$9,895.13	**Bob**	$67,913.01
	89.17		875.75		427.49		32,714.08
	92.92		396.02		327.92		92,913.09
	+ 38.47		+ 427.47		+ 8,911.15		+ 42,894.04

★ **Bonus Questions:** You will have noticed that each problem above has a name. I know this is strange but the reason for this will become clear as you answer the bonus questions below. (All bonus questions deal with the totals of the problems above.)

1. Bob married Esther. What is the total of their money? _____

2. Bill gave John $247.12 extra dollars. What is John's total now? _____

3. Wanda lent Al $409.00 to help buy a motor for his Corvette. How much does Al have now? _____

4. Karrie was given $327.00 by Tony to buy a horse. How much does Karrie have now? _____

5. Kathy gave her daughter $74.62 to get her flute fixed. How much does Christa have now? _____

Copyright © 2003 by John Wiley & Sons, Inc.

116. Subtracting Money

The secret to subtracting money correctly is to keep the decimal points all in a column as you subtract.

★ **Perform these calculations:**

Ziggy $409.49
    − 327.02

Jack $427.03
    − 318.01

Margaret $283.33
      − 250.95

Flossie $426.77
    − 340.48

Sir Clyde Manning

$2,918.16 − $327.09 = _____

Sonia

$11.79 − $8.40 = _____

Marlene

$12.32 − $9.67 = _____

Carol

$7.99 − $2.22 = _____

Henry $428.04
    − 343.44

Maria $871.12
    − 721.33

Bighampton $947.13
      − 47.22

Molly $362.44
    − 79.89

Copyright © 2003 by John Wiley & Sons, Inc.

★ **Bonus Questions:** You will have noticed that each problem above has a name. I know this is strange, but the reason for this will become clear as you answer the bonus questions below. (All bonus questions deal with the answers to the problems above.)

1. Sonia lent Marlene $2.40. How much does Sonia have now? _____

2. Jack dented Margaret's car. It cost him $74.00 to have it fixed. How much does Jack have left? _____

3. Henry lost $4.23. How much does he have left? _____

4. Bighampton sold Molly a "Game Person" for $72.94. How much does Molly have now? _____

5. Sir Clyde Manning played "Santa Claus." It cost him $23.75 for the beard. How much does he have left to buy presents? _____

NAME _____   DATE _____

117. Multiplying Money

The essential thing to remember when multiplying with money is to keep the decimal point in the correct position. There must always be two decimal places to the right of the decimal point, e.g., $37.<u>92</u>. If you find you have an answer like $27.4 when you calculate, you must place a zero after the 4, expressing $27.4 as $27.40. The dollar ($) sign must always be in the answer.

★   Calculate the following questions. A Choice Box is provided.

1. $327.42 × 3 =   2. $62.14 × 9 =   3. $48.12 × 7 =

4. $63.13
    ×   9

5. $6,412.14
    ×   22

6. $1,327.42
    ×   8

7. $64.21 × 9 =   8. $84.19 × 19 =   9. $42.52 × 11 =

10. $37.55
     ×   55

11. $81.11
     ×   19

12. $63.17
     ×   22

CHOICE BOX   (Why should you not have to calculate the last one?)

$559.26	$577.89	$982.26	$1,541.09
$2,065.25	$467.72	$1,389.74	$1,599.61
$141,067.08	$568.17	$336.84	$10,619.36

Copyright © 2003 by John Wiley & Sons, Inc.

118. Multiplying Money
with the Help of Mr. Washington

★ It was true that George Washington was a very honest man. The story is told that when the question was asked about who cut down a specific cherry tree, George replied, "I cannot tell a lie. It was I." Let's have a look at the event and some values and costs in today's money.

Copyright © 2003 by John Wiley & Sons, Inc.

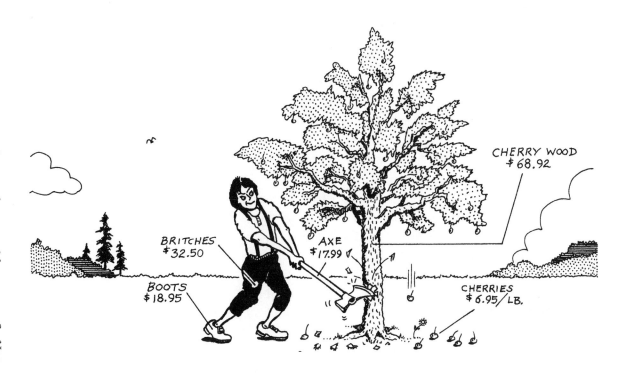

1. What is the value of 13 lbs. of cherries? _____

2. What is the value of the wood from 32 cherry trees? _____

3. You sold the wood from 11 cherry trees and 16 lbs. of cherries. You have _____.

4. What is the cost of 17 pairs of britches? _____

5. What is the cost of 39 pairs of boots? _____

6. What is the cost of 13 axes and 7 pairs of britches? _____

7. What is the cost of 3 pairs of boots and 9 axes? _____

8. What is the cost of 4 axes, 2 pairs of britches, and 2 pairs of boots? _____

9. You broke your axe on the cherry tree because the wood was so hard. How many pounds of cherries do you need to sell to pay for it? _____

10. Cherry wood has doubled in value. What is it now? _____

119. Multiplication and Subtraction with Money

QUICK ACCESS INFORMATION ➜ Here are some important definitions for you to know.

<u>Investment</u> is what you buy to resell.

<u>Your cost</u> is the amount of money you paid for the item.

<u>Multiplied by</u> is the number of *times* over your cost for which you were able to sell the item.

<u>The gross total</u> is the actual number of dollars for which you were able to sell your item.

<u>Net profit</u> is the amount of money you made after subtracting your original cost for the item.

★ One of the more joyous things in life is to see your money grow or multiply. In the chart below, you have purchased several items at a low price and are selling them for several times their value. Complete the chart. The first one is done to help you get started.

Investment	Your Cost	Multiplied By	Gross Total	Net Profit
Video Game System	$127.30	5 ×	$636.50	$509.20
Party Dress	$71.14	4 ×		
25 CDs	$237.20	2 ×		
Golf Clubs	$37.00	7 ×		
Football	$3.19	17 ×		
Comics	$0.05	32 ×		

Copyright © 2003 by John Wiley & Sons, Inc.

NAME _____   DATE _____

120. Multiplication with Money

★ Multiplying with money usually means multiplying with a whole number like 14, a decimal (.), and two numbers to the right of the decimal. (*Example:* $14.28 \times 3 = $42.84) Calculate the following problems. Draw a line from each problem to each correct answer.

$2.98 × 4 =	$171.36
$4.91 × 4 =	$263.27
$8.97 × 21 =	$214.41
$4.27 × 71 =	$303.17
$6.47 × 92 =	$595.24
$18.31 × 4 =	$8,952.52
$37.15 × 9 =	$548.94
$82.75 × 4 =	$554.40
$97.31 × 92 =	$334.35
$71.47 × 3 =	$73.24
$21.11 × 9 =	$189.99
$61.31 × 2 =	$122.62
$21.42 × 8 =	$460.85
$92.17 × 5 =	$331.00
$78.42 × 7 =	$5,091.41
$21.11 × 2 =	$19.64
$37.61 × 7 =	$42.22
$71.71 × 71 =	$188.37
$7.20 × 77 =	$3,012.75
$3.25 × 927 =	$11.92

Copyright © 2003 by John Wiley & Sons, Inc.

121. Dividing Money

★ There are essentially two different ways of dividing with money. The first is $8\overline{)\$17.36}$ and the second is $\frac{\$17.36}{8}$. The dollar sign must appear in your answer. Calculate these problems.

1. $8\overline{)\$17.36}$ 　　2. $9\overline{)\$19.62}$ 　　3. $7\overline{)\$15.05}$ 　　4. $4\overline{)\$128.48}$

5. $12\overline{)\$25.32}$ 　　6. $13\overline{)\$846.82}$ 　　7. $14\overline{)\$1,387.82}$ 　　8. $15\overline{)\$113.40}$

9. $\frac{\$16.89}{3} =$ 　　10. $\frac{\$227.97}{9} =$ 　　11. $\frac{\$36.48}{8} =$

OPTIONAL "TOUGH" EXTRA BONUS SPECIALS

12. Which two answers in the top row (1 to 4) when added together and divided by 2 equal $17.15? _____

13. Which two answers in the middle row (5 to 8) when added together and divided by 2 equal $36.35? _____

14. Which two answers in the bottom row (9 to 11) when added together and divided by 2 equal $15.48? _____

Copyright © 2003 by John Wiley & Sons, Inc.

122. Dividing Your Good Fortune

You have won the lottery. This is wonderful except you have discovered there are two problems with winning that much money:

You have so much you don't know what to do with it.

All your friends, relatives, and acquaintances have somehow showed up and would like to share in your good fortune.

★ **Fill in the chart to see where your money goes. You must divide the amount of money by the number of people. The first one is done for you.**

Amount	Who They Are	Number of People	Amount Each Will Get
$197,622.00	Closest friends	3	$65,874.00
$277,066.00	Parents	2	
$160,736.15	Brothers & Sisters	5	
$5,053.20	Classmates	24	
$102,588.88	2 Pairs of Grandparents	4	
$59,296.32	Long-lost relatives who suddenly remembered you	72	
$185,991.06	Worthwhile charities	327	
$224,143.14	Aunt Bernice, Cousin Juan, and all their children	402	
$17,354.75	Your neighbors	47	
$1,316.56	Shadow the cat & Comet the dog	2	

Copyright © 2003 by John Wiley & Sons, Inc.

123. Definition Puzzle on Money

★ Place the answers to this puzzle in their correct locations across or down. A Choice Box has been provided.

ACROSS

1. The amount of money deducted from your pay by your employer
3. Your ability to buy things
4. Charges for services or registrations
5. The amount of money left in your bank account
11. A fixed rate of payment for services on a regular basis
13. What an item is worth or what you have to pay
14. How much you make on a job— usually an amount per hour

DOWN

2. The actual money you have to spend
6. The amount of money you or your family members bring home
7. To obtain a loan
8. Money paid to the government to pay for roads, etc.
9. A set amount of money you have to live on
10. Money paid to a landlord
12. Extra time worked on a job outside the regular hours
15. An amount you lend to someone

CHOICE BOX

cost	borrow	loan	income	disposable
buying power	rent	fees	balance	budget
wage	salary	overtime	deductions	tax

Copyright © 2003 by John Wiley & Sons, Inc.

124. Skills Mastery Test—Money

★ **Read and answer each question carefully:**

1. The latest video game system costs $369.00. You make $6.00 per hour. How many hours must you work in order to pay for it? _____

2. $7.25 per hour for 40 hours per week = _____ wages per week

★ **Complete this chart:**

	Cost of Item	Down Payment	Principal or Amount Borrowed	Simple Interest Rate/Year	Period of Loan	Amount of Interest	Total to Be Repaid	Total Cost of Object Bought
3.	$1,000	$100	$900	7%	1 year			
4.	$1,200	$300	$900	4%	2 years			

5. $2.98 × 7 = _____

6. $4.91 × 9 = _____

7. $327.22 × 5 = _____

8. 4)$3.24 = _____

9. 5)$675.25 = _____

10. 8)$520.00 = _____

11. $327.42 + $879.45 = _____

12. $13.13 + $14.14 = _____

13. $12.72 + $847.91 = _____

14. $62.37 − $2.27 = _____

15. $137.11 − $49.12 = _____

16. $847.14 − $99.94 = _____

17. $9,246.10 − $327.40 = _____

18. $3.24 + $9.44 − $1.27 = _____

19. $6.94 + $96.74 − $0.27 = _____

20. $9.99 ÷ 3 + $3.94 = _____

21. $12.99 ÷ $4.33 + $42.71 = _____

22. $7.89 × 5 + $62.45 = _____

23. $6.22 × 3 + $98.25 = _____

★ **Read and answer each question carefully:**

24. Which is the better buy: 3 candies at 49¢ each or 4 candies for $1.99?

_____

25. Which is the better buy: 11 video games for $189.00 or 14 video games at $7.99 each? _____

Copyright © 2003 by John Wiley & Sons, Inc.

SECTION 6

GEOMETRY AND MEASUREMENT: FACTS AND INSIGHTS

125. Measure Math Match

★ When we measure objects, we use different types of measures to do different jobs. We could not use a yardstick to measure how much we weigh nor could we use the thrust of a rocket to measure ingredients for a chocolate cake. Your task is to place the number from the device or situation that needs to be measured on the left beside its correct measuring system on the right. Some measuring systems are used more than once.

1. Shoe size

2. The area of a dance floor

3. The sound of a bell

4. Cake ingredients

5. Test-tube contents

6. Height of a student

7. Olympic race track

8. Your weight

9. The shade or tint of a color

10. The capacity of a dump truck box

11. The weight of most medications (pills)

12. Container of milk

13. Length of a drag strip

14. Size of a school

15. Distance from Boise, Idaho to Juneau, Alaska

16. The power of a rocket

17. The power of a 1934 Ford hot rod

18. The size of a science lab beaker

19. The height of a flagpole

20. The cost of a chicken

_____ $\frac{1}{4}$ mile or 1,320 feet

_____ quarts or liters

_____ number of students

_____ square feet or square meters

_____ meters

_____ cubic yards or cubic meters

_____ miles or kilometers

_____ horsepower

_____ milliliter or centiliter

_____ feet or yards or meters

_____ dollars and cents

_____ pounds of thrust

_____ cups, teaspoons, tablespoons

_____ inches or centimeters

_____ milligrams

_____ decibels

_____ hue

_____ pounds or kilograms

Copyright © 2003 by John Wiley & Sons, Inc.

126. Geometry Angles

QUICK ACCESS INFORMATION ➡ Here are three different angles with their names.

Right angle

Acute angle

Obtuse angle

★ Use a protractor to measure the following angles and label the name of the angle. Match the correct letter of each figure with its size below to spell the name of the "Father of Geometry."

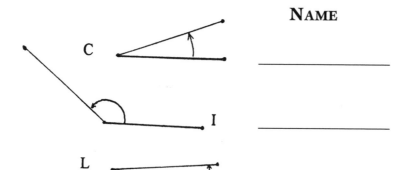

	NAME	**SIZE IN DEGREES**
C	_____	_____
I	_____	_____
L	_____	_____
E	_____	_____
D	_____	_____
U	_____	_____

Copyright © 2003 by John Wiley & Sons, Inc.

The "Father of Modern Geometry" is ___ ___ ___ ___ ___ ___.
                                     35° 120° 20° 5° 140° 90°

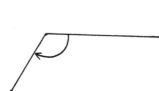

Teacher Note: To make sure every student has a protractor, photocopy several examples on a white sheet of paper, photocopy that sheet on overhead plastic, then cut out protractors for students' needs.

Copyright © 2003 by John Wiley & Sons, Inc.

127. Measuring Triangles

QUICK ACCESS
information

QUICK ACCESS INFORMATION ➜ The inside angles of all triangles total 180°.

★   Find the measure of the missing angles. Do not use a protractor.

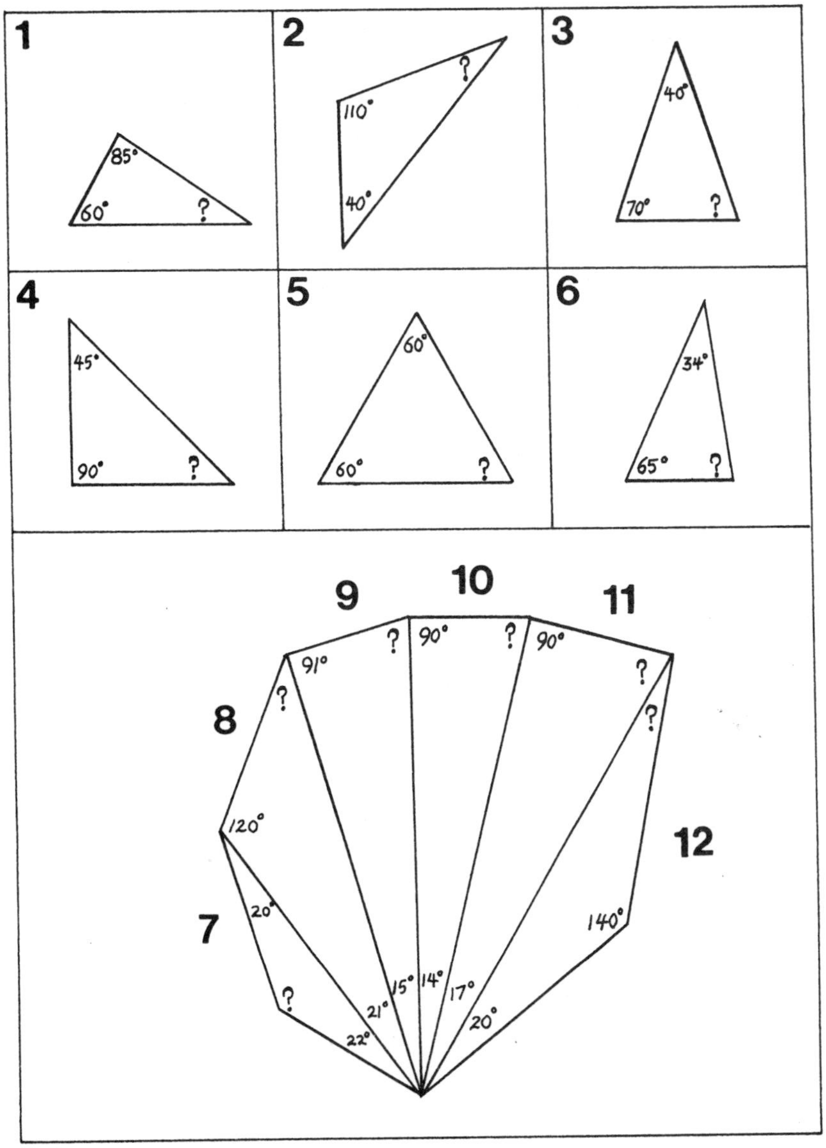

1. _____

2. _____

3. _____

4. _____

5. _____

6. _____

7. _____

8. _____

9. _____

10. _____

11. _____

12. _____

1

85°
60°   ?

2

110°
40°   ?

3

40°
70°   ?

4

45°
90°   ?

5

60°
60°   ?

6

34°
65°   ?

9   **10**   **11**

91°   ?   90°   ?   90°
?   ?

8   ?

120°

7

20°   **12**

140°

?
22° 21° 15° 14° 17° 20°

128. Complementary and Supplementary Angles

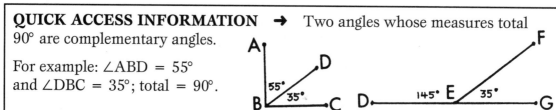

QUICK ACCESS INFORMATION ➡ Two angles whose measures total 90° are complementary angles.

For example: ∠ABD = 55° and ∠DBC = 35°; total = 90°.

Two angles whose measures total 180° are supplementary angles.
For example: ∠DEF = 145° and ∠FEG = 35°; total 180°.

★ Measure all angles with a protractor and tell whether they are complementary (comp.), supplementary (supp.), or neither.

MEASURES OF ANGLES   **NAME**

1.
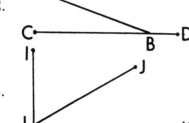

∠EFG _____ ∠GFH _____ _____

2.

∠ABD _____ ∠ABC _____ _____

3.
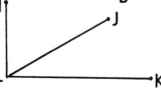

∠ILJ _____ ∠JLK _____ _____

∠MNO _____ ∠ONP _____ _____

4.

∠RTS _____ ∠QTS _____ _____

5.
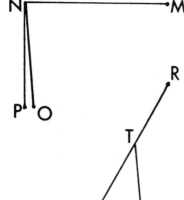

Copyright © 2003 by John Wiley & Sons, Inc.

129. Measuring Angles

QUICK ACCESS INFORMATION ➜
We need a tool called a protractor to measure angles. Most protractors have two sides or scales. One of the scales starts at 0° and is on the left; the other one starts at 0° and is on the right.

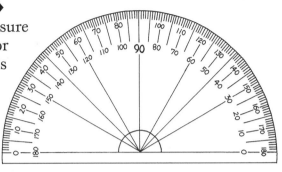

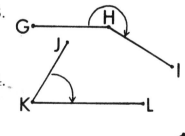

= ∠ JKL

Angles are named by their letters and use the ∠ symbol.

★ Name each angle and measure the degrees in the angle.

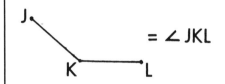

1.

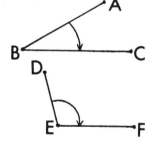

2.

DEGREES
(don't forget the degree symbol °)

NAME

_____   _____

3.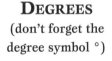

_____   _____

_____   _____

4.

_____   _____

5.

_____   _____

Copyright © 2003 by John Wiley & Sons, Inc.

130. Metric Measurement

★ Your task is to measure the lines below and write how long each line is in the space provided.

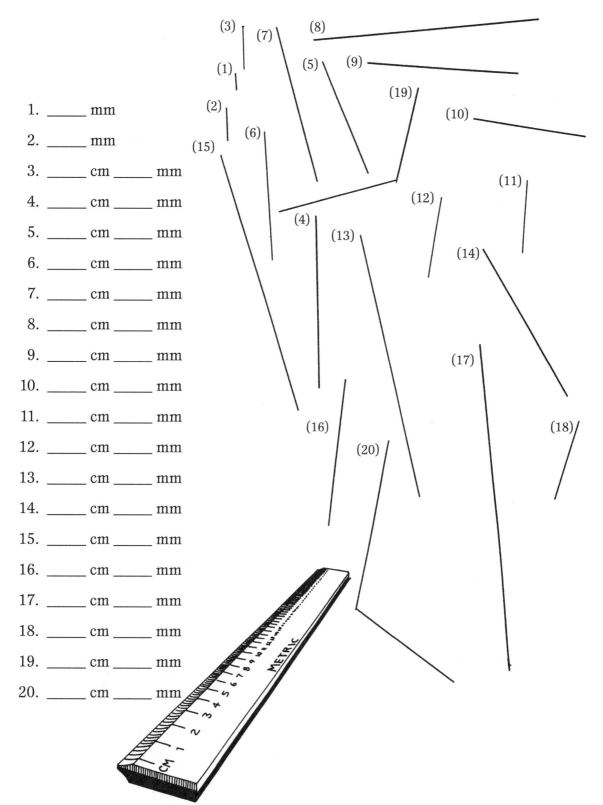

1. _____ mm

2. _____ mm

3. _____ cm _____ mm

4. _____ cm _____ mm

5. _____ cm _____ mm

6. _____ cm _____ mm

7. _____ cm _____ mm

8. _____ cm _____ mm

9. _____ cm _____ mm

10. _____ cm _____ mm

11. _____ cm _____ mm

12. _____ cm _____ mm

13. _____ cm _____ mm

14. _____ cm _____ mm

15. _____ cm _____ mm

16. _____ cm _____ mm

17. _____ cm _____ mm

18. _____ cm _____ mm

19. _____ cm _____ mm

20. _____ cm _____ mm

Copyright © 2003 by John Wiley & Sons, Inc.

131. Congruent Line Segments

QUICK ACCESS
information

QUICK ACCESS INFORMATION ➡ The word <u>congruent</u> means equal and is used most often in geometry. The symbol used to indicate that one thing is congruent to another is similar to the equal sign but with a wavy line above: ≅. The symbol used to indicate a segment is a straight line over the letter name of that segment: $\overline{AB}$.

★ Use a ruler to measure these line segments in order to find congruent pairs. The first one has been completed to get you started. (Use metric measure.)

Copyright © 2003 by John Wiley & Sons, Inc.

1. $\overline{AB} \cong \overline{XM}$

2. $\overline{CD} \cong$

3. ___ ≅

4. ___ ≅

5.

6.

7.

8.

9.

10.

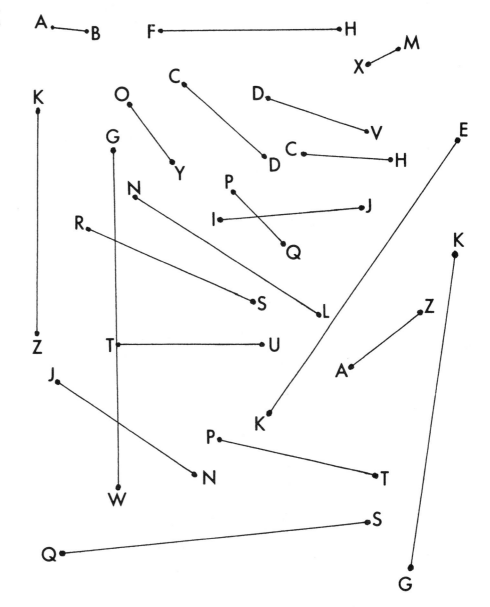

132. Congruent Angles

QUICK ACCESS
information

QUICK ACCESS INFORMATION ➜ The word <u>congruent</u> means equal and is used most often in geometry. The symbol used to indicate that one thing is congruent to another is similar to the equal sign but with a wavy line above: ≅. The symbol for angle is ∠.

★ Use a protractor to measure the angles of the figures to find congruent pairs. The first one has been completed to get you started.

1. ∠ABC ≅ ∠GHI

2. ∠DEF ≅ ∠

3.　　　≅

4.

5.

6.

7.

8.

9.

10.

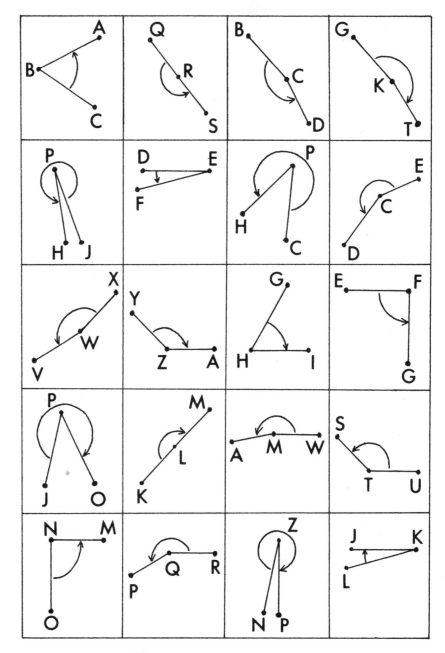

Copyright © 2003 by John Wiley & Sons, Inc.

133. Finding the Perimeter of Figures

Copyright © 2003 by John Wiley & Sons, Inc.

QUICK ACCESS INFORMATION → The perimeter of a figure is the distance around the figure. To discover the perimeter, you need to <u>add</u> the numbers around it.

Example: 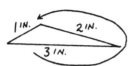   Perimeter of 6 inches

Sometimes a figure does not give the length of a side, so you need to arrive at the missing length or dimension by deduction. *Example:* The lengths of sides A and B are not given, but we see that length C = 2 ft. and length D = 1 ft. Because length C goes all the way to the top but length D doesn't, we need to subtract D (1 ft.) from C (2 ft.) = 1 ft., which is the length of A. Length of side B is found the same way. F = 7 ft.; E = 4 ft., we need F − E = 7 − 4 = 3 ft. Therefore, length B is 3 ft.

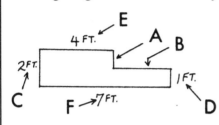

The total perimeter is found by adding A + B + C + D + E + F = 1 ft. + 3 ft. + 2 ft. + 1 ft. + 4 ft. + 7 ft. = 18 ft.

★ Find the perimeter of the following figures.

1

____

2

____

3

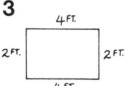

____

4

____

5

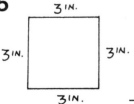

____

6

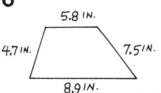

____

7

____

8

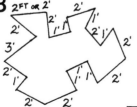

____

9

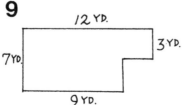

____

10

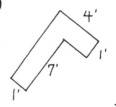

____

149

134. A Serious Perimeter!

★ Calculate the distance or perimeter around this figure. Be careful, though! It's not so easy as it looks. (All numbers are in feet.)

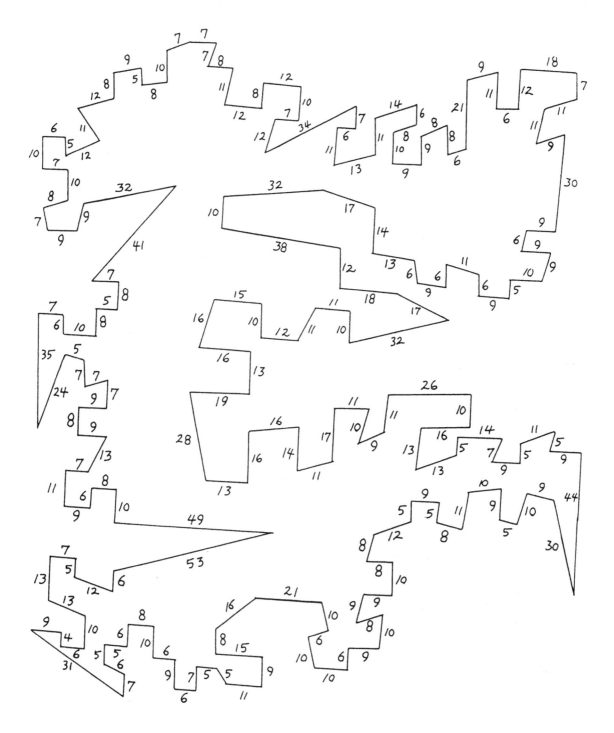

The answer is _____ feet.

Copyright © 2003 by John Wiley & Sons, Inc.

Copyright © 2003 by John Wiley & Sons, Inc.

NAME _____   DATE _____

135. Perimeter Questions About Shane's Hat

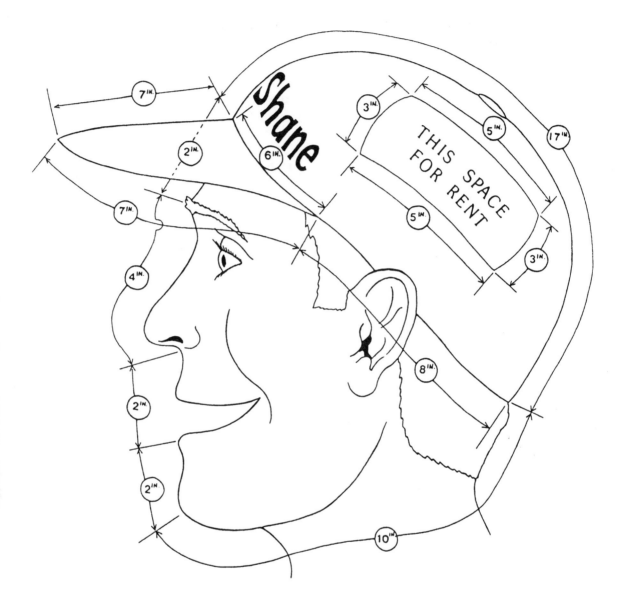

1. Starting with Shane's nose, calculate the perimeter of Shane's head with the hat on. Don't include the brim or peak. _____

2. Calculate the perimeter of Shane's hat alone. _____

3. Calculate the perimeter of the sign on Shane's hat. _____

4. Calculate the perimeter of the peak or brim on Shane's hat. _____

151

136. Finding Perimeters of Figures or Shapes

★ Here are several different figures and shapes. Some contain all the lengths of the sides you need to add, while others only have a few of the side lengths. You must deduce or figure out the lengths of the missing sides by subtracting and adding. The chart on the right has only part of the answers. Find the remainder of the answer and put the letter of the figure beside its location on the chart. The first one has been completed for you.

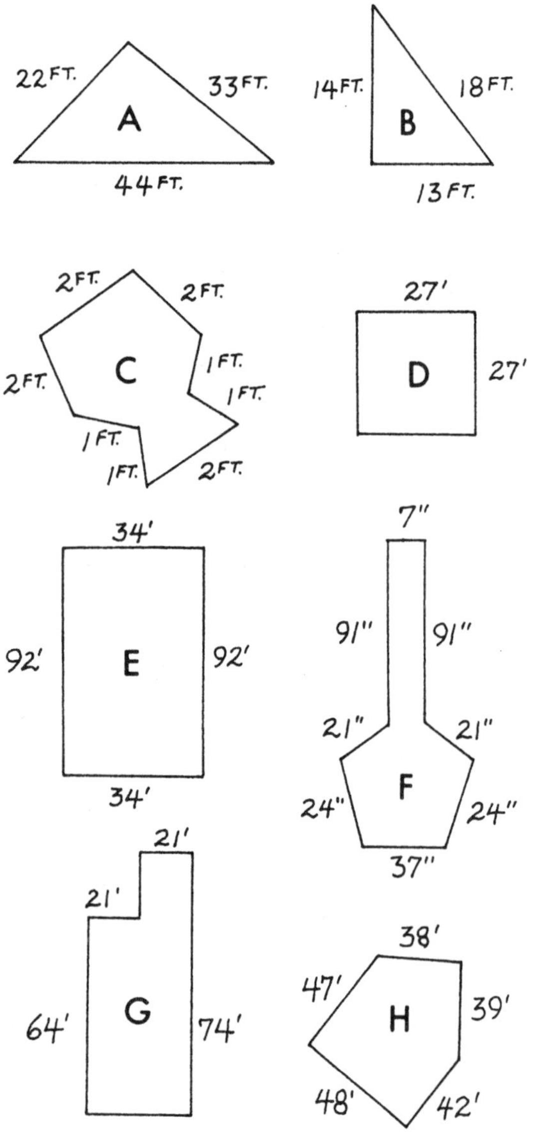

Figure Letter	Partial Answer
B	<u>4</u> 5 ft.
	_ _ 8 ft.
	_ 32 ft.
	_14 ft.
	_ _ 2 ft.
	1 _ ft.
	9 _ ft.
	3 _ _ in.
	3 _ 2 yd.
	1 _ _ yd.

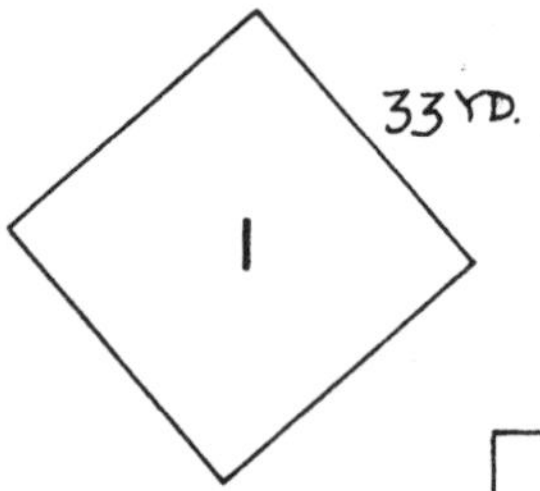

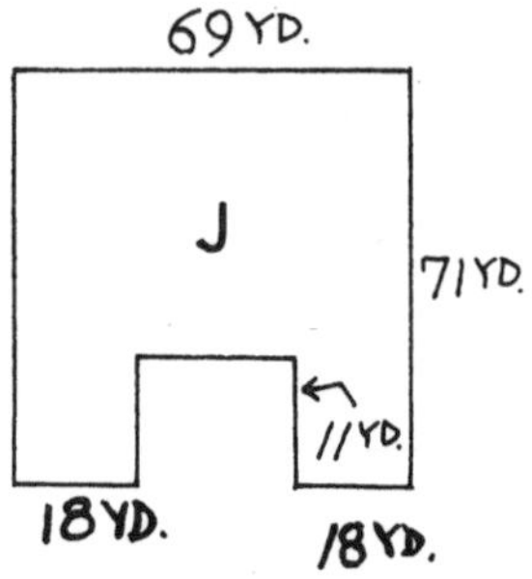

A: 22 FT., 33 FT., 44 FT.

B: 14 FT., 18 FT., 13 FT.

C: 2 FT., 2 FT., 2 FT., 1 FT., 1 FT., 1 FT., 1 FT., 2 FT.

D: 27', 27'

E: 34', 92', 92', 34'

F: 7", 91", 91", 21", 21", 24", 24", 37"

G: 21', 21', 64', 74'

H: 38', 47', 39', 48', 42'

I: 33 YD.

J: 69 YD., 71 YD., 11 YD., 18 YD., 18 YD.

Copyright © 2003 by John Wiley & Sons, Inc.

137. The Area of a Triangle

QUICK ACCESS information

QUICK ACCESS INFORMATION → In order to find the area of a triangle, we must use the following formula, which is much like using a recipe when baking cookies. We must use the formula $A = \frac{1}{2} b \times h$, which is $\frac{1}{2}$ the base of the triangle times the height.

For example:

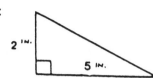

$A = \frac{1}{2} b \times h$

$A = \frac{1}{2} \times 5 \times 2$

$A = 5$ sq. in.

★ Find the areas of the following triangles. The first one is completed for you.

Copyright © 2003 by John Wiley & Sons, Inc.

1.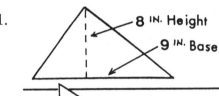

$A = \frac{1}{2} b \times h = \frac{1}{2} \times 8 \times 9$

$= \frac{1}{2} \times 72$

$= 36$ square inches

2.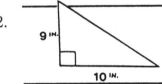

3.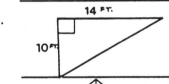

4.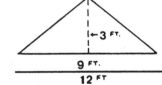

5.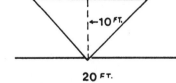

6.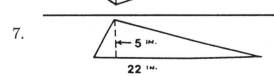

7.

138. The Area of Old MacDonald's Farm

★ Below is a recreation of Uncle Harry MacDonald's farm. He liked everything to be in squares or rectangles or a combination of the two. Study the diagram and answer the questions below. Don't forget to include sq. ft.

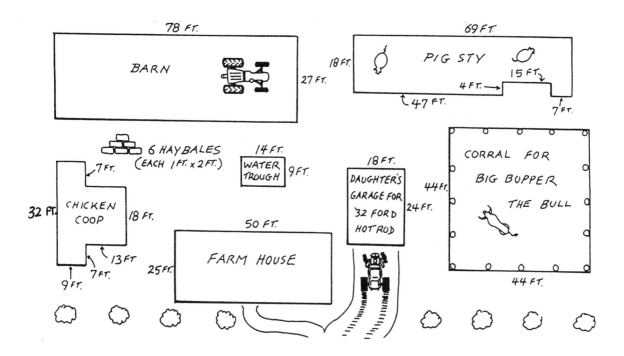

1. What is the area of Old MacDonald's house? _____

2. What is the area of his daughter's hot rod garage? _____

3. What is the area of the chicken coop? _____

4. What is the area of the pig sty and the barn together? _____

5. What is the space left inside the barn if the tractor occupied 12 sq. ft.? _____

6. Old MacDonald decided to double the area of his farm house. What would the area be if doubled? _____

7. What is the combined area of the water trough and Big Bopper's corral? _____

8. Old Harry MacDonald decided to expand his barn by 4,021 sq. ft. How big is it after the addition? _____

9. What is the total square footage of all the <u>buildings</u> on Old MacDonald's farm? _____

10. The chicken coop burned down. This reduced the square footage of the farm. What is the total now? _____

11. What is Old MacDonald's favorite saying? _____

Copyright © 2003 by John Wiley & Sons, Inc.

NAME _____ DATE _____

139. The Circumference of a Circle

★ Use the formula C = πD (where π = 3.14) to find the circumference (distance around the <u>outside</u>) of the following circles.

1. 7 IN.

2. 8 FT.

3. 5 IN.

4. 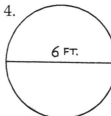 6 FT.

5. 7 FT.

6. 7.5 IN.

7. 8.5 YD.

8. 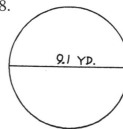 9.1 YD.

9. 1.02 YD.

10. 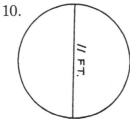 11 FT.

Copyright © 2003 by John Wiley & Sons, Inc.

PLACE YOUR ANSWERS BELOW.

1. _____   6. _____

2. _____   7. _____

3. _____   8. _____

4. _____   9. _____

5. _____   10. _____

HEAVY PIZZA, BIGHAMPTON?

140. The Area of a Circle

★ Use the formula A = πr² (where π = 3.14) to find the area (the region <u>inside</u>) of the following circles.

1.
3 FT.

2.
7 YD.

3.
9 FT.

4.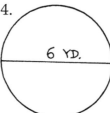
6 YD.

5.
3 IN.

6.
4.1 YD.

7.
7.5 IN.

8.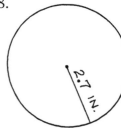
2.7 IN.

9.
11 FT.

10.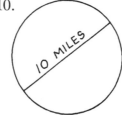
10 MILES

PLACE YOUR ANSWERS INSIDE THE CIRCLES.

1. _____

2. _____

3. _____

4. _____

5. _____

6. _____

7. _____

8. _____

9. _____

10. _____

Copyright © 2003 by John Wiley & Sons, Inc.

141. The Volume of Cubes and Rectangular Prisms

QUICK ACCESS
information

QUICK ACCESS INFORMATION ➜ The volume of an object is the measurement of the amount of room or space inside an object. That space or room is measured in cubic units or U^3. Units can be feet, inches, meters, etc.

★ Find the volume of each figure. The formulas are given below.

Volume of a cube = *side* × *side* × *side* = $s \times s \times s$

Volume of a rectangular prism = *length* × *width* × *height* = $l \times w \times h$

Copyright © 2003 by John Wiley & Sons, Inc.

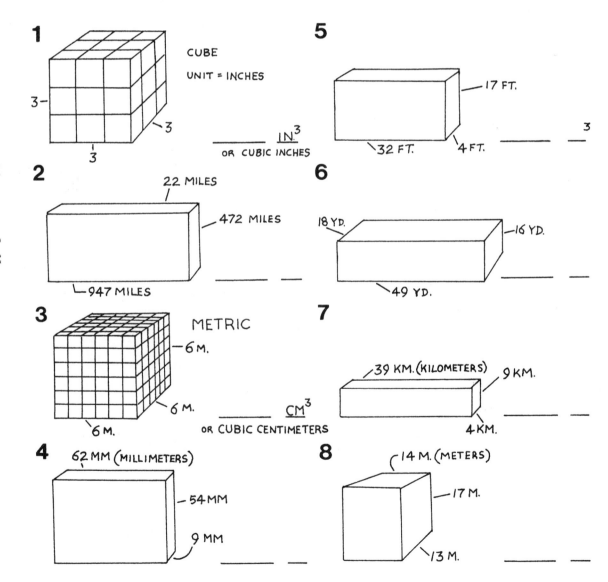

142. The Volume of Pyramids and Cones

QUICK ACCESS
information

QUICK ACCESS INFORMATION ➜ The volume of an object is a measurement of the amount of room or space inside an object. That space or room is measured in cubic units or U³. Units can be feet, yards, meters, etc. To find the volume of a pyramid or cone, use the formula:

$$\text{Area} = \tfrac{1}{3} \times \text{base} \times \text{height} \ or \ A = \tfrac{1}{3}\,b \times h$$

★ Calculate the volume of these pyramids and cones. You are given the area of the base in square units and the height in linear units or a straight line. Let's look:

EXAMPLE: 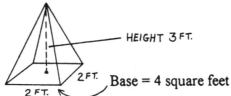 HEIGHT 3 FT.   2 FT.   2 FT.   2 FT.   Base = 4 square feet

$$4 \times 3 \times \tfrac{1}{3} = 4\text{FT}^3$$

1 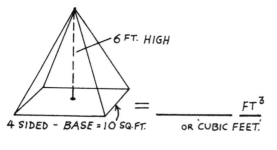 6 FT. HIGH   4 SIDED – BASE = 10 SQ. FT.   = _____ FT^3 OR CUBIC FEET.

4 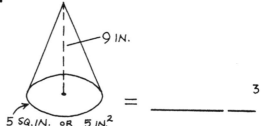 9 IN.   5 SQ. IN. OR 5 IN.²   = _____ ³

2 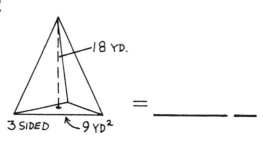 18 YD.   3 SIDED   9 YD²   = _____

5 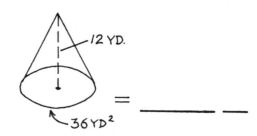 12 YD.   36 YD²   = _____

3 METRIC 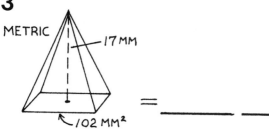 17 MM   102 MM²   = _____

6 METRIC 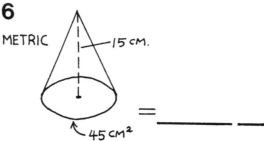 15 CM.   45 CM²   = _____

Copyright © 2003 by John Wiley & Sons, Inc.

143. Map Strategies: Part One

★ A map is a diagram drawn to help us find locations. Below is a map of a teenager's bedroom. This map has number–letter combinations across the bottom and up the side. You will see the map is divided into 4 parts.

Copyright © 2003 by John Wiley & Sons, Inc.

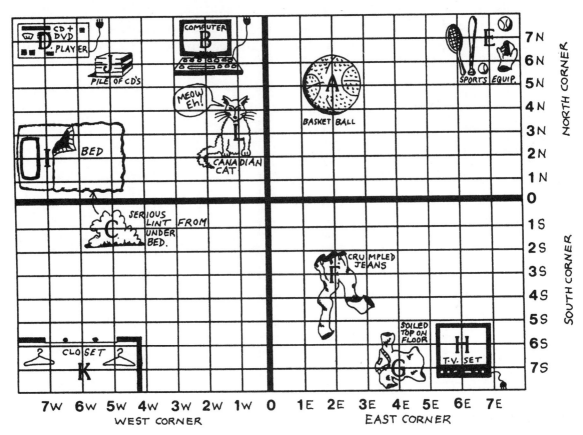

★ Find the location of these objects.

★ What is the letter and name of the objects at these locations?

Name of Object	Point Letter	Number Location		Number Location		Point Letter	Name of Object
		N or S	E or W	N or S	E or W		
Basketball	A	5N	2E	7S	4E	G	Soiled top on floor
TV set				6N	5W		
Crumpled jeans				3N	1W		
CD & DVD player				2N	7W		
Sports equipment				1S	5W		
Closet				7N	2W		

159

144. Map Strategies: Part Two

★ Many maps of the world are marked off in lines of latitude (sideways or horizontal) and lines of longitude (up and down or vertical). These lines are marked off in degrees and direction. Latitude is measured in degrees north or south of the equator (0°). Longitude is measured in degrees east or west of the Prime Meridian (0°). For example, 45°S means forty-five degrees south of the equator. In order to find a point, A, for example, we see that it is 150°W (west) and 45°S (south).

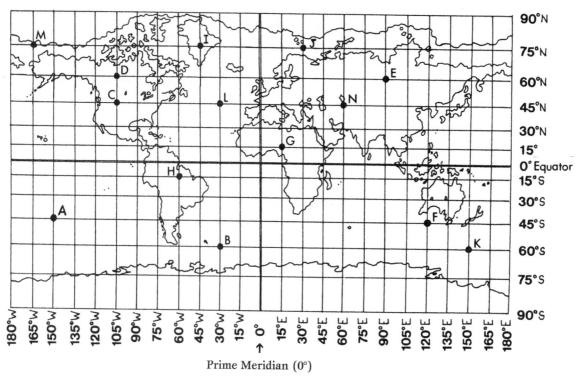

Copyright © 2003 by John Wiley & Sons, Inc.

★ Locate the following points.   ★ What is the letter at these points?

Point	Latitude	Longitude	Latitude	Longitude	Point
B			75°N	30°E	
H			45°N	60°E	
F			75°N	165°W	
L			45°N	105°W	
I			15°N	15°E	
E			60°N	105°W	
A			60°S	150°E	

145. Definition Puzzle on Geometry and Measurement Terms

★ Place the answers to this puzzle in their correct locations across or down. A Choice Box has been provided.

Copyright © 2003 by John Wiley & Sons, Inc.

ACROSS

1. The distance around a circle
5. A line from the center of a circle to a point on the circumference
6. A 4-sided figure with two pairs of parallel sides and four right angles
7. A 3-sided figure whose interior angles total 180°
9. To use a device like a ruler to see how long something is
10. The form of an object
13. The space inside a 2-dimensional figure
15. A diagram of an area drawn to scale

DOWN

2. A round figure
3. Figures that have exactly the same shape and size
4. A line segment that passes through the center of the circle and has both endpoints on the circle
8. The distance around any object with regular or irregular sides
11. A 4-sided figure with four congruent sides and angles
12. A closed figure with a round base and a curved surface that comes to a point—or a yummy ice cream holder
14. Two rays with a common endpoint

CHOICE BOX

area	angle	shape	square	congruent
perimeter	circle	cone	map	diameter
circumference	rectangle	triangle	measure	radius

146. Skills Mastery Test—Geometry and Measurement: Part One

★ Find the perimeter of each figure:

1.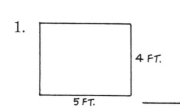
5 FT.   4 FT.

2.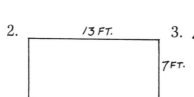
13 FT.   7 FT.

3.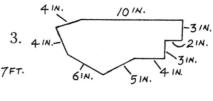
4 IN.   10 IN.   3 IN.   4 IN.   2 IN.   3 IN.   6 IN.   5 IN.   4 IN.

★ Find the area of each figure:

4.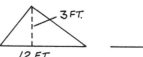
3 FT.   3 FT.

5.
17 IN.   8 IN.

6.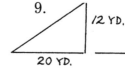
5 FT.   4 FT.   9 FT.   7 FT.

★ Find the area of each triangle:

7.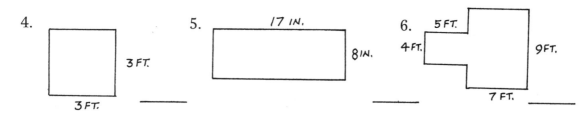
3 FT.   12 FT.

8. 4 IN.   11 IN.

9. 12 YD.   20 YD.

★ Draw a line from the device or situation to be measured on the left to units of measure on the right. (Some are used more than once.)

10. Sandal size   number of stories (or floors)

11. Height of an office building   milligrams

12. Height of your friend   horsepower

13. How heavy you are   dollars and cents

14. Weight of pills or medication   years

15. The power of a car motor   feet or yards

16. The cost of a turkey   quarts or liters

17. The age of your girl/boyfriend inches or centimeters

18. The length of your driveway   pounds or kilograms

19. Container of orange juice   cups, teaspoons, tablespoons

20. Recipe ingredients

Copyright © 2003 by John Wiley & Sons, Inc.

Copyright © 2003 by John Wiley & Sons, Inc.

NAME _____   DATE _____

147. Skills Mastery Test—Geometry and Measurement: Part Two

★ Find the circumference of the following circles:

1.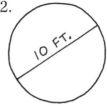
8 FT.

2.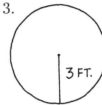
10 FT.

3.
3 FT.

★ Find the area of the following circles:

4.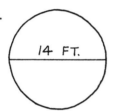
14 FT.

5.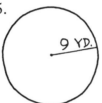
9 YD.

6.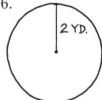
2 YD.

★ Measure these lines using the metric system:

7. ——————   8. ——————   9. ———————

★ Name these three angles:

10.

11.

12.

★ Measure the following angles using a protractor:

13.

14.

15.

★ Find the volume of these cubes:

16.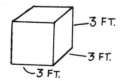
3 FT.
3 FT.
3 FT.

17.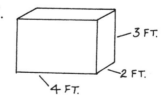
3 FT.
2 FT.
4 FT.

★ Find the volume of these pyramids and cones:

18.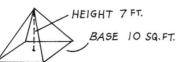
HEIGHT 7 FT.
BASE 10 SQ.FT.

19.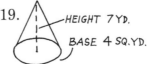
HEIGHT 7 YD.
BASE 4 SQ.YD.

20.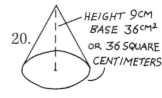
HEIGHT 9CM
BASE 36CM²
OR 36 SQUARE
CENTIMETERS

SECTION 7

CHARTS AND GRAPHS TO STIMULATE AND ENRICH

148. The Horizontal Bar Graph

★ Many bar graphs use bars that go up and down (vertical) but not all do. Some go sideways (horizontal). Each graph, no matter which way it goes, is a tool used for comparing and must be "read." Let's read the horizontal bar graph below by answering the questions. (All answers will be approximate.)

**The Value of 1934 Ford Hot Rods
with Modern V8 Motor and Automatic Transmission**

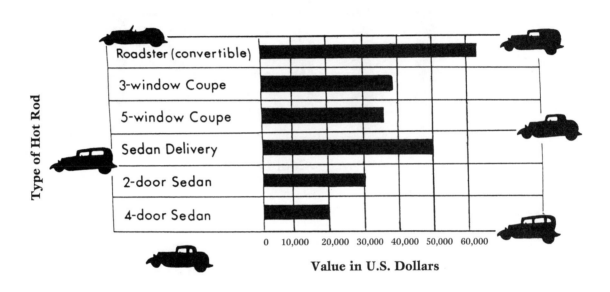

Copyright © 2003 by John Wiley & Sons, Inc.

1. What is the value of the 4-door sedan? _____

2. How much more is the value of the roadster than the value of the sedan delivery? _____

3. What is the value of the 3-window coupe? _____

4. What body style is closest in value to the 5-window coupe? _____

5. How much more in value is the sedan delivery than the 2-door sedan?

   _____

149. A Cool Bar Graph

★ Your task is to read the following bar graph and answer the questions below.

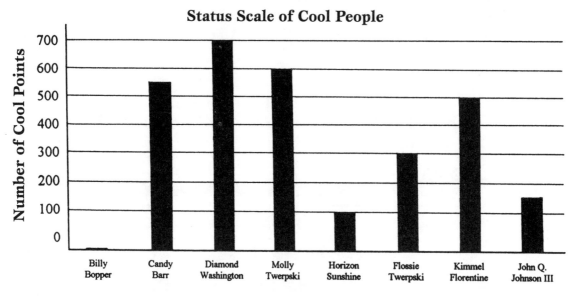

Status Scale of Cool People

1. The person with the most amount of

   cool is _____.

2. How many more "cool" points does Kimmel Florentine have than Billy Bopper?

   _____

3. Candy Barr states that she is so intelligent, she must be the "coolest" person of all. Is this true compared to Flossie Twerpski?

   _____

4. Name the cool person who is 50 points from Molly Twerpski.

   _____

5. The person with the least amount of cool is

   _____.

6. If Horizon Sunshine lost 50% of her coolness, how many points would she have

   left? _____

Copyright © 2003 by John Wiley & Sons, Inc.

NAME _____   DATE _____

150. A Cool Bar Graph (Continued)

★   Use the bar graph on worksheet 149 to answer these questions.

1. Which person is more cool, Candy Barr or Kimmel Florentine?
   _____

2. Molly Twerpski is going to lend her sister Flossie 100 cool points next week. How many points will Flossie have after this? _____ How many points will this leave Molly with? _____

3. What is the total amount of cool points shown for the top three cool people? _____

4. Candy Barr doesn't deserve the points she has. Take 35% of her points away. How many points does this leave her with? _____

5. Horizon Sunshine insulted Diamond Washington and therefore lost 73 cool points because Diamond was higher on the status scale. How many points does Horizon have now? _____

6. John Q. Johnson III thinks he should be equal to Kimmel Florentine because his name is "so cool." How many points does John Q. need to be equal to Kimmel Florentine? _____

7. Billy Bopper became the School President and gained 150 cool points. How many points does he have now? _____

8. Kimmel Florentine was the number-one choice of the Boston Bruins (the best NHL hockey team). This gives him 20% more points on the graph. He now has _____ points.

9. Molly Twerpski and Candy Barr rescued a child from the Speed River. Add 100 points to each of their graph scores. Molly now has _____ points. Candy now has _____ points.

10. Horizon Sunshine and John Q. Johnson III were seen wearing sneakers cut down to "Cheater Slippers." Add 140 points to their graph scores. Horizon now has _____ points. John Q. now has _____ points.

Copyright © 2003 by John Wiley & Sons, Inc.

151. The Picture Graph

★ The picture graph is another way to make quick comparisons by providing information visually. They are easy to read. Let's read the following picture graph.

The Number of Horses by Breed in the U.S.A.

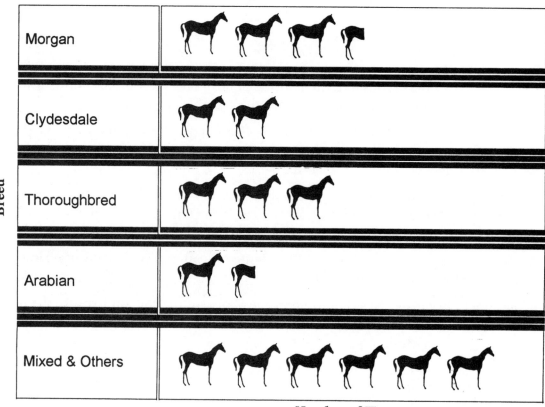

Number of Horses

Each horse = 10,000 animals

Copyright © 2003 by John Wiley & Sons, Inc.

1. Which horse *breed* has 35,000 horses? _____

2. Why do two of the breeds have half horses at the end?

_____

3. In the U.S., how many more Clydesdales are there than Arabians?

_____

4. Does this graph show the financial value of the horses? _____

5. What is the total number of Thoroughbreds, Morgans, and Arabians?

_____

Copyright © 2003 by John Wiley & Sons, Inc.

NAME _____   DATE _____

152. The Line Graph in Action

★ Line graphs are used to make comparisons. They consist of lines that reflect information. They usually show the up or down, the gain or loss, of an item, event, trend, or process! Use this line graph to answer these questions.

1. Between May and September, which activity had the greatest growth in popularity?

_____

2. Did the popularity of video games drop between March and July? _____

   If yes, by how much?

_____

3. During what months did the popularity of fashions and styles drop the most?

_____

4. What activities showed a decline in popularity from February to March?

_____

5. What two activities had the least amount of change?

_____

_____

6. Which activity was most popular in the summer?

_____

7. Which activity was the least popular in the winter?

_____

8. Is it possible to predict the time of popularity of certain activities by using the graph? _____

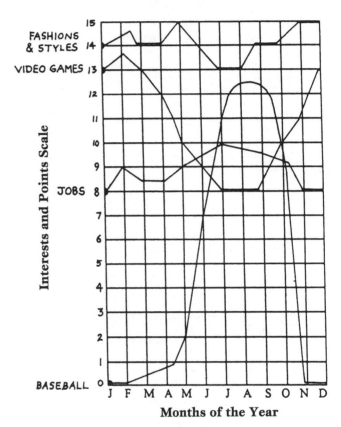

Teenage Interest for Different Months of the Year

171

153. Constructing a Line Graph

★ Place the following information from the table on the graph below. Plot the line graph. The number of sneakers worn in 1993 has been marked on the graph to get you started.

The Number of Pairs of Sneakers Worn by the Wonderful
Students Per Year at Cody High, Cody, Wyoming

Year	Number Worn	Year	Number Worn
1993	240	2000	370
1994	320	2001	320
1995	220	2002	200
1996	370	2003	270
1997	390	2004	320
1998	320	2005	220
1999	340	2006	200

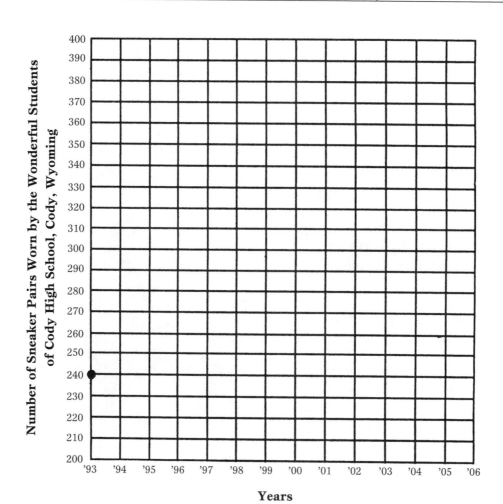

Copyright © 2003 by John Wiley & Sons, Inc.

154. Circle Graphs or Pie Charts

One of the most effective graphs or charts that can instantly give us a great deal of information is the Circle Graph or Pie Chart. The chart is separated into "pie pieces" that most often indicate the percent of an item or situation. It can also be used to indicate the exact number of something.

★   Study the circle graphs or pie charts below and answer the questions on worksheets 155 and 156.

Pies in America

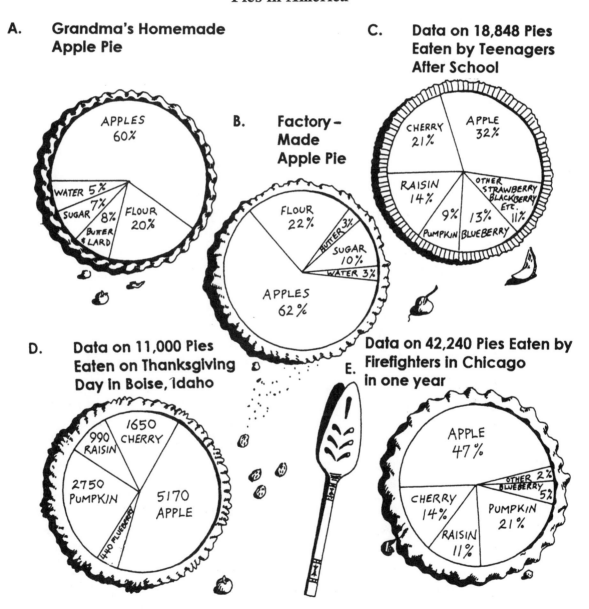

A.   Grandma's Homemade Apple Pie

APPLES 60%
WATER 5%
SUGAR 7%
8%
FLOUR 20%
BUTTER & LARD

B.   Factory-Made Apple Pie

FLOUR 22%
BUTTER 3%
SUGAR 10%
WATER 3%
APPLES 62%

C.   Data on 18,848 Pies Eaten by Teenagers After School

CHERRY 21%
APPLE 32%
RAISIN 14%
OTHER STRAWBERRY BLACKBERRY ETC.
9% 13% 11%
PUMPKIN BLUEBERRY

D.   Data on 11,000 Pies Eaten on Thanksgiving Day in Boise, Idaho

1650 CHERRY
990 RAISIN
2750 PUMPKIN
5170 APPLE
440 BLUEBERRY

E.   Data on 42,240 Pies Eaten by Firefighters in Chicago in one year

APPLE 47%
OTHER 2%
BLUEBERRY 5%
CHERRY 14%
PUMPKIN 21%
RAISIN 11%

Copyright © 2003 by John Wiley & Sons, Inc.

155. Circle Graphs or Pie Charts: Questions

★   In order to answer the questions below, you must "read" the graphs from
     worksheet 154.

1. What percent less flour is in Grandma's apple pie than factory-made apple pie?
    _____

2. By percent, how many more apple pies than blueberry pies were consumed by
    teenagers? _____

3. How many more pumpkin pies by percent were consumed by firefighters in
    Chicago in one year than blueberry pies? _____

4. In Boise, Idaho, how many more apple pies were eaten than pumpkin pies?
    _____

5. If 1,000 factory-made pies weigh 2,228 pounds, how much does each one weigh?
    _____

6. If 1,000 factory-made pies weigh 2,228 pounds, what is the weight of sugar
    used? _____

7. If Grandma's homemade apple pie weighs 40 ounces, how many ounces are
    water? _____

8. How much less sugar is in Grandma's apple pie than factory-made apple pie by
    percent? _____

9. What is the total percent of pies eaten by teenagers after school, not including
    "apple" and "other"? _____

10. The number of pumpkin pies eaten by firefighters in Chicago decreased by 4%.
    How many pies is this? _____

Copyright © 2003 by John Wiley & Sons, Inc.

156. Circle Graphs or Pie Charts: More Questions

★ **In order to answer the questions below, you must "read" the graphs from worksheet 154.**

1. By percent, how many more apple pies did the firefighters in Chicago eat than teenagers ate after school? _____

2. If factory-made pies use 920 pounds of ingredients for one batch, how many pounds of sugar, apples, and water are used? _____

3. On Thanksgiving Day in Boise, Idaho, how many fewer cherry pies were eaten than pumpkin pies? _____

4. How many raisin pies were eaten by firefighters in Chicago? _____

5. How many more apple pies were consumed by people in Boise, Idaho in one day than blueberry pies by firefighters in Chicago in a year? _____

6. What percent of the pies consumed in Boise on Thanksgiving Day were cherry? _____

7. How many more apple pies were consumed in Boise than blueberry and pumpkin together? _____

8. Firefighters in Chicago increased their apple pie consumption to 50% of the total of 42,240 pies. How many pies are they consuming now? _____

9. A factory pie costs $2.00 to make. If all ingredients cost the same, what is the cost of the flour? _____

10. What is *your* favorite kind of pie? _____

Copyright © 2003 by John Wiley & Sons, Inc.

157. Reading a Chart on Snowboarding

★   Here is a chart showing the data on snowboarding skills of seven teenagers. Read the chart and answer the questions that follow.

Name	Successful Runs	Completed but Wipeout Runs	Non-Completed Runs
Flipper Twerpski	272	74	63
Bighampton Jones	371	82	96
Billy Bopper	222	120	37
Candy Barr	372	4	2
Diamond Washington	229	96	16
Molly Twerpski	16	8	7
Horizon Sunshine	48	92	81

Copyright © 2003 by John Wiley & Sons, Inc.

1. How many runs in total did Bighampton Jones attempt? _____

2. Who is the best snowboarder? _____

3. How many more successful runs did Billy Bopper have than wipeout runs and non-completed runs? _____

4. How many more successful runs did Flipper Twerpski have than his sister Molly? _____

5. What is the total number of run attempts made by all the teenagers? _____

6. How many more wipeout runs did Diamond Washington have than Horizon Sunshine? _____

7. How many more completed runs did Candy Barr have than Flipper Twerpski? _____

8. Who had the largest number of wipeout and non-completed runs?
    _____

158. Definition Puzzle on Graphs and Charts

★ Place the answers to this puzzle in their correct locations across or down. A Choice Box has been provided.

Copyright © 2003 by John Wiley & Sons, Inc.

ACROSS

1. A line going sideways, not up and down
4. A way to organize and represent information
5. Judgment of two or more things
6. The final result of something
8. Placing data on a graph
10. Part of a line on a graph
11. An instrument used to measure weight
14. A circle graph piece

DOWN

2. A line going up and down, not sideways
3. A distance between two points
7. A caption on a map or chart
9. Information to be put on a graph
12. To use something with others
13. To keep track of something on a graph, or an old-fashioned music disk (different pronunciation)
15. A round figure

CHOICE BOX

segment	legend	vertical	outcome	record
circle	comparison	scale	share	pie
graph	horizontal	plot	line	data

159. Skills Mastery Test—Graphs and Charts

★ Read the bar graph and answer the questions below.

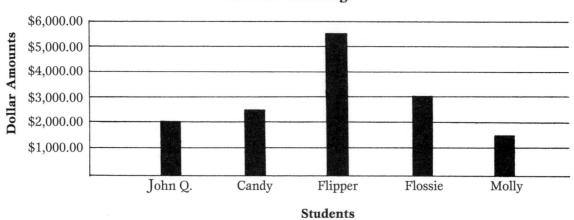

Summer Earnings

1. Which person made the most money? _____ How much more did

   she/he earn than the next highest earner? _____

2. How much money did Molly and Candy make together? _____

3. How much more money did Flipper make than John Q.? _____

4. How much money did Flipper and Flossie make together? _____

5. Which two people had the least amount of income for the summer?

   _____ and _____

6. Flossie is going to lend Molly half of her income. How much will Molly have

   now? _____ How much will Flossie have left? _____

7. Take 10% of John Q.'s money and give it to charity. How much does he have

   left? _____

8. How much money will it take for Candy to be equal to Flipper?

   _____

Copyright © 2003 by John Wiley & Sons, Inc.

SECTION 8

HOOKED ON RATIO, PROBABILITY, AND AVERAGE

LEARNING

Copyright © 2003 by John Wiley & Sons, Inc.

NAME _____   DATE _____

160. Probability: Ten Thinking Questions

★ What is the probability or the chance of the following situations occurring? Place answers in lowest terms.

WHAT IS THE PROBABILITY OF:

1. Having 7 worms of 7 different lengths in a cup and picking out the longest one on the first try? _____

2. Finding a good skateboard location on the first try if there are 8 good places in town but only 2 are open today? _____

3. Competing for the 1 position left in the Extreme Snowboard Competitions if there are 72 people—including yourself—trying to qualify? _____

4. Picking a green ball on the first try out of a barrel of 3 green, 1 blue, and 5 red balls? _____

5. Picking a cool person to model at the fashion show from your class of 28 cool students? _____

6. You have 5 alphabet blocks in a sack. Each block has 6 sides. The 26 letters of the alphabet are on the sides painted blue; 4 letters are repeated, but they are on the sides painted red. What is the probability of seeing a red repeated letter first when you look into the sack? _____

7. Rolling a 4 on a single die? _____

8. Picking a queen out of a deck of cards that are face down? _____

9. Flipping a coin and getting heads the first time? _____

10. The sun rising in the morning? _____

OPTIONAL OPINION/DISCUSSION QUESTION:

What is the probability of UFOs being real alien spacecraft and extraterrestrial beings landing on Earth? _____ (Discuss after you have answered.) If your opinion changed after the discussion, write your new answer here._____

161. Probability: Reading Story Problems

★ **What is the probability or the chance of the following situations occurring? Write the answers mathematically, for example: 3 out of 11 or $\frac{3}{11}$. If you have an answer like 5 out of 10 or $\frac{5}{10}$, simplify this to: $\frac{5}{10} = \frac{1}{2}$ or 1 out of 2.**

1. You have 5 DVDs mixed up in your school bag. What is the probability of reaching in once and pulling out the one you want? _____

2. Your best friend couldn't find the 2 video magazines you need, so you stick your hand into his messy pile of 48 magazines and draw only 1 out. What is the probability of it being one of the ones you want? _____

3. Your best friend can't find your 7 super-expensive cashmere sweaters in her pile of 455 pieces of strewn clothing (sound familiar?) in her closet. What is the probability of finding one of your sweaters by taking the one on top of the pile?

   _____

4. You are a cool person because your wonderful sister/brother is buying you one of the latest style tops as a gift. Your sister/brother must choose from 3 brown tops, 2 red tops, 1 yellow top, and 1 pink top. You, however, only want a brown or yellow top. What is the probability your brother/sister will buy you one of the tops you want? _____

5. Your best friend asks you for a dime. You have 3 dimes, 4 nickels, 2 quarters, and 1 penny in your pocket. You thrust your hand into your pocket and pull out the first coin you touch. What is the probability of it being a dime? _____

OPTIONAL OPINION/DISCUSSION QUESTION:

What is the probability of your sister/brother lending you his/her new $82,407 Viper sports car the first day you get your driver's license? You live in a quiet neighborhood without much traffic, but it took you 17 tries (or attempts) to get your license. _____ (Discuss after you have answered.) If your opinion changed after the discussion, write your new answer here. _____

Copyright © 2003 by John Wiley & Sons, Inc.

Copyright © 2003 by John Wiley & Sons, Inc.

162. The Application of Average or Mean

QUICK ACCESS INFORMATION ➜ In order to find the average of a set or group of numbers, you must add the numbers and divide by the number of numbers in the set. For example, if you have 3 numbers—27, 32, and 19—and you add them to total 78, you must divide by 3 to find the average, which is 26. This average is often called the *mean*.

Kelvington Cones—The Serious Ice Cream Stand
People Served for One Week

Server	S	M	T	W	T	F	S	Totals
Tony	113	141	147	225	68	171	38	
Kevin	107	182	149	147	42	221	91	
Karrie	118	191	121	298	191	141	111	
Dave	120	228	130	120	247	240	142	
Ruth	327	73	328	35	211	362	271	
Totals								

★ **Use the chart above to answer these questions. Give answers to two decimal places.**

1. Add the totals for each column, both vertically and horizontally. Write the totals in the chart.

2. What was the average or mean number of people served on Friday by each server? _____

3. What was the average or mean number of people served by Tony per day for the week? _____

4. On average, how many more people were served by Dave than by Kevin per day for the week? _____

5. What was the average or mean number of people served on Monday by each server? _____

6. On average, how many people did Karrie serve per day for the week? _____

7. On average, how many people did Ruth serve per day for the week? _____

8. There were 35 "salesperson days" available in which to buy cones. How many were bought on 1 "salesperson day"? _____

163. Mean, Mode, and Median

QUICK ACCESS
information

QUICK ACCESS INFORMATION ➜

The *mean* of a group of numbers is the average. To find the mean or average, we must first add our numbers, then divide by the number of numbers. Our total of the example set is 105, and there are 5 numbers, so we divide 105 by 5: 105 ÷ 5 = 21. The *mean* or average of the example set is 21.

The *mode* in a set or group of numbers is the one that occurs most often. The number 14 occurs most often in our example set, so 14 is the *mode*.

The *median* is the middle number in a set or group of numbers. When those numbers are arranged from largest to least or from least to largest, 23 is our middle number in the example set, so it is the *median*. In columns or sets of numbers that have an even number of numbers, you need to add the two central numbers and divide by 2 to get the median.

Example Set
14
14
23
24
30
105

★ Find the mean, mode, and median of these sets of numbers. If an answer is not available, put N/A.

1. 15   Mean _____
   15
   21   Mode _____
   24
   25   Median _____

2. 350   Mean _____
   327
   283   Mode _____
   Median _____

3. 32   Mean _____
   19
   19   Mode _____
   6
   Median _____

4. 32   Mean _____
   33
   35   Mode _____
   35
   35   Median _____

5. 37   Mean _____
   28
   14   Mode _____
   12
   11   Median _____
   11
   6

6. 1   Mean _____
   2
   3   Mode _____
   4
   5   Median _____
   5
   5
   6
   5

Copyright © 2003 by John Wiley & Sons, Inc.

Copyright © 2003 by John Wiley & Sons, Inc.

NAME _____   DATE _____

164. Alpha-Numerical Puzzle

★ Your task is to calculate the problems in order. The answer to each problem will correspond with a letter of the alphabet. Write each letter on the lines below in order to reveal an important truth. Some letters are used more than once. The first one is done to help you get started.

8	23	55	45	7	44	75	69	11	71	72	86	87	9	1	19	32	40	78	25	33	37	34	91	37	22
A	B	C	D	E	F	G	H	I	J	K	L	M	N	O	P	Q	R	S	T	U	V	W	X	Y	Z

$$\overset{T}{\underline{\quad}}\ \underline{\quad}\ \underline{\quad}\qquad \underline{\quad}\ \underline{\quad}\ \underline{\quad}\ \underline{\quad}\qquad \underline{\quad}\ \underline{\quad}\ \underline{\quad}\ \underline{\quad}\ \underline{\quad}\ \underline{\quad}\qquad \underline{\quad}\ \underline{\quad}$$

(Question #s)   1   2   3   4   5   6   7   8   9   10   11   12   13   14   15

$$\underline{\quad}\ \underline{\quad}\ \underline{\quad}\ \underline{\quad}\qquad \underline{\quad}\ \underline{\quad}\ \underline{\quad}\qquad \underline{\quad}\ \underline{\quad}\ \underline{\quad}\ \underline{\quad}\ .$$

(Question #s)   16   17   18   19   20   21   22   23   24   25   26

1. 5×5

2. $621 \div 9$

3. Subtract 1145 from the sum of 897 and 255

4. $327 - 304$

5. The average of 12, 4, and 5

6. $97 - 19$

7. $75 - 50$

8. The number of 10's in 252

9. 23×3

10. $159 - 69 + 6 - 85$

11. 3^2

12. 15×5

13. $21 + 57$

14. The average of 14, 12, and 7

15. $81 \div 9$

16. $5074 \div 59$

17. $721 - 710$

18. $327 - 283$

19. $258 - 251$

20. $327 - 319$

21. $62 - 22$

22. $45 \times 5 - 218$

23. $350 - 306$

24. $5 \times 62 - 270$

25. $298 + 74 - 365$

26. $6547 - 6540$

185

165. Introduction to Ratios

QUICK ACCESS information

QUICK ACCESS INFORMATION ➔ We use ratios to compare one thing to another. For example, you can compare the number of people who came to a party (22) to the number of people invited (41).

These numbers are called the terms of the ratio.

(Number of people who came) **22 : 41** (Number of people invited)

This symbol means "compared to."

★ Write a ratio in simplest form to compare the number of things below.

1. Bangs to Bucks _____ : _____

2. DVDs to Pigs _____ : _____

3. Cows to DVDs _____ : _____

4. Pigs to Bucks _____ : _____

5. Cows to Pigs _____ : _____

6. Cows to Bucks _____ : _____

7. Bucks to DVDs _____ : _____

8. Bangs to Pigs _____ : _____

9. Bangs to Cows _____ : _____

10. DVDs to Bangs _____ : _____

Copyright © 2003 by John Wiley & Sons, Inc.

NAME _____   DATE _____

166. Ratio Word Problems

★   **Write the ratio in the space provided for each part of every question.**

1. Flipper Twerpski bought 7 of the new video game programs out of the 10 that were available.

   a.   What is the ratio of the number bought to the number available?
   _____

   b.   What is the ratio of the number *not* bought to the number available?
   _____

   c.   What is the ratio of the number *not* bought to the number bought?
   _____

2. Flossie Twerpski (Flipper's sister) went bowling with Candy Barr. She got a strike 9 out of 15 attempts.

   a.   What is the ratio of strikes to attempts?   _____

   b.   What is the ratio of missed strikes to attempts?   _____

   c.   What is the ratio of strikes to missed strikes?   _____

3. Thirty-eight students with unusual and wonderful names (like Betty Bopalouper) attend Cody High School. There are 20 girls and 18 boys in this group.

   a.   What is the ratio of girls to boys?   _____

   b.   What is the ratio of boys to girls?   _____

   c.   What is the ratio of girls to the total number of students?   _____

   d.   What is the ratio of boys to the total number of students?   _____

4. Old McGillicutty and his wife had 17 children. The first ten children had normal names like Ted; however, seven of the children were named after a number like "Number 11" or "Number 17."

   a.   What is the ratio of those with number names to those with regular names?
   _____

   b.   What is the ratio of those with normal names to the total?   _____

   c.   **Trick Question:** What is the ratio of those with number names to the number of people in the family?   _____

Copyright © 2003 by John Wiley & Sons, Inc.

167. Three-Term Ratios

QUICK ACCESS information

QUICK ACCESS INFORMATION ➔ The ratio 4:7 is a two-term ratio comparing two things. However, if we use 3:4:7, we are now comparing three things. The money in your pocket or wallet, for example, could be a comparison of pennies to nickels to dimes. 3:4:7 could then be 3 pennies to 4 nickels to 7 dimes.

We can make two-term ratios out of three-term ratios by separating them into groups of two's. For example, the ratio of the number of pennies to nickels is 3:4, the number of nickels to dimes is 4:7, and the number of pennies to dimes is 3:7.

Remember, simplify all ratios.

Letters can also be used with or instead of numbers.

★ Make three different two-term ratios in simplest form from *each* three-term ratio. The first one has been completed to get you started.

1.   4:1:9
     4:1
     1:9
     4:9

2.   7:8:4
     _____
     _____
     _____

3.   9:11:22
     _____
     _____
     _____

4.   17:34:68
     _____
     _____
     _____

5.   4:5:20
     _____
     _____
     _____

6.   A:14:28
     _____
     _____
     _____

7.   B:4:G
     _____
     _____
     _____

8.   4:7:X
     _____
     _____
     _____

9.   Y:X:2
     _____
     _____
     _____

10.   A:B:C
     _____
     _____
     _____

Bonus: Make three different 2-word phrases or compound words from the following:

kick, drop, off

_____

_____

_____

man, show, floor

_____

_____

_____

Copyright © 2003 by John Wiley & Sons, Inc.

168. Understanding Forms
(Ratio, Fraction, and Written)

★ Math concepts can take different forms but still have the same value. Here we see ratios, fractions and written forms of the same number. Fill in the following chart. The first two have been completed to help you get started.

Ratio Form	Fraction Form	Written Form	Ratio Form Using "To"
2:5	$\frac{2}{5}$	two-fifths	2 to 5
7:8	$\frac{7}{8}$	seven-eighths	7 to 8
	$\frac{2}{3}$		
			1 to 4
		five-eighths	
1:7			
			4 to 5
4:9			
	$\frac{3}{7}$		
			7 to 11
		three-fifths	
	$\frac{1}{10}$		
5:9			
		four-elevenths	

Copyright © 2003 by John Wiley & Sons, Inc.

169. Proportions Explained

QUICK ACCESS INFORMATION ➜   The directions on the pancake box require certain ingredients. You can use a ratio to compare the number of cups of pancake mix to the number of cups of milk.

<u>For 1 batch of pancakes:</u>
   Number of cups of pancake mix → 2:3 ← Number of cups of milk
<u>For 2 batches of pancakes:</u>
   Number of cups of pancake mix → 4:6 ← Number of cups of milk

The ratios 2:3 and 4:6 are known as equivalent ratios. When an equation shows two ratios are equivalent, it is known as a proportion and is written like this:
$$2:3 = 4:6$$

To obtain equivalent ratios (proportions), you must multiply both sides by the same number. For example, 7:4 → multiply each by 3 (or both by any other number), which equals $7 \times 3 = 21$ and $4 \times 3 = 12$ so the equivalent ratio to $7:4 = 21:12$.

★   Make two proportions from the following ratios by multiplying them by the number 2, 3, 4, 5, or 7. The first one has been done for you.

1. 3:4 =   **9:12** (multiplied by 3)
             6:8 (multiplied by 2)

2. 7:2 =   _____

              _____

3. 9:4 =   _____

              _____

4. 17:4 = _____

              _____

5. 12:7 = _____

              _____

6. 2:9 =   _____

              _____

7. 1:2 =   _____

              _____

8. 1:8 =   _____

              _____

9. 1:4 =   _____

              _____

10. 4:11 = _____

              _____

11. 2:7 = _____

              _____

12. 7:11 = _____

              _____

13. 9:5 = _____

              _____

14. 3:5 = _____

              _____

15. 4:7 = _____

              _____

Copyright © 2003 by John Wiley & Sons, Inc.

170. Definition Puzzle
on Ratios, Probability, and Average

★ Place the answers to this puzzle in their correct locations across or down. A Choice Box has been provided.

Copyright © 2003 by John Wiley & Sons, Inc.

ACROSS

1. The likelihood that something will occur
3. You make this when you judge two or more things together
6. When things get bigger or larger
7. The shape or style of something
9. When things are equal, they are _____
10. When you add a column of numbers and divide by the number of numbers
13. The middle number in a set or column of numbers (when ordered least to greatest or greatest to least)
14. What something is worth
15. %

DOWN

2. 3:5:7 is a three-_____ ratio
4. When you lose something, it is a _____
5. A name given when two ratios are equal
8. A regular form or shape
11. The average of a set or column of numbers
12. The number that occurs most often in a set or column of numbers

CHOICE BOX

increase	mean	mode	loss	median
equivalent	probability	proportion	forms	value
pattern	term	comparison	average	percent

171. Skills Mastery Test—Ratio, Probability, and Average

★   Write these ratios in simplest form:

1. 2:4 = _____   2. 6:24 = _____   3. 7:28 = _____   4. 25:75 = _____

★   Put these ratios in simplest fraction form:

5. 4:10 = _____   6. 10:200 = _____   7. 14:21 = _____   8. 6:8 = _____

★   Make three different two-term ratios from each three-term ratio:

9. 5:1:7 = _____   10. A:B:Z = _____

_____   _____

_____   _____

★   Make two proportions from the following ratios by multiplying by the number 2, 3, 4, 5, or 7:

11. 5:1 = _____, _____   12. 3:7 = _____, _____

★   What is the mean, mode, and median of these sets of numbers?

13. 14   mean _____   14. 353   mean _____
    14   350
    23   mode _____   284   mode _____
    24
    25   median _____   median _____

★   Answer this question:

15. What is the probability of picking a nickel out of a jar on the first try if there are 10 nickels, 5 dimes, and 2 pennies in the jar? _____

Copyright © 2003 by John Wiley & Sons, Inc.

SECTION 9

PRE-ALGEBRA AND EARLY ALGEBRA SKILL BUILDERS

172. Understanding "N" and "X" in Math

QUICK ACCESS
information

> **QUICK ACCESS INFORMATION** ➜ In math the letters "N," "X," etc., often take the place of numbers. When multiplying by 4, for example, we write the form 4N or 4(N), 4X or 4(X). This form is used for two reasons: (1) To write 4XN or 4XX would cause confusion with the letter X. To write 4 times N or 4 times X would be too long in order to write math questions.

★ Calculate the problem above each box and place the answer in the box below the problem. The first set has been completed for you.

Copyright © 2003 by John Wiley & Sons, Inc.

SET 1

N = 234

2N or 2(N)

468

3N or 3(N)

702

2N + 3N

1170

SET 2

N = 428

3N or 3(N)

2N or 2(N)

3N − 2N

SET 3

X = 327

4X or 4(X)

2X or 2(X)

4X − 2X

SET 4

X = 375

5X or 5(X)

3X or 3(X)

5X − 3X

173. Using the Word "of" in Math

QUICK ACCESS INFORMATION ➡ When used in a fraction problem or equation, the word "of" means to multiply together the numbers on either side of it. For example, $\frac{1}{2}$ of $50 = \frac{1}{2} \times 50 = 25$.

★ Calculate the equation above each box and place the answer in the box below the equation. The first one has been started for you.

SET 1

N = 60

$\frac{1}{2}$ of N

| 30 |

$\frac{1}{3}$ of N

| |

$\frac{1}{2}N - \frac{1}{3}N$

| |

SET 2

N = 100

$\frac{2}{5}$ of N

| |

$\frac{3}{5}$ of N

| |

$\frac{3}{5}N - \frac{2}{5}N$

| |

SET 3

N = 49

$\frac{2}{7}$ of N

| |

$\frac{6}{7}$ of N

| |

$\frac{6}{7}N - \frac{2}{7}N$

| |

SET 4

X = 72

$\frac{1}{8}$ of X

| |

$\frac{3}{8}$ of X

| |

$\frac{1}{8}X + \frac{3}{8}X$

| |

SET 5

X = 48

$\frac{1}{4}$ of X

| |

$\frac{1}{2}$ of X

| |

$\frac{1}{4}X + \frac{1}{2}X$

| |

Copyright © 2003 by John Wiley & Sons, Inc.

NAME _____   DATE _____

174. Balance in Algebra

QUICK ACCESS
information

QUICK ACCESS INFORMATION ➜   There are certain rules we must follow when we begin to work with algebra. They are:

1. The value of the letter in a problem or equation is what we are looking for.

2. What you do to one side of the equation, you must do to the other side in order to keep balance.

3. The letters X and Y are the most commonly used letters in algebra. Other letters are used to a lesser extent.

★   Solve the following equations in the space below. Then find the answer in the mixed-up list on the right and write the equation's number on the appropriate line. The first one has been done for you.

1. $5 + X = 8$ _____ X = 20

2. $X + 3 = 13$ _____ Y = 9

3. $X + 7 = 12$ _____ Y = 6

4. $Y + 5 = 13$ _____ X = 2

5. $X + 8 = 19$ _____ X = 12

6. $X - 3 = 17$ _____ Y = 8

7. $X + 2 = 19$ __1__ X = 3

8. $5 + Y = 14$ _____ Y = 29

9. $7 + Y = 42$ _____ X = 11

10. $11 + Y = 17$ _____ X = 5

11. $7 + X = 31$ _____ Y = 35

12. $X + 9 = 11$ _____ X = 24

13. $X - 5 = 7$ _____ X = 17

14. $-3 + X = 41$ _____ X = 10

15. $-5 + Y = 24$ _____ X = 44

Copyright © 2003 by John Wiley & Sons, Inc.

175. The Order of Operations

QUICK ACCESS INFORMATION ➡ In order to calculate equations, there must be an order by which they are completed. If a surgeon needs to operate on a person with multiple problems, the surgeon will do the most necessary operation first. These rules are very important in algebra because once you substitute for the variable (replace the letter with a number), you must use the proper order of operations.

Memorize this order of operations:

1. Do the work in brackets or parentheses first (7×2).

2. Calculate the values of the powers (5^2, the value of expressions with exponents).

3. Do multiplication or division in the order they appear.

4. Do addition or subtraction in the order they appear.

★ Solve the equations below. The equations in Set 2 use the same numbers as the equations in Set 1, but brackets and numbers with exponents have been changed. Do you get the same answers?

SET 1	SET 2
1. $71 \times 4 + (2 - 1) =$ _____	1. $71 \times (4 + 2) - 1 =$ _____
2. $(18 + 7) - 4 \times 2 =$ _____	2. $18 + (7 - 4) \times 2 =$ _____
3. $22 + (19 - 8) \times 2 =$ _____	3. $22 + (19 - 8) \times 2^2 =$ _____
4. $(22 + 9) + (5 \times 4) =$ _____	4. $22 + 9 + (5 \times 4^2) =$ _____
5. $(32 + 19) + (8 \times 4) =$ _____	5. $32 + (19 + 8) \times 4 =$ _____
6. $99 \times 2^2 + (9 - 7) =$ _____	6. $99 \times (2 + 9) - 7 =$ _____
7. $(28 - 24) - (4 \div 2) =$ _____	7. $28 - (24 - 4) \div 2 =$ _____
8. $(16 \div 2) + 22 \div 11 =$ _____	8. $(16 \div 2^2) + 22 \div 11 =$ _____
9. $(33 \div 3) + 9 + 11 =$ _____	9. $33 \div 11 + 3 + 9 =$ _____
10. $49 \div 7 + (7 \times 7) =$ _____	10. $(49 \div 7) + (7^2 \times 7) =$ _____

Copyright © 2003 by John Wiley & Sons, Inc.

176. A Look at the Language of Algebra

QUICK ACCESS INFORMATION ➔ When beginning to look at algebraic terms, it is necessary to understand the language used.

<u>Topic 1:</u> "3 increased by a number." We don't know what the number is, so we call it N or some other letter. If 3 is increased by a number, this means 3 + N. If we knew what the value of N was, we would not need to use the letter. If N = 2, we can then say 3 + N = 3 + 2 = 5.

<u>Topic 2:</u> The expression 4X is a common way of writing a number with a variable, but what does this mean? The 4 is a whole number and the X is an unknown number or variable. They are placed close together or are placed in brackets 4(X) or (4)(X) to indicate that they are to be multiplied together. If we say 4X or 4(X) or (4)(X) when X = 5, we can say (4)(5) or 4(5) = 20. This is done to avoid confusion with the multiplication sign and the letter X.

★ **Complete the following problems. Write what they mean in numbers, signs, and letters. The first one is done to help you get started.**

1. 4 increased by a number = **4 + N**

2. 3 decreased by a number =

3. 2 times a number =

4. 3 times a number decreased by 4 =

5. 7 multiplied by X =

6. 12 decreased by a number =

7. 12 increased by 2 times a number =

8. 13 decreased by a number squared =

9. 7 decreased by 2N =

10. 14 decreased by 3X =

11. Reduce N by 7 =

12. N less 4 =

13. X times 7 =

14. 17 times 3X =

15. 17 added to 17N =

16. 34 multiplied by 7X =

17. 21 reduced by 6X =

18. 47 decreased by 2M =

19. 20 decreased by 4X plus 7 squared =

20. 18 plus 2M decreased by 3B =

Copyright © 2003 by John Wiley & Sons, Inc.

177. What Are Exponents?

QUICK ACCESS information

> **QUICK ACCESS INFORMATION** ➡ When dealing with exponents, using a number like 5^2, the base number is 5 and the exponent is the little 2. This, in effect, means that $5^2 = 5 \times 5 = 25$ or 5 times itself; and 5^4 means $5 \times 5 \times 5 \times 5 = 625$ or 5 times itself 4 times.

★ Calculate the values of these numbers with exponents. The first one in each row has been completed for you.

1. $2^2 = $ **2 × 2 = 4**

2. $3^2 = $

3. $2^4 = $

4. $2^5 = $

5. $2^3 = $

6. $5^3 = $

7. $5^1 = $

8. $9^2 = $

9. $9^3 = $

10. $10^2 = $

11. $3^2 + 2^2 = $
    3 × 3 + 2 × 2 =
    9 + 4 = 13

12. $5^3 - 4^2 = $

13. $3^3 - 3^2 = $

14. $2^2 + 3^4 = $

15. $7^2 - 3^2 = $

16. $9^2 - 7^2 = $

17. $12^2 - 11^2 = $

18. $10^3 - 9^2 = $

19. $7^3 - 2^3 = $

20. $2^7 - 3^2 = $

21. $75 - 4^3 = $ **75 − 64 = 11**

22. $13 - 3^2 = $

23. $96 - 7^2 = $

24. $99 - 4^3 = $

25. $22 - 2^2 = $

26. $8 - 2^2 = $

27. $9 - 2^2 = $

28. $242 - 14^2 = $

29. $97 + 32^3 = $

30. $194{,}482 - 21^4 = $

Copyright © 2003 by John Wiley & Sons, Inc.

178. Substitution Box Questions in Early Algebra

★ Complete the following box questions. Then solve the
puzzle below. One is done for you.

Copyright © 2003 by John Wiley & Sons, Inc.

When x = 4
1. $5(x)$ =
2. $5x$ =
you

When B = 7
7. $2B + B$ =
8. $4B - 3B$ =
owe

When M = 8
13. $M + M$ =
14. $2M + M$ =
save

When x = 7
3. $2x - 1$ =
4. $3x - 2$ =
life

When A = 9
9. $A - 7$ =
10. $A + 4$ =

When N = 3
15. $3N - 2N$ =
16. $3N - N^2$ = 0
The

When y = 2
5. $7y + 2$ =
6. $3y - 4$ =

When x = 5
11. $2x - 7$ =
12. $3x - 10$ =
money

When x = 10
17. $x^2 - 2x$ =
18. $x^2 + 3x$ =
may

Look at the number below each line, go to your answers from the box questions, and
place the word on the line that corresponds or is in the same box as that answer.

___The___   _____   _____   _____   _____   _____
    0   19   20   24   130   21

_____   _____ .
    20   5

201

179. Basic Equations: Side Balancing

QUICK ACCESS information

> **QUICK ACCESS INFORMATION** ➜ When working with algebraic equations, it is important to know that "what you do to one side of the equation, you must do to the other side." *Example:* To solve $N - 3 = 4$ you must add the same number, 3, to both sides: $N - 3 + 3 = 4 + 3$. Therefore, $N = 7$.

★ Solve these equations to find the value of the letters.

1. $R - 3 = 7$

2. $A - 4 = 7$

3. $U - 4 = 18$

4. $N - 2 = 7$

5. $P + 7 = 14$

6. $Y - 3 = 4$

7. $S - 19 = 8$

8. $L + 5 = 11$

9. $F + 3 = 4$

10. $N + 2 = 39$

11. $5 + T = 13$

12. $4 + B = 18$

13. $K - 8 = 2$

14. $C - 4 = 9$

15. $E + 34 = 98$

16. $Y + 15 = 18$

17. $9 + G = 32$

18. $D - 2 = 21$

19. $H - 4 = 2$

20. $T - 1 = 1$

> **Bonus:** Place in order the letters used on the left into the sentence below to reveal a wonderful thing to do.
>
> ___each ___ro___nd
>
> a___d ___at
>
> ___our___e___ ___
>
> o___ ___he ___ac___
>
> be___aus___ ___ou
>
> fi___ure___ t___is
>
> ou___.

Copyright © 2003 by John Wiley & Sons, Inc.

180. Different Forms of Basic Equations
(Number Sentences)

★ Find the value of the variables (letters). The answers are somewhere in the answer barrel. Check them off as you complete each equation. (Two of the answers in the barrel are not used.)

1. $Y - 9 = 15$

2. $\dfrac{M}{8} = 8$

3. $3X = 45$

4. $\dfrac{X}{9} = 4$

5. $X - 6 = 15$

6. $3Y = 75$

7. $X - 17 = 3$

8. $\dfrac{N}{5} = 10$

9. $B - 5 = 14$

10. $7T = 49$

11. $\dfrac{X}{7} = 4$

12. $7X = 42$

13. $9T = 27$

14. $6 + X = 14$

15. $11 + M = 12$

16. $8 + M = 22$

17. $\dfrac{X}{4} = 11$

18. $7Y = 63$

3 64 22 15 36 24 25 21 44 9 20 6 8 10 7 50 19 28 14 1

I DARE ME TO OPEN THE LID.

Copyright © 2003 by John Wiley & Sons, Inc.

181. Quick Algebra, Right Now

★   Look at each equation and write the value of the letter in the space
    provided. Try to work as quickly—and accurately—as you can!

1. $N - 9 = 7$ _____	$X - 4 = 3$ _____	$X + 4 = 12$ _____	$12 - X = 7$ _____	$17 + N = 42$ _____
2. $22 + 5 = B$ _____	$37 + 9 = X$ _____	$X + 5 = 13$ _____	$M + 2 = 7$ _____	$B - 17 = 32$ _____
3. $X + 12 = 25$ _____	$7 + 7 = B$ _____	$14 - 5 = X$ _____	$14 - X = 3$ _____	$92 - Y = 68$ _____
4. $3 + X = 14$ _____	$9 - X = 3$ _____	$8 + 14 = B$ _____	$17 - X = 8$ _____	$32 + Y = 47$ _____
5. $18 - X = 4$ _____	$42 + B = 61$ _____	$34 - B = 7$ _____	$18 - 12 = M$ _____	$22 - 22 = Y$ _____
6. $19 - 5 = B$ _____	$19 + X = 32$ _____	$X - 4 = 17$ _____	$B - 12 = 9$ _____	**Free** **(How nice!)**

Copyright © 2003 by John Wiley & Sons, Inc.

182. Translating from Words to Numbers

★ A very necessary skill is the ability to translate (change and understand) what is written as words into math action. Below are pre-algebra questions that must be "translated" to number form and then completed.

1. This number is 3 less than the sum of 18 and 24. _____

2. This number is 14 more than the difference between 62 and 12. _____

3. When this number is divided by 3, it is $\frac{1}{3}$ of the number or 5. _____

4. Four times a number is equal to the average of 31 and 33. _____

5. Five times a number is equal to the average of 37 and 63. _____

6. Five times this number is $\frac{2}{5}$ of 150. _____

7. When multiplied by 4, this number is equal to the difference between 60 and 20. _____

8. 92 is 18 less than twice this number. _____

9. The square of this number is 4 less than the difference between 271 and 231. _____

10. Three times this number is $\frac{1}{3}$ of 36. _____

11. Twice the product of 4 and 8 is 5 less than this number. _____

12. This number is $\frac{7}{8}$ of 4^2 plus the product of 2 and 4. _____

Copyright © 2003 by John Wiley & Sons, Inc.

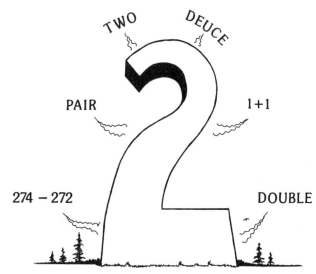

TWO   DEUCE

PAIR   1 + 1

274 − 272   DOUBLE

183. Positive and Negative Numbers

★ Let's put a thermometer on its side to learn about positive and negative numbers.

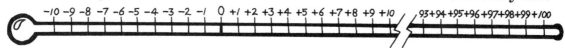

Seriously Cold   **Seriously Hot**

A form of numbers was needed to indicate values below zero as well as to indicate values above zero, so − and + signs were added to give these numbers a special form, style, or distinction, such as −2 and +7.

★ **A. Use > or < to make true statements below. The first two are completed to get you started.**

1. +2 ⊙ −2
   (+2 is warmer than −2)

2. −2 ⊙ −3
   (−2 is warmer than −3)

3. −7 ◯ −8

4. +2 ◯ −7

5. +3 ◯ +4

6. −11 ◯ −12

7. +14 ◯ −2

8. −1 ◯ +3

9. +4 ◯ +11

10. −1 ◯ +12

11. −17 ◯ −110

12. −110 ◯ +110

★ **B. Study the thermometer and then arrange these numbers from least (coldest) to greatest (warmest).**

1. +5, +6, +4, +1, 0
   _____

2. −8, −6, −10, 0, −3, −4
   _____

3. −3, −2, −5, +7, +6, +4
   _____

4. −5, +3, 0, −7, +8
   _____

5. −22, +14, −9, +82, −1
   _____

6. +97, −91, +94, −37, +91
   _____

7. +17, −1, 0, +32, +19
   _____

8. +14, −1000, +9200
   _____

9. +47, +55, −4, +19, −84
   _____

10. +19, −14, −11, −2, −17, −4, −1
    _____

Bonus Research Question: What is the temperature at Absolute Zero?

_____C° or _____F°

Copyright © 2003 by John Wiley & Sons, Inc.

184. Perimeter Expressions

We can write the perimeter of a figure by first making an expression and then simplifying it.

For example:

Expression → S + S + S + S
Simplified Expression → 4S

★ Write an expression for the perimeter of each figure. Place the simplified answer on the line.

1.
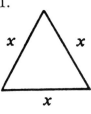

_____

2. **2b**

_____

3.
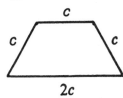

_____

4. **a**
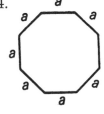

_____

5. **3a**
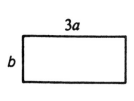

_____

6. **3m**
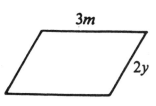

_____

7.
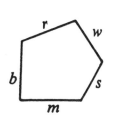

_____

8. **4b**

_____

9. **m**
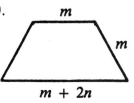

_____

10. **2r + 1**
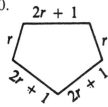

_____

11.
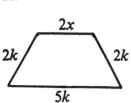

_____

12. **c + 2a**
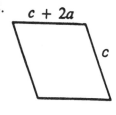

_____

Copyright © 2003 by John Wiley & Sons, Inc.

185. Understanding Integers

QUICK ACCESS
information

QUICK ACCESS INFORMATION ➜ An integer is another name for an ordinary number that is part of a set of numbers. An integer can be +4 and its opposite, −4. In this case, 0 is also an integer.

Here is a set of integers: . . . −4, −3, −2, −1, 0, +1, +2, +3, +4 . . .

★ Look at the blocks below. Choose integers from the boxes to construct your own equations. Construct three equations from each box. Two have been given to get you started.

  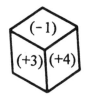 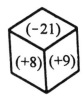

1. (+2) + (−3) = −1   4. _____ + _____   7. _____ − _____   10. _____ − _____

2. (−3) − (+2) = −5   5. _____ − _____   8. _____ + _____   11. _____ + _____

3. _____ + _____   6. _____ + _____   9. _____ − _____   12. _____ − _____

  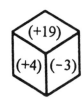 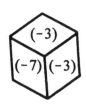 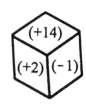

13. _____ + _____   16. _____ − _____   19. _____ + _____   22. _____ − _____

14. _____ − _____   17. _____ + _____   20. _____ − _____   23. _____ + _____

15. _____ + _____   18. _____ − _____   21. _____ + _____   24. _____ − _____

Copyright © 2003 by John Wiley & Sons, Inc.

186. Locating Integers on a Number Plane
(Grid)

QUICK ACCESS
information

QUICK ACCESS INFORMATION → In order to locate the point, we must know that the first number in the ordered pair means you move first right or left that number of spaces from the center 0. The second number means you then move up or down that number of spaces. For example, (+3, +2): We first move to the right 3 spaces, then we move up 2 spaces. This will give us the point on the grid we are looking for. We then label that point (+3, +2).

Copyright © 2003 by John Wiley & Sons, Inc.

③ Ordered pairs of integers here will have a − sign first and a + sign second, e.g., (−3, +2). Move 3 to the left from the center 0, then 2 up.

① Ordered pairs of integers (numbers) in this corner will have 2 + signs, e.g., (+ 3, + 2). To find this point, first move right 3 lines from the center 0, then 2 up from the black line at + 3.

④ Ordered pairs of integers here will have 2 − signs, e.g., (−3, −2). Move 3 to the left from center 0, then 2 down.

② Ordered pairs of integers (numbers) in this corner will have a + sign first and a − sign second, e.g., (+ 3, −2). Move 3 to the right and 2 down.

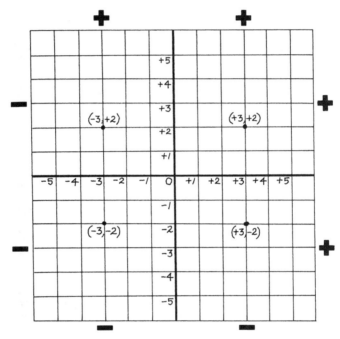

★ Find the ordered pairs listed below on the grid. Put a dot on the grid and label like those already there.

1. (+4, +2)   2. (+3, +4)   3. (+4, −1)   4. (+5, −5)

5. (−5, +5)   6. (−1, +5)   7. (−2, −4)   8. (−5, −4)

187. Square and Square Root Made Easy

QUICK ACCESS
information

> **QUICK ACCESS INFORMATION** ➜ In order to square a number, you must multiply the number by itself, e.g., $7 \times 7 = 49$ (49 is the square of 7). In order to find the square root of a number, you must find what number multiplied by itself equals the number you are working with. $\sqrt{\ }$ is the symbol used to indicate that square root is needed, e.g., $\sqrt{81}$. What number times itself is 81? We know that $9 \times 9 = 81$, so 9 is the square root of 81.

★ Study and complete the chart below. (Keep this completed chart for later use.)

Number or Square Root	Number times itself	Square
1	1×1	1
2	2×2	
	3×3	9
4		
		25
6		36
	7×7	
8		
9		81
		100
	11×11	121
12		
13		
14		
	15×15	
		256
		289
	18×18	
	19×19	
20		

Copyright © 2003 by John Wiley & Sons, Inc.

Copyright © 2003 by John Wiley & Sons, Inc.

188. Definition Puzzle on Pre-Algebra and Early Algebra Terms

★ Place the answers to this puzzle in their correct locations across or down. A Choice Box has been provided.

ACROSS

1. A number sentence like 7 − X = 20
4. A form of math using variables
5. When things do not agree
10. The process of doing something
11. A number like 5² with 5 as the base and ² as the exponent
13. A number that shows the number of times a base number is to be used as a factor
16. These are used to represent a number
17. When two or more things have some of the same properties

DOWN

2. An unknown represented by a letter
3. The arranging of numbers in a square
6. When you replace one thing with another
7. A word used to mean multiply
8. This tells you where to go or what to do
9. Signs used to enclose words, symbols, or figures ( )
12. What something is worth
14. When one side is the same value as another side
15. When something is by itself

CHOICE BOX

order	difference	power	algebra	operation
similarity	value	variable	substitute	sign
brackets	balance	of	exponent	alone
equation	letters			

189. Skills Mastery Test—Pre-Algebra and Early Algebra: Part One

★ **Write the value of the letter:**

1. $X - 7 = 4$ $X = $ _____
2. $N - 2 = 11$ $N = $ _____
3. $X + 7 = 12$ $X = $ _____
4. $13 + B = 15$ $B = $ _____

★ **Add these:**

5. $(+2) + (+1) = $ _____
6. $(+4) + (-3) = $ _____
7. $(-9) + (-7) = $ _____
8. $(-4) + (+2) = $ _____

★ **Use > or < to make true statements:**

9. $+7$ ◯ $+8$ 10. -7 ◯ $+8$ 11. -7 ◯ -8 12. $+7$ ◯ -8

★ **Arrange these thermometer readings from coldest to warmest:**

13. $-3, +2, -7, 0, +8$ _____ , _____ , _____ , _____ , _____

14. $+9, -10, +11, -12, -4, -9$ _____ , _____ , _____ , _____ , _____ , _____

★ **Answer the following, where N = 18, Y = 15, B = 16:**

15. $\frac{1}{2}$ of N = _____   16. $\frac{1}{3}$ of Y = _____   17. $\frac{1}{4}$ of B = _____

★ **Calculate these using the correct "Order of Operations":**

18. $22 + (12 - 8) \times 2 = $ _____   19. $14 \times (1 + 7) - 9 = $ _____

20. $(75 \div 5^2) + 4 \div 2 = $ _____

★ **Write a number sentence where the number is N:**

21. 4 increased by a number = _____   22. 2 times a number plus 11 = _____

★ **Calculate the value of these numbers:**

23. $5^2 = $ _____   24. $9^2 = $ _____   25. $19 - 4^2 = $ _____

Copyright © 2003 by John Wiley & Sons, Inc.

190. Skills Mastery Test—Pre-Algebra and Early Algebra: Part Two

★ Solve the following equations:

1. $(+2) + (-4) + (+8) =$ _____

2. $(+18) + (-14) + (+7) =$ _____

3. $(+7) + (-4) + (+8) =$ _____

4. When X = 4

   $3X =$ _____

5. When N = 9

   $4N =$ _____

6. When X = 5

   $3X - 4 =$ _____

7. When N = 2

   $2N + 7 =$ _____

8. When N = 8

   $2N - 14 =$ _____

9. When N = 7

   $N^2 + 7 =$ _____

★ Complete these equations to find the values of the letters alone:

10. $R - 4 = 7$

    $R =$ _____

11. $K + 7 = 19$

    $K =$ _____

12. $B - 9 = 1$

    $B =$ _____

13. $X - 3 = 4$

    $X =$ _____

14. $Y + 6 = 11$

    $Y =$ _____

15. $B + 2 = 29$

    $B =$ _____

16. $3X = 45$

    $X =$ _____

17. $4Y = 100$

    $Y =$ _____

18. $\frac{X}{5} = 10$

    $X =$ _____

19. $9X = 27$

    $X =$ _____

20. $11 + B = 12$

    $B =$ _____

21. $4B = 20$

    $B =$ _____

★ Rewrite these equations:

22. $-(+9) =$ _____

23. $-(2x + 7) =$ _____

24. $-(-5y + 9x) =$ _____

25. $-(4y - 2b) + 9 =$ _____

Copyright © 2003 by John Wiley & Sons, Inc.

SECTION 1   ESSENTIAL STRATEGIES FOR WHOLE NUMBER SKILLS

1.   The Math Completion Puzzle

1803	(11)	1052	(3)	1038	(1)
823	(6)	1761	(18)	1897	(9)
1845	(14)	1263	(2)	2360	(12)
1630	(13)	2168	(10)	1031	(16)
2897	(8)	1148	(4)	2475	(15)
1929	(17)	1842	(7)	914	(5)

2.   Adding Sweet 7's Through the Grid

7	0	9	3	7	6	4	5	3	2	1	5	7	8	1	3	0	2	4	3
3	1	6	7	0	3	2	0	9	1	5	4	6	8	9	1	9	1	2	6
4	3	4	2	1	0	9	1	4	3	3	6	8	0	2	1	1	0	1	3
1	3	2	2	6	8	9	3	5	6	7	8	8	1	4	4	1	3	9	8
5	6	8	7	3	4	7	5	6	4	0	9	1	2	3	2	3	1	2	5
6	7	3	5	2	2	9	2	4	7	2	1	7	8	2	1	1	9	4	6
5	8	5	1	0	4	8	6	7	5	4	2	1	5	8	1	4	7	9	0
0	1	3	4	2	5	8	4	8	6	5	1	8	1	0	5	0	1	4	7
1	3	7	5	3	6	4	8	4	0	2	9	1	4	9	3	5	9	1	0
2	4	6	8	9	1	3	2	7	9	1	5	7	6	3	0	1	5	2	3
7	9	3	2	1	7	8	9	4	5	3	9	0	3	0	1	4	1	5	8
8	0	1	4	5	3	7	9	4	3	5	9	5	3	3	0	2	8	6	1
9	1	8	2	7	5	6	3	9	3	9	3	6	8	7	5	3	4	5	1

3.   Adding Sweet 8's Through the Grid

8	7	3	5	3	0	1	6	2	3	5	4	2	3	1	8	9	3	4	5
0	1	4	3	5	7	5	6	8	0	9	6	1	2	0	3	5	8	5	8
4	6	2	4	3	8	1	4	3	5	9	2	3	2	1	2	4	3	1	9
5	3	3	3	5	4	4	5	7	4	2	1	4	9	2	2	0	1	0	4
7	5	8	2	4	0	9	0	1	2	1	1	7	4	8	9	3	4	2	3
9	0	3	9	1	7	9	2	8	1	2	4	5	1	0	2	5	7	6	2
2	4	5	4	6	5	2	0	6	9	0	7	8	7	3	4	6	5	7	1
3	0	8	2	6	9	8	6	2	1	7	6	1	4	4	1	5	2	1	8
8	9	3	7	2	8	8	9	6	2	6	9	3	7	3	9	1	8	5	4
5	3	2	1	5	4	7	8	0	3	2	5	8	9	2	6	6	4	3	1
4	3	1	5	7	8	9	0	5	3	2	6	1	0	0	1	2	1	8	5
1	0	9	1	5	6	3	4	8	5	6	7	2	4	3	5	4	2	0	5
3	7	5	8	3	6	2	5	1	0	7	8	6	5	3	1	0	2	0	0

4.   Addition Number Boxes (Answers may vary. These are suggestions.)

1.

2	3	4
4	2	7
7	1	1
4	1	2

2.

7	6	3
4	9	2
9	7	1
9	8	1

3.

2	1	9
4	2	8
5	3	7
7	1	7

4.

3	7	1
2	9	2
9	1	7
4	1	3

5.

2	4	6
2	9	8
8	8	2
7	9	1

6.

6	3	2
1	7	1
8	4	2
9	7	1

7.

5	10	11
14	6	12
3	18	9
17	7	8

8.

14	17	20
13	10	1
4	9	2
10	8	10

9.

19	21	16
22	17	18
14	23	25
16	14	9

5. The Wonderful Addition Puzzle

¹⁵1	8	6	3	4	7	8	9	⁶2	0	7	8	4	3	²⁰8	5	⁵2	
6	3	1	5	2	⁹8	4	3	2	5	⁷2	⁴4	6	8	9	1	7	4
¹⁹1	0	7	0	4	6	7	9	5	0	2	1	6	4	8	0	6	
3	4	¹1	0	5	0	3	2	1	7	4	0	1	1	3	0	3	
2	4	8	8	2	6	7	9	1	4	7	3	2	¹⁰7	1	3	2	
¹⁶3	0	9	8	¹⁸9	5	1	3	5	8	8	9	4	¹²1	5	6	2	
8	2	¹³5	1	0	9	²1	8	7	⁸9	0	¹¹2	3	8	0	2	3	
1	3	6	9	¹⁴2	4	8	0	1	9	0	7	3	1	1	4	5	
7	9	1	4	4	5	7	9	3	9	3	6	1	2	5	6	8	
3	5	6	9	1	3	2	¹⁷1	5	1	6	2	0	9	5	4	3	

1. 1050	5. 2463	9. 860	13. 561	17. 1516
2. 1879	6. 2251	10. 713	14. 2480	18. 951
3. 1264	7. 2247	11. 2380	15. 1863	19. 1070
4. 2117	8. 999	12. 1812	16. 1817	20. 818

6. Subtraction Number Boxes (Answers may vary. These are suggestions.)

1.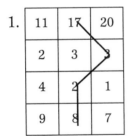

2.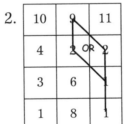

3.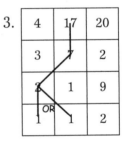

4.

5.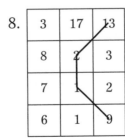

6.

7.

8.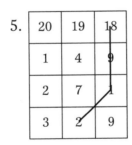

9.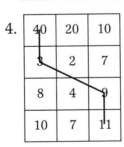

7. The Wonderful Subtraction Puzzle: Part One

9	5	7	6	8	4	3	1	2	4	9	0	2	4	3	7	9
4	3	3	0	4	5	7	6	4	8	0	9	1	9	5	5	5
6	7	8	0	4	1	9	4	1	8	5	6	6	1	0	0	2
7	9	1	5	3	7	8	3	6	6	0	1	5	4	4	3	0
1	2	3	5	8	6	4	5	6	4	9	2	7	8	6	5	2
4	6	9	9	3	2	8	6	0	5	8	4	2	3	4	4	9
9	5	1	0	0	1	9	1	5	9	1	0	4	0	5	7	6
6	7	5	3	1	2	9	8	9	1	3	1	3	2	0	4	5
4	5	1	9	0	1	2	3	8	5	3	4	6	7	3	5	9
5	1	5	4	3	1	0	9	5	6	3	5	1	9	0	7	8

1. 643	6. 612	11. 344	16. 298
2. 418	7. 648	12. 520	17. 515
3. 492	8. 555	13. 304	18. 657
4. 195	9. 618	14. 474	19. 762
5. 504	10. 302	15. 605	20. 586

8. The Wonderful Subtraction Puzzle: Part Two

9	5	2	2	5	4	3	1	2	4	9	0	2	4	3	5	9
4	3	3	9	0	9	7	6	4	8	3	9	1	9	5	5	5
6	7	8	8	5	1	6	5	7	2	5	6	6	1	0	5	2
7	9	1	6	0	1	1	3	6	4	5	1	4	2	9	0	0
1	2	3	5	8	6	4	5	3	6	9	8	0	9	6	5	2
4	6	9	9	3	2	2	8	7	0	8	4	2	9	4	4	9
7	3	4	3	8	9	9	1	7	0	1	0	4	8	0	1	3
6	7	5	9	1	2	9	5	9	9	5	5	7	5	0	4	5
4	5	1	4	4	0	3	3	8	5	3	4	6	7	3	5	9
5	1	5	7	3	1	0	9	5	6	3	5	1	9	0	7	8

1. 6011	6. 6572	11. 2998	16. 3947
2. 2896	7. 4600	12. 4290	17. 8013
3. 5950	8. 5995	13. 5550	18. 4389
4. 6142	9. 3779	14. 3999	19. 4403
5. 2870	10. 809	15. 7343	20. 5575

9. Being Careful in Math

1. 5	3. 15	5. 4	7. 8	9. 11
2. 7	4. 8	6. 11	8. 0	10. 82

10. Math Connections

1. 565152	5. 92541
2. 235625	6. 95202
3. 581972	7. 645498
4. 180635	8. 114597

11. The Wonderful Multiplication Puzzle

9	9	3	3	5	1	7	2	5	7	2	5	8	6	3	[2]8	1	0	2	8
3	0	7	0	2	3	3	4	3	5	7	6	1	3	9	4	8	6	3	5
7	9	8	4	8	0	1	2	4	3	8	2	[1]2	2	8	9	7	3	1	6
2	3	1	0	8	[12]3	7	5	8	3	3	1	[4]2	1	8	7	3	5	4	0
8	7	4	6	4	5	3	1	7	[3]1	7	0	8	2	[5]2 [10]	2	7	0	3	1
2	3	5	3	3	6	2	9	3	6	0	9	6	5	4	3	5	8	3	9
6	9	4	2	[13]2	4	5	7	4	8	[16]2	7	2	0	5	8	[18]2 [15]5		[19]2	0
9	0	3	5	0	6	0	2	9	7	[11]3	6	1	8	0	5	4	3	1	7
3	[20]2	5	7	[14]1	9	2	0	1	4	3	8	7	1	9	1	5	0	3	8
7	1	2	3	5	8	4	3	[6]1	5	9	[9]2 [8]9	9	9	6	0	6	1	5	6
2	1	3	4	8	4	0	8	3	7	3	1	0	5	9	4	4	2	4	3
9	4	0	3	3	1	[7]1	7	6	0	2	4	6	3	2	[17]1	7	0	4	3
6	8	6	5	6	9	7	3	0	4	8	5	3	0	6	5	8	4	2	9

1. 2289	5. 2450	9. 2145	13. 2457	17. 1704
2. 849	6. 1360	10. 2270	14. 1920	18. 2456
3. 1708	7. 1760	11. 3618	15. 2520	19. 2135
4. 2862	8. 2996	12. 3564	16. 2720	20. 2114

12. Shady Division

Divisible by 7

14	13	35	65	42	61
21	9	99	81	79	56
33	86	63	69	7	88
19	70	81	31	77	18
84	14	34	32	33	19
13	33	20	17	22	28

Divisible by 4

20	83	36	61	91	24
44	77	95	8	73	71
45	41	4	9	40	97
47	12	62	32	67	69
55	82	7	86	89	93
28	10	48	81	1	16

Divisible by 2

7	19	2	1	9	20
9	22	35	4	15	61
11	45	75	17	12	67
13	77	6	79	99	73
10	31	65	81	37	8
25	39	14	83	16	18

Divisible by 3

3	11	7	8	6	10
68	67	21	41	22	27
23	9	37	38	33	47
18	35	40	43	44	15
13	9	12	2	1	20
24	65	36	64	30	46

Divisible by 5

15	46	71	17	16	20
44	69	45	52	74	35
30	72	54	73	10	48
55	51	5	77	47	50
49	18	91	25	76	92
93	60	19	21	53	40

Divisible by 9

81	94	52	9	89	72
42	43	18	41	27	83
37	49	14	7	3	99
38	36	44	90	1	20
47	69	46	48	45	40
63	50	79	39	51	54

Divisible by 6

12	46	31	18	45	36
39	72	2	1	10	9
38	32	42	40	41	24
30	43	44	9	66	7
37	47	48	8	54	3
34	49	33	6	35	60

Divisible by 8

72	15	14	31	37	81
25	11	8	69	56	52
9	80	20	88	53	51
24	2	32	17	16	19
1	12	87	33	83	34
13	96	10	40	91	48

Divisible by 10

68	94	10	2	1	8
90	67	73	30	74	84
78	27	20	81	80	83
60	32	14	9	7	3
18	70	81	40	76	79
77	85	21	75	50	89

13. Logical Deductive Reasoning

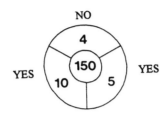

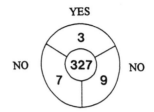

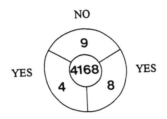

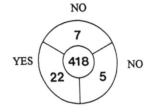

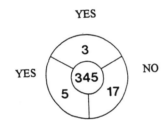

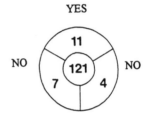

14. The Wonderful Division Puzzle: Part One

0	11,12 6	5	4	0	9	3	4	3	2	8	6	0	4	2	1	0
1	9	7	3	1	8	2	1 4	8 1	6	3	4	6 3	2	5	7	6
9	3	1	2	1	0	9	2	4	7 5	7	6	3	9	4	0	7
2	7	5	19 5	2	3	0	4 7	7	1	6	8	9 8	4	1	9	0
2	5	2	2	6	3	8	8	9	6	16 4	3	7	6	14 5	4	7
8	5	3	2	1	5 4	5	9	0	3	6	0	2 2	7	0	2	1
8	4	2	1	0	15 1	9	8	0	1	5	1	3	8	10 9	3	5
0	9	3	3 1	0	5	3	2	17 5	7	8	1	13 2	5	6	1	0
7	5	4	3	1	9	2	5	8	5	3	9	7	2	7	3	1
2	20 5	9	7	0	1	3	4	9	2	18 6	9	8	6	8	9	0

1. 416	6. 325	11. 693	16. 465
2. 232	7. 516	12. 654	17. 589
3. 1053	8. 147	13. 258	18. 698
4. 789	9. 841	14. 547	19. 523
5. 459	10. 987	15. 159	20. 597

15. The Wonderful Division Puzzle: Part Two

0	3	0	1	[17]8	7	3	0	2	1	5	0	[4]8	[15]9	0	[19]4	0
2	0	1	7	8	5	3	8	4	0	8	9	[13]4	8	1	7	1
9	1	[5]3	5	0	2	[1]2	3	[3]6	[2]9	0	0	3	0	2	6	2
0	6	0	0	2	4	6	7	0	6	0	0	[18]7	7	0	[16]5	5
9	0	1	2	8	9	3	6	5	0	0	3	3	4	5	1	0
[11]6	2	0	1	3	[7]5	7	0	3	1	[12]5	0	7	2	0	0	3
0	1	2	4	0	6	0	2	0	9	4	9	0	[8]5	2	4	0
2	3	1	0	9	0	2	0	[10]6	0	0	0	9	0	7	6	[9]9
0	1	0	[6]5	4	6	4	0	1	3	[14]4	3	1	[20]3	2	0	1
0	9	1	2	5	3	0	0	7	2	1	4	5	0	0	2	1

1. 26
2. 96
3. 69
4. 89
5. 35
6. 54
7. 57
8. 52
9. 91
10. 61
11. 62
12. 54
13. 48
14. 41
15. 98
16. 51
17. 88
18. 77
19. 47
20. 32

16. The Wonderful Division Puzzle: Part Three

[15]5	3	[16]5	0	1	2	4	6	[1]9	7	8	[14]2	5	9	5	6	[18]8
5	7	2	1	0	1	7	5	8	3	4	0	0	9	0	1	4
5	0	3	2	[8]2	1	4	3	7	6	0	[17]1	1	0	5	2	4
8	[2]7	7	[7]8	5	7	6	9	1	0	9	2	3	5	4	7	2
9	5	[4]6	5	4	3	7	4	[9]3	2	1	2	7	9	3	4	[10]6
1	4	5	2	0	9	3	7	4	6	0	3	[3]9	5	1	1	2
3	2	2	1	5	6	6	[5]3	7	8	[12]5	4	2	0	0	8	0
[19]3	2	7	8	1	0	8	5	0	5	4	0	[13]6	5	3	9	3
2	8	9	1	3	[6]6	8	7	5	0	7	8	8	4	2	1	0
3	3	5	4	8	2	3	1	[20]2	8	3	7	0	1	[11]8	4	1

1. 987
2. 754
3. 951
4. 654
5. 357
6. 687
7. 852
8. 254
9. 321
10. 620
11. 841
12. 547
13. 653
14. 259
15. 555
16. 523
17. 722
18. 844
19. 327
20. 283

17. Multiplication and Division Crossnumber Puzzle

¹8	²9	■	³4	⁴9	⁵2	⁶3	■	■
9	3	■	⁷6	5	4	7	9	⁸3
6	■	⁹4	8	■	■	¹⁰9	6	2
¹¹7	¹²3	8	0	■	¹³8	2	■	7
■	¹⁴2	2	■	¹⁵9	4	■	¹⁶7	1
¹⁷9	7	■	¹⁸3	■	■	¹⁹3	8	■
8	■	²⁰9	8	7	2	7	2	■
7	²¹2	■	²²9	9	3	6	8	9
5	5	■	²³4	8	9	8	5	0

18. Rounding Off Whole Numbers

Number	Nearest Thousand	Nearest Hundred	Nearest Ten
4,745	5,000	4,700	4,750
4,586	5,000	4,600	4,590
8,488	8,000	8,500	8,490
6,715	7,000	6,700	6,720
13,546	14,000	13,500	13,550
2,732	3,000	2,700	2,730
1,184	1,000	1,200	1,180
2,272	2,000	2,300	2,270
4,111	4,000	4,100	4,110
9,477	9,000	9,500	9,480
14,557	15,000	14,600	14,560
15,139	15,000	15,100	15,140

19. Prime Number Gaps

8	1	6	4	1	6	4	9	8	6	7↓ 9	1	0	1	4
0	6	1	6→ 6	1	⑤	8	4	6	8	4	0	9	8	1
9	2↓ 6	9	0	6	4	8	0	1	9	⑦	8	4	6	0
9	9	1	8	6	9	1→ ③	②	⑦	6	②	0	1	4	8
0	1	6	8	4	9	0	1	9	4	6	4	3↓ 6	0	9↓ ⑦
1	⑦	4	4→ ③	1	9	⑦	6	8	9	1	6	⑦	8	1
8	4	6	1	8	9	8	4	1	8↓ 8	4	1	②	1	9
4	8	4	6	5→ ③	9	1	②	0	1	1	0	⑤	9	③
8	6	0	1	8	0	9	4	1	②	0	9	4	8	0
10→ 8	③	8	⑤	6	4	1	8	6	1	9	8	8	1	9

1. 3276	3. 6725	5. 3912	7. 9472	9. 7193
2. 6917	4. 3197	6. 6158	8. 8121	10. 8385

20. The Prime Number Division Chart

Numbers	Can the number on the left be divided evenly by these prime numbers? (Yes or No)					
	2	3	5	7	11	13
26	YES	NO	NO	NO	NO	YES
56	YES	NO	NO	YES	NO	NO
27	NO	YES	NO	NO	NO	NO
33	NO	YES	NO	NO	YES	NO
44	YES	NO	NO	NO	YES	NO
52	YES	NO	NO	NO	NO	YES
30	YES	YES	YES	NO	NO	NO
105	NO	YES	YES	YES	NO	NO
42	YES	YES	NO	YES	NO	NO
154	YES	NO	NO	YES	YES	NO
143	NO	NO	NO	NO	YES	YES
195	NO	YES	YES	NO	NO	YES

21. Composite Number Gaps

5⟳(6)	(8)	5	1	1	9⟳(4)	3	5	(6)	5	3	7	3↓(4)	2	1
1	3	2	3	5	1	7	5	3	1	2	5	7	1	3
6↓2	5	7	5	5	7	1	3	7	2	10↓7	1	7	2	5
5	1	1	2	1⟳7	5	(4)	(9)	5	3	1	2	(4)	3	5
(6)	2	5	3	2	1	5	3	2	1	(8)	5	7	5	3
3	1	3	7	5	2	3	3	2↓5	2	(4)	3	5	4↓2	7
1	3	5	5	7	3	2	5	(4)	5	3	5	3	(4)	2
5	7⟳(4)	(4)	2	5	3	5	2	(8)	2	5	3	1	(9)	5
2	3	5	1	3	5	2	5	5	7	3	2	5	2	3
1	5	2	8⟳3	(8)	(8)	7	7	7	2	1	5	3	7	1

1. 7549   3. 4774   5. 6851   7. 4425   9. 4356
2. 5485   4. 2492   6. 2563   8. 3887   10. 7184

22. Greatest Common Factor and Least Common Multiple

A. 1. 3   4. 5
   2. 6   5. 3
   3. 5   6. 6

B. 1. 20   4. 75
   2. 60   5. 48
   3. 30   6. 60

23. The Rhyming Variety Page

1. 1048   6. 216   11. 298   16. 19
2. 18   7. 129   12. 708   17. 18
3. 1974   8. 1048   13. 19   18. 116
4. 1048   9. 116   14. 129   19. 1974
5. 379   10. 529   15. 1048   20. 708

As I was <u>going</u> to <u>St. Ives</u>
I <u>met</u> a <u>man</u> with <u>seven</u> <u>wives</u>.
Each <u>wife</u> had <u>seven</u> sacks.
Each sack had <u>seven</u> <u>cats</u>.
Each cat had <u>seven</u> <u>kits</u>.
<u>Kits</u>, <u>cats</u>, <u>sacks</u>, and <u>wives</u>.
How <u>many</u> were <u>going</u> to <u>St. Ives</u>?

Bonus Question: One (because only <u>I</u> was going to St. Ives)

24. The Partially Completed Choice Puzzle

	8	9	10	11	12	13	14
1	3	1	5	8	6	4	3
2	8	0	2	3	0	5	4
3	6	5	5	2	5	6	5
4	4	6	2	1	8	1	8
5	7	1	4	1	4	7	0
6	4	8	1	2	3	1	0
7	2	1	3	2	7	6	7

25. The Number Match Game

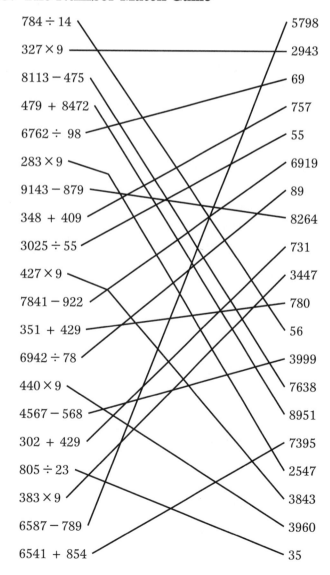

26. Take Your Pick

1. 44
2. 766
3. 203
4. 340
5. 888
6. 81
7. 187
8. 567
9. 558
10. 815
11. 617
12. 228
13. 348
14. 745
15. 983

0	9	7	6	¹4	3	1	1	9	8
⁵8	2	4	3	4	5	7	0	1	2
8	0	9	1	4	1	0	2	4	¹⁴7
8	¹¹6	1	7	5	9	7	5	2	4
0	7	9	3	2	⁴3	4	0	0	5
2	6	7	5	7	0	8	3	4	5
0	1	³2	0	3	3	5	⁸5	1	9
¹²2	7	2	¹⁵9	8	3	6	6	2	0
2	8	5	4	2	1	5	7	2	1
8	5	²7	6	6	5	2	3	0	9
9	1	0	6	7	0	2	¹³3	4	8
2	5	9	⁹5	5	8	0	1	3	5
4	3	0	2	9	1	¹⁰8	3	⁶8	6
8	0	⁷1	8	7	0	1	7	1	5
3	6	9	1	2	1	5	2	4	3

27. Vertical and Horizontal Calculations

A	B	C	D	E	
4	7	3	2	9	25
8	7	5	0	2	22
9	2	4	2	2	19
7	3	4	8	7	29
8	7	4	7	1	27
36	26	20	19	21	122

F					
8	7	9	8	4	36
G 7	7	2	3	7	26
H 3	4	5	4	4	20
I 8	7	0	2	2	19
J 1	2	2	7	9	21
27	27	18	24	26	122

28. The James Q. Dandy (Jim Dandy) Variety Puzzle

3	5	9	8	1	3	7	7	5	7	1	3	4	8	2	3	4	8	9	7
5	9	7	3	5	6	8	2	7	4	6	2	8	4	8	8	5	1	6	3
5	9	7	6	0	1	2	5	7	8	6	4	8	4	6	5	4	2	8	5
5	8	0	3	1	0	9	5	3	1	9	2	3	5	3	9	5	8	3	6
1	5	9	6	3	4	2	9	7	0	2	1	5	8	4	0	1	3	8	6
2	6	4	3	1	6	9	2	0	9	0	5	8	5	1	5	6	3	8	7
0	3	8	3	8	1	8	0	5	1	9	3	8	9	5	6	2	3	7	1
7	7	1	7	2	6	3	9	5	1	5	6	1	8	5	9	5	1	2	0
5	9	1	4	5	8	6	7	9	7	5	2	8	9	6	1	4	3	1	7
8	5	6	1	4	0	1	3	8	3	2	8	3	1	2	4	5	4	6	0
8	9	6	2	3	5	5	8	1	2	3	5	1	3	5	9	9	0	8	2
5	0	3	6	5	3	2	4	6	8	1	0	9	0	1	7	1	6	0	0
0	2	3	1	5	7	2	6	8	3	1	2	5	9	5	9	6	1	2	1
1	3	8	1	7	4	1	5	3	6	9	8	5	4	4	1	3	5	9	2
2	2	4	0	2	6	6	4	1	5	4	3	6	8	9	7	5	6	6	8
8	6	8	6	3	2	0	7	3	1	0	5	9	7	3	4	8	8	9	0
5	0	2	8	8	5	6	1	9	3	3	8	3	8	6	5	6	4	4	0
9	5	7	6	5	2	1	3	8	9	8	1	3	3	5	6	4	1	1	3
8	9	6	2	5	4	8	8	6	4	4	2	8	5	7	2	1	0	6	4
0	5	4	8	3	4	5	9	4	3	0	2	9	6	3	4	7	3	8	5

1. 573	5. 546	9. 653	13. 353	17. 442
2. 7,348	6. 548	10. 841	14. 302	18. 800
3. 159	7. 725	11. 1095	15. 1106	19. 121
4. 58	8. 502	12. 171,600	16. 7,385	20. 867

29. Math Puzzle Boxes

Grid 1:

[1] 1	6	■	■
[2] 1	2	9	[3] 9
[4] 2	3	■	3
[5] 5	2	■	7

Grid 2:

[1] 1	2	5	■
[2] 2	0	4	8
[3] 4	3	7	9
■	[4] 8	9	1

Grid 3:

■	[1] 1	0	[2] 7
[3] 4	9	■	9
8	■	[4] 7	9
[5] 2	9	4	■

The Long Box

685	678	678	853	830	701	4425

30. Center Math Vocabulary

```
C E N T I M E T E R A L C B V W E L L I P S E R I O L C
U R Y T P L F Q W R E X C O A M I N T E R S E C T P O M
M N E R A T F W N A P L Y M U L A S E U N E V Q U R T
R E U P C H W O G I K M U L T I P L E S U P O R N F G U
C V B T O S A T R E O I N F D E G H I P V N P T R E R T
L L O C K B H P E R P E N D I C U L A R E R K Y U M C Z
B R A V I V E M B R A N G L E R G M H W P O E S U T B O
V A S C U K L E                       B O L T Y B M F
T N A V I S T W                       E D U T I T A L
I T N B I G W O                       L N M I L O P R
P G K U N J O T                       O B M K D E R S
M H I L I G H L                       N S T H G I R
R N R T N I O P                       G O T N J I N J
T M W I P O N J                       I N B M E X T R
I K T Y O L D L                       T O L B D J I Y
V L E R M I C O                       U M O N E Y E W
P O R B V A E M                       D R I U N M E R
C P R I A P S K                       E X T V E R A W
Q L D E R E L P                       B E R U S A E M
U E P E G L K I                       P E R T I C M L
U C J M I K R E                       L D U M B R E T
I M E B U P L S                       C T I D E W B R
O N O I T A R S                       J O H V N S T R
T P G U L P A W                       I V B M I U R Y
G I S U M H J A                       N P O K L S E W
G H I J D L F K D E O P R N O M W A S M M A S R T Y O W
P O W E R W E E G H I V U M B E N A L P B A T N R O V R
P R T Y M N G R G P F M S A T B V R U T I M T R E W R T
R R E N K R L R T Y B B T W Q U E S Y O L U B H A S T R
E T T I E M V N A E S T E L E L G N A I R T N B G H E L
Y E R E M B T Y R E R G K H I L P O N W E T V C R E L P
N O S T R E M S B C F M A R I T H M E T I C N E T I R B
```

31. Definition Puzzle on Whole Number Terms

	[15]C	A	L	C	U	L	A	T	E		[12]C	O	M	P	L	E	T	E	
															[5]V			[4]Q
			[2]P			[13]C	O	R	R	E	C	T	E					U
[7]I	N	T	E	R	E	S	T						R					O
[10]L			I					[9]D			T					T
O			[1]M	U	[8]L	T	I	P	L	I	C	A	T	I	O	N		I
G			E		O	[14]A		V			C					E
I				C	N		I			A					N
C				A	S		S			L					T
A				T	W		I							
L				E	E	[3]C	O	M	P	O	S	I	T	E	
					R		N							
[6]N	U	M	E	R	I	C	A	L		[11]H	O	R	I	Z	O	N	T	A	L

32. Skills Mastery Test—Whole Numbers: Part One

1. 28
2. 1489
3. 1711
4. 178
5. 374
6. 104
7. 6633
8. 16093
9. 22272
10. 85
11. 6
12. 98

13. Answers can vary. Here is one possibility.

7	9	14
8	4	13
3	2	7
2	9	1

14.

5	21	95	25
11	10	36	92
64	19	7	200
60	65	70	20
15	75	84	18

15. 9985
16. 3443
17. 439504
18. 1166529
19. 2520
20. 341549
21. 152
22. 78
23. 23
24. 3323
25. 38033

33. Skills Mastery Test—Whole Numbers: Part Two

1. 3   2. 5   3. 4   4. 14   5. 24   6. 135

7. 5,000   4,500   4,540

8. 8,000   8,300   8,320

9. 19

10. 681,658,408

11.

36	14	60	99
84	32	96	98
86	24	48	72
89	94	62	144

12. ⑦ ⑪ 14, ⑲ ② ③ 88, ⑰ 9, ⑤

13. 3   10   9

SECTION 2   GETTING TO THE POINT WITH DECIMALS

34. Adding Decimals

1. 112.9	3. 255.381	5. 84.156	7. 123.645	9. 90.987
2. 31.027	4. 18.075	6. 746.433	8. 92.752	10. 179.04

35. True or False Decimals

1. NO   .27   NO   75.60   2. YES, YES   3. NO   771.500   YES
                .83   67.010
              74.50   7.625

36. Move the Gears: Part One (Addition of Decimals)

1. 13.281	4. 380.38	7. 505.609	10. 355.51
2. 983.6	5. 349.54	8. 337.07	11. 12
3. 558.5	6. 509.11	9. 630.52	12. 12.11

37. Subtracting Decimals

1. .731	3. 19.581	5. 27.96	7. 99.982	9. 452.2181
2. 5.351	4. 6.221	6. 229.25	8. 576.253	10. 15.717

38. Move the Gears: Part Two (Subtraction of Decimals)

1. 7858.69	4. .97	7. 13.74	10. 3.17
2. 4.73	5. 2.84	8. .648	11. 4.97
3. 1.19	6. 51.229	9. 4.64	12. 1.491

39. Multiplying Decimals

1. 71.94	4. 7313.2	7. 38883.57	10. 2092.188	13. 2.3606
2. 15.372	5. 10.1108	8. 90.4638	11. 303.702	14. 6.7252
3. 769.23	6. 34906.64	9. 4229.631	12. 8.6686	15. 76.713

40. Move the Gears: Part Three (Multiplication of Decimals)

1. 18.86	3. 28.49	5. 12.61	7. 69.52	9. 18.96	11. 39.69
2. 49.98	4. 14.03	6. 78.57	8. 24.82	10. 14.58	12. 29.26

41. Double-Up Decimals

1. 431.2	4. 321.55	7. 777.04	10. 14198.7
2. 4029.6	5. 7687.8	8. 2920.88	11. 988.56
3. 53.9	6. 135.4	9. 1643.4	12. 60614.88

DOUBLE-UP PROBLEMS:

1. 60668.78	3. 22021.9	5. 8	7. 1277.48
2. 13210.14	4. 7366.25	6. 11717.4	8. 1419.76

42. Dividing Decimals

1. 770	3. 7.5	5. 89	7. 70.7	9. .88
2. 350	4. .99	6. .51	8. .97	10. .35

43. Move the Gears: Part Four (Division of Decimals)

1. $48.72 \div 5.6 = 8.7$
2. $35.49 \div 3.9 = 9.1$
3. $38.48 \div 7.4 = 5.2$
4. $87.12 \div 8.8 = 9.9$
5. $12.04 \div 4.3 = 2.8$
6. $5.75 \div 2.3 = 2.5$
7. $21.15 \div 4.5 = 4.7$
8. $35.28 \div 4.2 = 8.4$
9. $13.72 \div 9.8 = 1.4$
10. $33.06 \div 5.8 = 5.7$
11. $6.75 \div 2.5 = 2.7$
12. $28.49 \div 3.7 = 7.7$

44. Rounding Off and Comparing Decimal Numbers

1. 3.5; >
2. 2.95; >
3. 8.9; <
4. 14.4; =
5. 122.0; <
6. 127.74; <
7. 409.349; <
8. 1272; <
9. 750.0; =
10. 327.3; <

Bonus Question: Power tools are used.

45. Expressing Decimals as Fractions: Part One

1. $7\frac{1}{10}$ 4. $9\frac{1}{4}$ 7. $7\frac{3}{4}$ 10. $4\frac{1}{2}$ 13. $\frac{1}{5}$

2. $8\frac{27}{100}$ 5. $7\frac{3}{10}$ 8. $\frac{2}{5}$ 11. $\frac{9}{10}$ 14. $7\frac{9}{10}$

3. $9\frac{1}{2}$ 6. $9\frac{1}{5}$ 9. $3\frac{3}{4}$ 12. $27\frac{2}{5}$ 15. $8\frac{23}{25}$

Bonus Question:

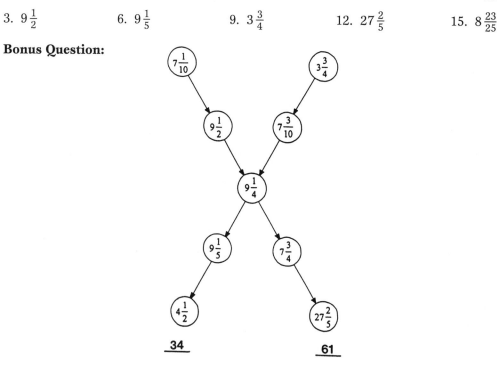

46. Expressing Decimals as Fractions: Part Two

A.   1. $7\frac{1}{3}$ 3. $7\frac{1}{2}$ 5. $7\frac{2}{3}$ 7. $8\frac{1}{50}$ 9. $7\frac{1}{8}$

2. $7\frac{31}{100}$ 4. $7\frac{1}{4}$ 6. $3\frac{9}{10}$ 8. $4\frac{1}{2}$ 10. $3\frac{3}{5}$

B.

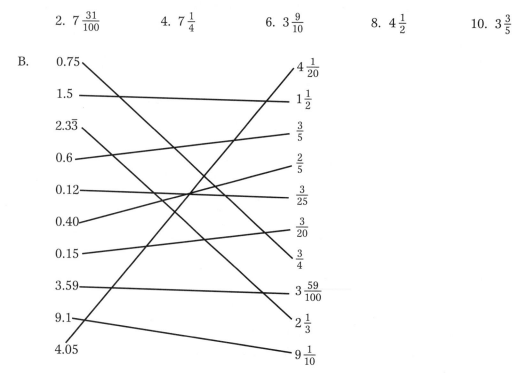

47. Humans vs. Aliens: Metric Comparison/Conversion

1. 123.64 lbs.
2. 90.42 lbs.
3. 149.82 lbs.
4. 113.74 lbs.
5. Human Male by 26.18 lbs.
6. Alien Female by 23.32 lbs.
7. 16,416 kg.; 36,115.2 lbs.
8. 11.16 mph (Alien)
9. 3.1 mph (Human)
10. 31,126.48 mph
11. 22 lbs.

48. The Great Overlapping Math Puzzle

Set A	Set B	Set C
56,275	75,855	55,824
51,574	74,344	44,708
69,112	12,564	64,369
31,536	36,424	24,918
22,890	90,325	25,804
38,285	85,035	35,789
45,747	47,296	96,744
25,284	84,772	72,284

Set A			Set B					Set C		
5	6	2	7	5	8	5	5	8	2	4
5	1	5	7	4	3	4	4	7	0	8
6	9	1	1	2	5	6	4	3	6	9
3	1	5	3	6	4	2	4	9	1	8
2	2	8	9	0	3	2	5	8	0	4
3	8	2	8	5	0	3	5	7	8	9
4	5	7	4	7	2	9	6	7	4	4
2	5	2	8	4	7	7	2	2	8	4

49. Four-Function Crossnumber Puzzle

¹6	²5	³4	■	■	■	■	⁴4	⁵7	⁶1
⁷3	4	7	■	■	■	■	⁸2	2	2
⁹8	6	2	¹⁰2	■	■	¹¹3	7	8	5
■	¹²2	4	¹³6	■	¹⁴9	2	■	■	■
■	■	¹⁵4	8	¹⁶4	3	9	■	■	■
■	■	■	¹⁷8	3	2	■	■	■	■
■	■	¹⁸7	4	2	4	¹⁹9	■	■	■
■	²⁰3	4	7	■	²¹8	2	²²4	■	■
²³8	²⁴8	9	8	■	■	²⁵7	3	²⁶9	²⁷2
²⁸7	1	8	■	■	■	■	²⁹9	0	8
³⁰2	9	4	■	■	■	■	³¹8	0	3

50. Cruising Route 66 with Math

55	−	5	÷	16	=	GAS	×	3	−	8	+	4
−			3			+		7.4				=
5			÷			16.5		+				GAS
+	9	−	7	÷	3		7	−	2	−	17	+
4			+			14		÷				8.7
=			2					3				=
GAS	−	7	+	8	÷	8	+	26	+	30	−	GAS
−			17			÷		9				
13.2			−			2		÷				11
+	7	−	17	+	GAS	=	10	+	2	×	22	
2						GAS		=				17
4			3			+		GAS				−
GAS	×	8	+	2	+	23	=	GAS	+	79	−	45
−			9			−		8				
14			÷			8		−				34
+	7	÷	74	+	2	−	9	+	14	÷	2	=
												66

Bonus Question: 19

51. Pirate Math

1. $14.49
2. $63,279.88; 1,691.76 lbs.; 11,189.76 lbs. or 5.59488 tons
3. 13.78 or 14 pieces of eight
4. 39,482.7 nautical miles
5. $123,276.37
6. 796.1033 ft.
7. 3.95 ft. longer; .01 ft. wider

52. More Pirate Math

8. 79 pieces of eight
9. 14.25¢ or $.1425
10. $3.93
11. 12,429 lbs. or 6.2145 tons
12. 46.02 hours
13. 53.34 lbs.
14. 263.66 lbs.; yes

53. Decimal Stew: Tenths Place

1. 9.4	4. 44.6	7. 7.12	10. 4.3	13. 26.4
2. 19.5	5. 9.1	8. 20.02	11. 8.7	14. .88
3. 21.5	6. 48.9	9. 9.4	12. 16.2	15. 38.5

54. Decimal Stew: Hundredths Place

1. 33.75	4. 6.11	7. 11.58	10. 4.38	13. 11.8326
2. 21.12	5. 408.01	8. 9.75	11. 31.11	14. 16.67
3. 30.84	6. 14.76	9. 14.77	12. 290.07	15. 14.76

55. Decimal Stew: Thousandths Place

1. 14.464	4. 11.211	7. 96.688	10. 94.382	13. 255.551
2. 9.634	5. 5.562772	8. 25.034	11. 28.133	14. 430.139071
3. 2.217828	6. 12.582	9. 342.184	12. 8,914.327	15. 505.926

56. The Velocity Page

1. 60 mph	2. 72 mph	3. 80 mph	4. 40 mph	5. 72 mph

57. Definition Puzzle on Decimals

				[19]C				[4]H	U	N	D	R	E	D	T	H	S	
				O														
[11]S				M												[15]T		
Y				P		[10]M		[5]P	[3]R	O	C	E	D	U	R	E		
M		[12]S	P	A	C	E			O							N		
B				R		[1]T	H	O	U	S	A	N	D	T	H	S		[9]H
O		[6]T		I		R			N									U
L		E		N		I			D	[8]L	O	C	A	T	I	O	N	N
		N		G		C			I									D
		T							N									R
		H							[13]G	E	A	R	S					E
		S																D
				[14]O	N	E	S			[7]T	H	O	U	S	A	N	D	S

58. Skills Mastery Test—Decimals: Part One

1.
$$\begin{array}{r} 3.250 \\ .629 \\ +\,47.300 \\ \hline 51.179 \end{array}$$

2.
$$\begin{array}{r} 773.290 \\ -\,49.979 \\ \hline 723.311 \end{array}$$

3. 52.59

4. 52.6

5. 289.5
6. 70.8
7. 122.32

8. 71.17
9. 326.845
10. 1,807.54

11. 22.07
12. 54.45
13. 389.1

14. 44.3730
15. <
16. <

17. >
18. 16 kg

19. 8.068 km per second

20. 11.13 chickens (or about 11 chickens)

59. Skills Mastery Test—Decimals: Part Two

1. 22.89
2. 12.81
3. 15.9
4. 162.8
5. 234.89

6. 89.46
7. 145.52
8. $8\frac{11}{50}$
9. $9\frac{1}{2}$
10. $\frac{3}{4}$

11. $\frac{4}{5}$
12. $3\frac{7}{50}$
13. $7\frac{1}{4}$
14. $\frac{1}{2}$
15. $\frac{1}{10}$

16. 23.52 lbs.
17. 9.3
18. .1
19. 11.9
20. 1.08

21. 4.52 tons
22. $27,603.84
23. 503.999
24. 3.618
25. 158.438

SECTION 3   FRACTIONS IN THE LEARNING PROCESS

60. The Eight-Piece Fraction Puzzle: Part One

A. $\frac{4}{9}$	C. $1\frac{1}{2}$	E. $1\frac{3}{8}$	G. $\frac{11}{14}$
B. $1\frac{1}{9}$	D. $\frac{25}{36}$	F. $\frac{19}{20}$	H. $1\frac{3}{20}$

61. The Eight-Piece Fraction Puzzle: Part Two

A. $10\frac{3}{4}$	C. $8\frac{1}{10}$	E. $4\frac{5}{8}$	G. $16\frac{3}{8}$
B. $2\frac{28}{33}$	D. $16\frac{13}{20}$	F. $5\frac{5}{24}$	H. 9

62. Finding the Value of Names: Part One

1. $1\frac{1}{4}$	5. $\frac{9}{34}$	9. $\frac{7}{8}$	13. $\frac{3}{5}$	17. $\frac{7}{12}$
2. $1\frac{1}{4}$	6. $\frac{7}{16}$	10. $\frac{5}{14}$	14. $1\frac{7}{20}$	18. $1\frac{1}{7}$
3. $\frac{5}{8}$	7. $1\frac{1}{3}$	11. $\frac{3}{4}$	15. $1\frac{1}{10}$	19. $\frac{25}{34}$
4. $\frac{5}{18}$	8. $\frac{11}{18}$	12. $\frac{13}{28}$	16. $1\frac{1}{8}$	20. $\frac{13}{42}$

63. Finding the Value of Names: Part Two

1. $4\frac{1}{4}$	5. $3\frac{3}{14}$	9. $5\frac{1}{4}$	13. $24\frac{5}{8}$	17. $5\frac{3}{8}$
2. $6\frac{3}{4}$	6. $21\frac{3}{10}$	10. 4	14. $12\frac{3}{8}$	18. $13\frac{11}{16}$
3. $6\frac{15}{16}$	7. $8\frac{1}{4}$	11. $18\frac{5}{14}$	15. $33\frac{11}{16}$	19. $30\frac{11}{20}$
4. $4\frac{3}{7}$	8. $12\frac{1}{2}$	12. $6\frac{1}{8}$	16. $21\frac{19}{40}$	20. $10\frac{7}{9}$

64. Cool Name Fractions

Flipper Twerpski $= 1\frac{2}{3}$

Candy Barr $= 1\frac{1}{2}$

Billy Bopper $= 1\frac{3}{4}$

Vinny Kool $= 1\frac{1}{6}$

Agulik Eskimo $= 1\frac{3}{8}$

Sunbeam Love $= 1\frac{3}{10}$

Butch Kelvington $= 1\frac{11}{20}$

Jimmy Dandy $= 1\frac{5}{6}$

Molly Golly $= \frac{13}{30}$

Kimmel Yaggy $= 1\frac{1}{12}$

King Buckingham $= 3\frac{1}{2}$

Lovespace Joy $= 16\frac{1}{2}$

Joan Joan Jones $= 9\frac{1}{12}$

Buck Shynkaruk $= 14\frac{6}{7}$

Horizon Sunshine $= 10\frac{17}{24}$

Bonus Questions

1. $10\frac{3}{4}$ 2. $18\frac{1}{20}$ 3. $2\frac{23}{60}$ 4. $2\frac{4}{15}$ 5. $2\frac{11}{12}$

65. Subtraction with Common Denominators: Part One

1. $\frac{11}{15}$ 4. $\frac{5}{8}$ 7. $\frac{1}{6}$ 10. $2\frac{3}{8}$ 13. $2\frac{15}{22}$

2. $\frac{1}{3}$ 5. $\frac{7}{10}$ 8. $\frac{1}{8}$ 11. $1\frac{3}{10}$ 14. $3\frac{1}{15}$

3. $\frac{1}{2}$ 6. $\frac{1}{8}$ 9. $1\frac{1}{4}$ 12. $3\frac{11}{14}$ 15. $7\frac{7}{10}$

66. Subtraction with Common Denominators: Part Two

1. $1\frac{3}{4}$ 3. $1\frac{13}{18}$ 5. $1\frac{1}{2}$ 7. $1\frac{4}{7}$ 9. 2

2. $6\frac{3}{8}$ 4. $6\frac{7}{10}$ 6. $2\frac{8}{9}$ 8. $8\frac{3}{8}$ 10. $\frac{3}{4}$

67. Subtraction with Common Denominators: Part Three

1. $2\frac{13}{18}$ 3. $1\frac{10}{21}$ 5. $2\frac{14}{45}$ 7. $1\frac{32}{33}$ 9. $\frac{17}{60}$

2. $1\frac{9}{20}$ 4. $1\frac{11}{14}$ 6. $1\frac{11}{28}$ 8. $\frac{17}{24}$ 10. $6\frac{9}{14}$

68. Addition, Subtraction, and Substitution Using Fractions

1. $1\frac{7}{8}$ 3. $2\frac{1}{8}$ 5. $1\frac{5}{8}$ 7. $1\frac{1}{8}$ 9. $\frac{1}{4}$

2. $\frac{11}{30}$ 4. $1\frac{1}{4}$ 6. $\frac{13}{30}$ 8. $\frac{7}{30}$ 10. $1\frac{1}{8}$

69. Boxing Up the Multiplication of Fractions

1. $\frac{1}{8}$ 5. $\frac{7}{40}$ 9. $2\frac{2}{3}$ 13. $5\frac{1}{4}$ 16. $\frac{4}{25}$

2. $\frac{1}{6}$ 6. $\frac{4}{25}$ 10. $\frac{7}{32}$ 14. $\frac{1}{2}$ 17. $\frac{4}{45}$

3. $\frac{1}{10}$ 7. $1\frac{1}{3}$ 11. $\frac{1}{5}$ 15. $\frac{27}{40}$ 18. 12

4. $\frac{2}{15}$ 8. 2   12. $\frac{7}{40}$

70. Interesting Name Math

1. $22\frac{1}{6}$ 3. $1\frac{7}{8}$ 5. $11\frac{1}{4}$ 7. $16\frac{11}{12}$ 9. $69\frac{2}{3}$

2. $53\frac{1}{6}$ 4. $10\frac{5}{6}$ 6. $42\frac{3}{4}$ 8. $4\frac{1}{16}$ 10. $3\frac{1}{2}$

71. Bubble-Bath Math

1. $2\frac{1}{4}$ 5. $1\frac{1}{8}$ 9. 1   13. $3\frac{1}{16}$ 17. $12\frac{11}{16}$

2. $5\frac{1}{4}$ 6. $1\frac{5}{16}$ 10. 6   14. $8\frac{3}{4}$ 18. $5\frac{1}{2}$

3. 3   7. $2\frac{7}{10}$ 11. $\frac{7}{16}$ 15. $1\frac{2}{5}$ 19. $8\frac{1}{6}$

4. $13\frac{1}{2}$ 8. $1\frac{2}{3}$ 12. $2\frac{5}{8}$ 16. $4\frac{3}{8}$ 20. $\frac{7}{20}$

72. The Zippy Way to Equivalent Fractions

$\frac{5}{10}$, $\frac{21}{28}$, $\frac{63}{72}$, $\frac{77}{121}$, $\frac{16}{20}$, $\frac{3}{9}$, $\frac{12}{54}$, $\frac{6}{10}$, $\frac{45}{54}$, $\frac{24}{64}$

73. Division of Fractions: Part One

1. $1\frac{1}{7}$ V   3. $5\frac{1}{3}$ D   5. $1\frac{3}{7}$ O   7. $1\frac{7}{8}$ A   9. $1\frac{1}{3}$ E

2. 3 I   4. $3\frac{1}{2}$ E   6. $\frac{16}{21}$ G   8. $2\frac{6}{7}$ M   10. $3\frac{1}{5}$ S

Message: VIDEO GAMES

74. Division of Fractions: Part Two

1. $1\frac{1}{8}$ A   3. $1\frac{4}{9}$ T   5. $3\frac{5}{11}$ M   7. $\frac{1}{2}$ B   9. $1\frac{11}{17}$ L

2. $1\frac{2}{3}$ U   4. $\frac{44}{65}$ O   6. $1\frac{1}{3}$ O   8. $1\frac{9}{35}$ I   10. $\frac{5}{8}$ E

Message: AUTOMOBILE

75. Dividing Whole Numbers and Mixed Numbers by Fractions

1. 27   3. 72   5. $8\frac{1}{6}$ 7. $2\frac{1}{4}$ 9. 10   11. $2\frac{13}{16}$

2. $10\frac{2}{3}$ 4. $37\frac{4}{5}$ 6. $13\frac{1}{5}$ 8. $31\frac{1}{2}$ 10. 21   12. 5

76. Fraction Squares

Set 1: $1\frac{1}{6}$ $1\frac{1}{2}$ $\frac{15}{56}$ Set 2: $\frac{19}{35}$ $\frac{1}{7}$ $\frac{7}{12}$

          $\frac{19}{24}$ $\frac{1}{4}$

Set 3: $\frac{3}{16}$ $\frac{2}{5}$ $\frac{3}{10}$ Set 4: $\frac{1}{2}$ $1\frac{1}{15}$ $\frac{4}{7}$

          $\frac{8}{15}$ $1\frac{1}{3}$

77. Fractions Are a Breeze

1. 92 mph   3. 4 mph   5. $\frac{1}{2}$ 7. 15 mph   9. $\frac{21}{25}$

2. 25 mph   4. 12 mph   6. $\frac{31}{75}$ 8. $\frac{1}{19}$ 10. Breeze

78. Life Span Math Questions: Part One

1. 3; $\frac{1}{4}$ of a year

2. 6; $\frac{1}{2}$ of a year

3. 9; $\frac{3}{4}$ of a year

4. 6; 0.5 of a year

5. 3; 0.25 of a year

6. 4; $0.3\overline{3}$ of a year

7. 24; 2 years

8. 30; $2\frac{1}{2}$ years

9. 33; $2\frac{3}{4}$ years

10. 8; $0.6\overline{6}$ of a year

11. 39; $3\frac{1}{4}$ years

12. 45; $3\frac{3}{4}$ years

13. 27; $2\frac{1}{4}$ years

14. 54; $4\frac{1}{2}$ years

15. 210; 17.5 years

16. 261; 21.75 years

79. Life Span Math Questions: Part Two

1. 8 mo.

2. 159 mo.

3. 534 mo.

4. 162 mo.

5. 28.75 years

6. 24.25 years

7. 873 mo.

8. 1,470 mo.

9. 24 years

10. Same age

80. Expressing Fractions as Decimals: Part One

A. 1. 0.75 3. 7.5 5. 0.05 7. 0.9 9. 0.1

2. 0.25 4. 2.8 6. 0.375 8. $0.444\overline{4}$ 10. 0.625

B.

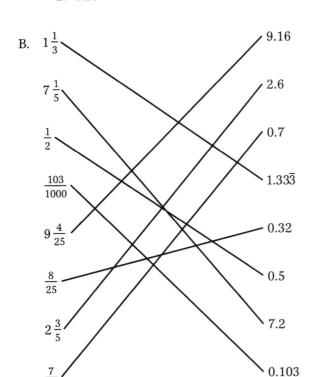

$1\frac{1}{3}$ 9.16

$7\frac{1}{5}$ 2.6

$\frac{1}{2}$ 0.7

$\frac{103}{1000}$ $1.33\overline{3}$

$9\frac{4}{25}$ 0.32

$\frac{8}{25}$ 0.5

$2\frac{3}{5}$ 7.2

$\frac{7}{10}$ 0.103

81. Expressing Fractions as Decimals: Part Two

1. 3.1
2. 4.25
3. 0.33$\overline{3}$
4. 4.2
5. 3.25
6. 2.125
7. 2.75
8. 2.9
9. 7.6
10. 14.1
11. 3.5
12. 2.4
13. 7.3
14. 8.7

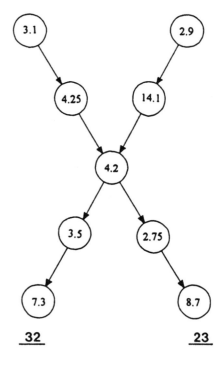

32   **23**

82. The Fraction Name Game

1. 242 lbs.

2. $\frac{9}{24}$, $\frac{3}{8}$

3. $\frac{12}{24}$, $\frac{1}{2}$

4. $\frac{5}{10}$, $\frac{1}{2}$

5. $\frac{11}{44}$, $\frac{1}{4}$

6. $\frac{18}{63}$, $\frac{2}{7}$

7. $\frac{5}{10}$, $\frac{1}{2}$

8. $\frac{78}{242}$, $\frac{39}{121}$

83. Simplifying Fractions

Name	Body Weight (in Pounds)	Pounds Needed to Lose	Fraction	"Reduced" Fraction
Flipper Twerpski	200 lbs.	50 lbs.	$\frac{50}{200}$	$\frac{1}{4}$
Akira Tsutsumi	350 lbs.	200 lbs.	$\frac{200}{350}$	$\frac{4}{7}$
Kimmel Florentine	168 lbs.	18 lbs.	$\frac{18}{168}$	$\frac{3}{28}$
Molly Sousa	132 lbs.	22 lbs.	$\frac{22}{132}$	$\frac{1}{6}$
Bighampton Butler Jones	260 lbs.	65 lbs.	$\frac{65}{260}$	$\frac{1}{4}$
Wonder Skyblue Jones	148 lbs.	30 lbs.	$\frac{30}{148}$	$\frac{15}{74}$
Marylou Pettigrew	225 lbs.	75 lbs.	$\frac{75}{225}$	$\frac{1}{3}$
Clyde Manning	98 lbs.	2 lbs.	$\frac{2}{98}$	$\frac{1}{49}$
Horizon Sunshine	286 lbs.	98 lbs.	$\frac{98}{286}$	$\frac{49}{143}$
Moira Moonbeam	175 lbs.	3 lbs.	$\frac{3}{175}$	$\frac{3}{175}$

84. Definition Puzzle on Fraction Terms

											[6]H	I	G	H	E	S	T			
		[14]O	V	E	R															
					[12]U	[3]N	L	I	K	[2]E				[10]M	[4]I	X	E	D		
	[11]L		[9]R			U				Q					M					
	O		E			M		[8]C		U					P					
	W		D		[1]D	E	N	O	M	I	N	A	T	O	R	[7]P				
	E		U			R		M		V					O	A				
	S		C			A		M		A					[5]P	R	O	P	E	R
[15]W	T		E			T		O		L					E	T				
H			D			O		N		E	[13]S				R					
O						R				N	E									
L										T	T									
E											S									

85. Skills Mastery Test—Fractions: Part One

1. 1
2. $\frac{1}{2}$
3. $1\frac{1}{2}$
4. $\frac{7}{8}$
5. $1\frac{17}{24}$
6. $\frac{41}{45}$
7. 6
8. $5\frac{3}{4}$
9. $3\frac{7}{8}$
10. $9\frac{1}{2}$
11. $17\frac{9}{10}$
12. $10\frac{5}{6}$
13. $\frac{1}{2}$
14. $\frac{2}{5}$
15. $\frac{1}{14}$
16. $\frac{1}{2}$
17. $\frac{3}{8}$
18. $\frac{21}{64}$
19. 2
20. $6\frac{1}{2}$
21. 1
22. $2\frac{1}{8}$
23. $1\frac{1}{4}$
24. $2\frac{3}{11}$
25. $17\frac{9}{16}$

86. Skills Mastery Test—Fractions: Part Two

1. $\frac{1}{3}$
2. $\frac{5}{8}$
3. $\frac{1}{6}$
4. $\frac{2}{3}$
5. $\frac{1}{6}$
6. $\frac{7}{16}$
7. $\frac{7}{8}$
8. $6\frac{3}{8}$
9. 2
10. 3
11. $4\frac{5}{7}$
12. $1\frac{2}{25}$
13. 0.5
14. 0.4
15. 2.25
16. 7.2
17. 21
18. 44
19. 4
20. 30
21. $\frac{5}{6}$
22. $\frac{4}{35}$
23. $\frac{5}{8}$
24. $\frac{9}{14}$
25. $1\frac{19}{30}$

SECTION 4   UNDERSTANDING PERCENT
FOR SKILL DEVELOPMENT

87. Percent Basics (Fractions to % and % to Decimals)

A. 1. 23%   3. 99%   5. 117%   7. 11%   9. 34%
    2. 37%   4. 24%   6. 96%   8. 29%   10. 32%

B. 1. 0.12   3. 0.07   5. 0.64   7. 0.90   9. 0.99
    2. 0.49   4. 0.98   6. 0.37   8. 0.14   10. 1.42

Message: THEIR FRIENDS

88. Understanding Values Less than 1%

A. 1. 0.003   5. 0.00009   9. 0.007
    2. 0.0003   6. 0.0009   10. 0.0000007
    3. 0.004   7. 0.009   11. 0.00007
    4. 0.0004   8. 0.005   12. 0.0007

B. 1. 0.9%   5. 0.92%   9. 0.808%
    2. 0.09%   6. 0.842%   10. 0.0004%
    3. 0.009%   7. 0.037%   11. 0.123%
    4. 0.5%   8. 0.73%   12. 0.0029%

C. Answers will vary as to location of shading. Just be sure 53 spaces are shaded.

89. Fraction, Decimal, and Percent Equivalents

Fraction	Decimal	Percent	Fraction	Decimal	Percent
$\frac{1}{2}$	0.5	50%	$\frac{1}{4}$	0.25	25%
$\frac{3}{4}$	0.75	75%	$\frac{1}{6}$	$0.16\bar{6}$	$16\frac{2}{3}\%$
$\frac{1}{8}$	0.125	$12\frac{1}{2}\%$	$\frac{1}{10}$	0.1	10%
$\frac{1}{3}$	$0.33\bar{3}$	$33\frac{1}{3}\%$	$\frac{5}{8}$	0.625	$62\frac{1}{2}\%$
$\frac{1}{5}$	0.2	20%	$\frac{3}{10}$	0.3	30%
$\frac{7}{10}$	0.7	70%	$\frac{5}{6}$	$0.83\bar{3}$	$83\frac{1}{3}\%$
$\frac{3}{5}$	0.6	60%	$\frac{4}{5}$	0.8	80%

90. Greater than 100%

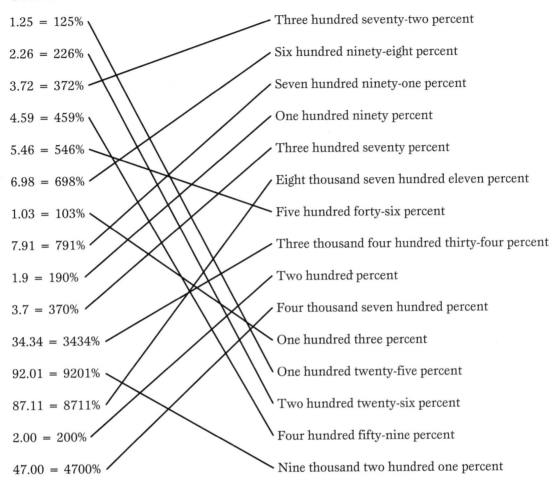

1.25 = 125%

2.26 = 226%

3.72 = 372%

4.59 = 459%

5.46 = 546%

6.98 = 698%

1.03 = 103%

7.91 = 791%

1.9 = 190%

3.7 = 370%

34.34 = 3434%

92.01 = 9201%

87.11 = 8711%

2.00 = 200%

47.00 = 4700%

Three hundred seventy-two percent

Six hundred ninety-eight percent

Seven hundred ninety-one percent

One hundred ninety percent

Three hundred seventy percent

Eight thousand seven hundred eleven percent

Five hundred forty-six percent

Three thousand four hundred thirty-four percent

Two hundred percent

Four thousand seven hundred percent

One hundred three percent

One hundred twenty-five percent

Two hundred twenty-six percent

Four hundred fifty-nine percent

Nine thousand two hundred one percent

91. Percent Stew

1. 90%	7. $75\frac{1}{2}$%	13. 180%	19. 87%
2. 143%	8. 275%	14. 700%	20. 350%
3. 50%	9. 325%	15. 257%	21. 112%
4. 75%	10. 250%	16. 1%	22. 350%
5. $27\frac{1}{2}$%	11. 203%	17. 370%	23. 100%
6. 75%	12. 122%	18. 900%	24. 217%

92. Relating Percent to Diagrams

1. separated: 800; left: 3,200

2. separated: 900; left: 8,100

3. separated: 152.5; left: 2,897.5

4. separated: 2,176; left: 3,264

5. separated: 34.4; left: 1,685.6

6. separated: 15; left: 360

7. separated: 45; left: 135

8. separated: 360; left: 2,040

9. separated: 62.3; left: 827.7

10. separated: 11,200; left: 16,800

93. Presidential Percentages

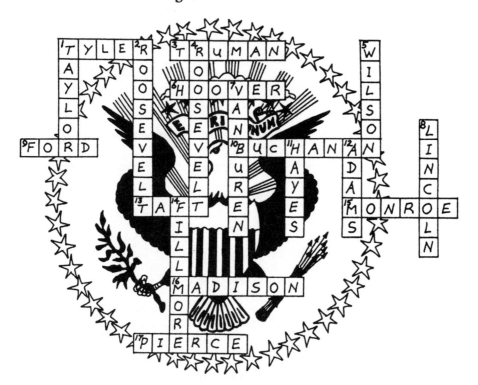

94. Percent of a Hot Rod by Weight

1. 3200 lbs.	3. 5%	5. $27\frac{1}{2}$%	7. 7%	9. $7\frac{1}{2}$%
2. 11%	4. 20%	6. 35%	8. 4%	10. 3%

95. Geo Math

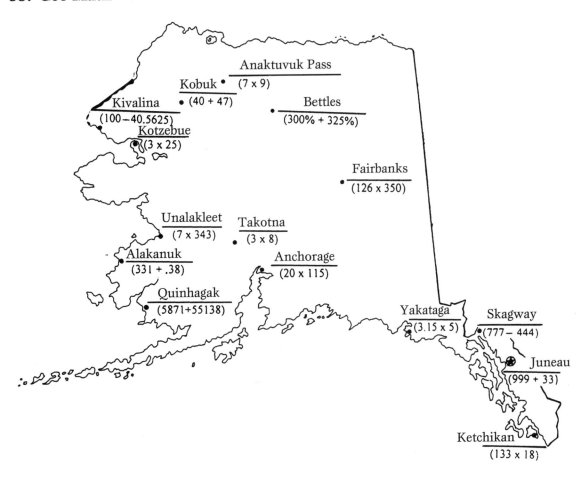

96. Monster Math

1. 10%	3. 150%	5. 390 lbs.	7. 0
2. 25%	4. 1,430 lbs.	6. 12.5% Land, 33.3% Water	8. 1,573 lbs.

97. Calculating Percent of Gain or Increase

1. 656 more calories, 713%

2. 14 amphibians, 18%

3. 57 lbs., 475%

4. 51 hrs., 134%

5. 255 days, 381%

98. Calculating Percent of Loss or Decrease

1. 10; 29%
2. 109 mph; 56%
3. 310 bales; 74%

4. 2 inches; 29%
5. 40 hours; 83%
6. 36 people; 84%

99. Understanding Percent from the Decimal Place

1. 3%   5
2. 0.8%   7
3. 9%   2
4. 0.9%   8
5. 0.3%   10
6. 11%   11
7. 1.9%   12
8. 6.3%   13
9. 0.72%   15
10. 0.34%   14
11. 8.43%   9
12. 1.37%   6
13. 0.1%   1
14. 0.01%   4
15. 2.74%   3

100. Definition Puzzle on Percent

[12]S																			
P												[8]D	E	[3]C	R	E	A	[6]S	E
A				[13]M		[9]P								O				U	
[11]C	O	M	P	A	R	E		[2]V						R			[5]H	C	
E				T		R		A						R			U	C	
						[1]C	A	L	C	U	[15]L	A	T	E			N	E	
				H		E		U			O			C			D	S	
	[14]P					N		E			W			T			R	S	
[10]C	O	N	V	E	R	T					E						E		
	I										S						D		
	N							[7]P	A	T	T	E	R	N			T		
	T																H	[4]O	F

101. Skills Mastery Test—Percentage

1. 19.6
2. 49
3. 34.3
4. 122.5
5. 161.7
6. 196
7. 41%

8. 64%
9. 80%
10. 10%
11. 220%
12. 425%
13. 175%
14. 250%

15. 1%
16. 42%
17. 137%
18. 0.03%
19. 319%
20. 3%
21. $7\frac{1}{2}\%$

22.

Fraction	Decimal	Percent
$\frac{3}{4}$	0.75	75%
$\frac{1}{5}$	0.2	20%

SECTION 5   MONEY CONCEPTS
FOR THE MODERN CLASSROOM

102.   The Monthly Budget

Answers will vary.

103.   Better Buying Power—Division of Money

1. 6 yd. for $270.00; $5.00 saved on each yard

2. 5 lbs. for $115.00; $12.00 saved on each pound

3. 18 ft. for $432.00; $1.00 saved on each foot

4. 8 ft. for $57.92; $0.01 or 1¢ saved on each foot

5. 3 yd. for $2.94; $2.14 saved on each yard

6. 7 lbs. for $43.75; $0.75 or 75¢ saved on each pound

7. 8 ft. for $40.00; $0.25 or 25¢ saved on each foot

8. 2 yd. for $5.50; $0.25 or 25¢ saved on each yard

9. 88 yd. for $78.32; $0.01 or 1¢ saved on each yard

10. 12 oz. for $25.20; $0.05 or 5¢ saved on each ounce

11. 17 lbs. for $8.33; $0.01 or 1¢ saved on each pound

12. 6 ft. for $2.40; $0.01 or 1¢ saved on each foot

13. 15 yd. for $7.20; $0.02 or 2¢ saved on each yard

14. 12 oz. for $17.88; $0.03 or 3¢ saved on each ounce

15. 30 yd. for $4,950.00; $5.00 saved on each yard

16. 16 ft. for $54.40; $0.10 or 10¢ saved on each foot

17. 7 lbs. for $364.00; $2.00 saved on each pound

18. 10 oz. for $1.00; $1.00 saved on each ounce

19. 11 lbs. for $2.42; $0.03 or 3¢ saved on each pound

20. 827 ft. for $537.55; $1.35 saved on each foot

104.   The True Cost of an Item—Hours of Work Required

1. 21
2. 29
3. 13
4. 4
5. 32
6. 23
7. 25
8. 22
9. 160
10. 1,551
11. 4,629

105. Wages, Deductions, and Taxes

A. Based on a 4-Week Month
   Hours per month = 160
   Gross Income per month = $1,080.00
   Income tax per month = $55.36
   Social Security per month = $70.20
   Health per month = $47.00
   Net Income or Disposable Income After
      Deductions = $907.44

B. Based on a 4-Week Month
   Hours per month = 176
   Gross Income per month = $1,223.20
   Income tax per month = $69.88
   Social Security per month = $79.52
   Net Income or Disposable Income After
      Deductions = $1,073.80

C. Based on a 4-Week Month
   Regular Hours per month = 160
   Overtime hours per month = 68
   Gross Income per month = $2,096.00
   Income tax per month = $193.84
   Social Security per month = $136.24
   Net Income or Disposable Income After
      Deductions = $1,765.92

106. Money Stew (+, −): Part One

A.
1. $9.18	5. $3.05	9. $12.53	13. $3.13
2. $12.08	6. $1.26	10. $4.40	14. $148.65
3. $4.24	7. $3.81	11. $21.49	15. $79.84
4. $10.18	8. $4.25	12. $4.98	

B.
1. $7.43	2. $8.91	3. $131.18	4. 0

   5. A fool and his money are soon parted.

107. Money Stew (+, −, ×, ÷): Part Two

A.
1. $18.10	5. $52.68	9. $17.70	13. $6.42
2. $1,584.44	6. $28.53	10. $3.33	14. $16.74
3. $39.37	7. $9.20	11. $27.88	15. $15.69
4. $33.75	8. $80.85	12. $49.72	

B.
1. $1,592.21	2. $39.85	3. $70.85	4. $425.34

   5. A penny saved is a penny earned.

108. The Real Cost of Borrowing

Cost of the Car	Down Payment	Principal or Amount Borrowed	Simple Interest Rate Per Year	Period of the Loan	Amount of Interest	Total Amount to Be Repaid	Total Cost of Your Cool Car
$900	$100	$800	7%	1 year	$56.00	$856.00	$956.00
$1,000	$300	$700	6%	1 year	$42.00	$742.00	$1,042.00
$1,400	$300	$1,100	9%	2 years	$198.00	$1,298.00	$1,598.00
$2,000	$400	$1,600	10%	3 years	$480.00	$2,080.00	$2,480.00
$12,000	$700	$11,300	$5\frac{1}{2}\%$	1 year	$621.50	$11,921.50	$12,621.50
$12,000	$200	$11,800	$7\frac{1}{2}\%$	$1\frac{1}{2}$ years	$1,327.50	$13,127.50	$13,327.50

109. The Cost of a Tiger

1. $1,918.20
2. $297.52
3. $17,572.19
4. $3,350.28

5. $287.39
6. $98,555.80
7. $312.44
8. $2,197.39

9. $5,912.51
10. Answers will vary.

110. The Cost of a Dump Truck

COST OF RUBBER PARTS
Hoses	$642.75
Tires	$1,647.00
Spacers & body mounts	$379.20

COST OF METAL PARTS
Truck body	$7,321.70
Truck box	$8,460.89
Frame	$6,991.29
Bumpers	$1,203.58

COST OF ENGINE AND DRIVE TRAIN
Engine	$8,090.37
Transmission	$5,927.30
Rear axle	$3,270.94

COST OF INTERIOR PARTS
Seats	$892.47
Dash gauges, knobs, etc.	$2,024.71
Mats, rug, etc.	$1,797.40

COST OF FLUIDS
Oil	$100.32
Antifreeze	$39.40
Transmission fluid	$39.41

COST OF MISC. ITEMS
Electrical	$2,947.32
Glass	$901.79
Fuel	$327.92

TOTAL COST OF DUMP TRUCK: $53,005.76

111.   Comparing the U.S. Dollar to Other Currencies

Item	U.S. Price	Canadian Price	United Kingdom (British) Price	European Countries (Euro) Price
Football	$22.95	$36.95	£18.82	€26.39
CD	$15.95	$25.68	£13.08	€18.34
Makeup	$37.50	$60.38	£30.75	€43.13
Dress	$72.98	$117.50	£59.84	€83.93
Pen	$0.79	$1.27	£0.65	€0.91
Haircut	$24.95	$40.17	£20.46	€28.69
Gallon of Gas	$1.25	$2.01	£1.03	€1.44
Sneakers	$84.32	$135.76	£69.14	€96.97
Watch	$14.95	$24.07	£12.26	€17.19
Rock Concert Tickets	$40.00	$64.40	£32.8	€46.00

112.   Making Change (Answers will vary. These are suggestions.)

Item	Cost of Item	Amount given in payment	$50	$20	$10	$5	$1	25¢	10¢	5¢	1¢	Total Change Received
Dress	$98.20	$100.00					1	3		1		$1.80
Football	$32.98	$50.00			1	1	2				2	$17.02
Video game	$14.20	$20.00				1		3		1		$5.80
Video game magazine	$4.99	$5.00									1	$0.01
Calculator	$14.62	$50.00		1	1	1		1	1		3	$35.38
Stapler	$3.95	$5.00					1			1		$1.05
Fast-food burger	$4.21	$10.00				1		3			4	$5.79
Entrance to zoo	$4.00	$20.00			1	1	1					$16.00
Pen	$2.49	$10.00				1	2	2			1	$7.51
Trail ride on horse	$179.40	$200.00		1				2	1			$20.60
CD	$12.49	$20.00				1	2	2			1	$7.51
Makeup	$17.37	$50.00		1	1		2	2	1		3	$32.63
Airplane ride	$50.52	$100.00		2		1	4	1	2		3	$49.48
Popcorn	$0.39	$100.00	1	2		1	4	2	1		1	$99.61
Lollipop	$0.29	$50.00		2		1	4	2	2		1	$49.71

113.   The Good Ol' Days, 1934

1. per day, $2.88; per week, $17.28;
   per month, $69.12

2. $.70 or 70¢

3. 4,121 hours

4. $6.25

5. $252.00

6. $7.74

7. 4.5 hours

8. $8.00

114.   The More Recent Good Ol' Days, 1955

1. $12.40

2. $6.00, $1.20

3. $1.56

4. 1,694 hours

5. $1.68

6. $1,176.00

7. $37.20

8. $4.17

115.   Adding Money

Ted—$2.23	Christa—$238.78	Wanda—$409.65	Karrie—$2,370.58
Molly—$13.46	John—$346.70	Bill—$664.61	Esther—$19,561.69
Kathy—$176.62	Al—$1,660.26	Tony—$547.98	Bob—$236,434.22

Bonus Questions:

1. $255,995.91   2. $593.82   3. $2,069.26   4. $2,697.58   5. $313.40

116.   Subtracting Money

Ziggy—$82.47	Marlene—$2.65
Jack—$109.02	Carol—$5.77
Margaret—$32.38	Henry—$84.60
Flossie—$86.29	Maria—$149.79
Sir Clyde Manning—$2,591.07	Bighampton—$899.91
Sonia—$3.39	Molly—$282.55

Bonus Questions:

1. $.99 or 99¢   2. $35.02   3. $80.37   4. $209.61   5. $2,567.32

117.   Multiplying Money

1. $982.26

2. $559.26

3. $336.84

4. $568.17

5. $141,067.08

6. $10,619.36

7. $577.89

8. $1,599.61

9. $467.72

10. $2,065.25

11. $1,541.09

12. $1,389.74

By the process of elimination. If all answers are correct, the answer remaining is the answer to the last problem.

118. Multiplying Money with the Help of Mr. Washington

1. $90.35	3. $869.32	5. $739.05	7. $218.76	9. 2.59 or 3 lbs.
2. $2,205.44	4. $552.50	6. $461.37	8. $174.86	10. $137.84

119. Multiplication and Subtraction with Money

Investment	Your Cost	Multiplied By	Gross Total	Net Profit
Video Game System	$127.30	5 ×	$636.50	$509.20
Party Dress	$71.14	4 ×	$284.56	$213.42
25 CDs	$237.20	2 ×	$474.40	$237.20
Golf Clubs	$37.00	7 ×	$259.00	$222.00
Football	$3.19	17 ×	$54.23	$51.04
Comics	$0.05	32 ×	$1.60	$1.55

120. Multiplication with Money

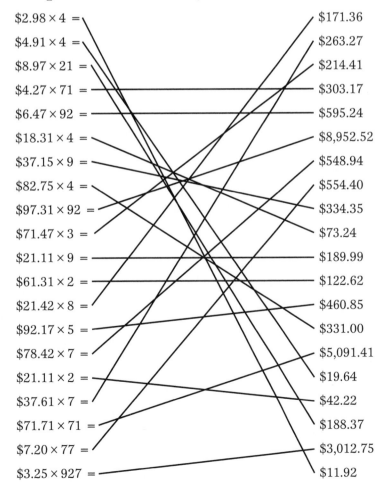

$2.98 × 4 =	$171.36
$4.91 × 4 =	$263.27
$8.97 × 21 =	$214.41
$4.27 × 71 =	$303.17
$6.47 × 92 =	$595.24
$18.31 × 4 =	$8,952.52
$37.15 × 9 =	$548.94
$82.75 × 4 =	$554.40
$97.31 × 92 =	$334.35
$71.47 × 3 =	$73.24
$21.11 × 9 =	$189.99
$61.31 × 2 =	$122.62
$21.42 × 8 =	$460.85
$92.17 × 5 =	$331.00
$78.42 × 7 =	$5,091.41
$21.11 × 2 =	$19.64
$37.61 × 7 =	$42.22
$71.71 × 71 =	$188.37
$7.20 × 77 =	$3,012.75
$3.25 × 927 =	$11.92

121. Dividing Money

1. $2.17	4. $32.12	7. $99.13	10. $25.33
2. $2.18	5. $2.11	8. $7.56	11. $4.56
3. $2.15	6. $65.14	9. $5.63	

Bonus: 12. 2 and 4   13. 6 and 8   14. 9 and 10

122. Dividing Your Good Fortune

Amount	Who They Are	Number of People	Amount Each Will Get
$197,622.00	Closest friends	3	$65,874.00
$277,066.00	Parents	2	$138,533.00
$160,736.15	Brothers & Sisters	5	$32,147.23
$5,053.20	Classmates	24	$210.55
$102,588.88	2 Pairs of Grandparents	4	$25,647.22
$59,296.32	Long-lost relatives who suddenly remembered you	72	$823.56
$185,991.06	Worthwhile charities	327	$568.78
$224,143.14	Aunt Bernice, Cousin Juan, and all their children	402	$557.57
$17,354.75	Your neighbors	47	$369.25
$1,316.56	Shadow the cat & Comet the dog	2	$658.28

123. Definition Puzzle on Money

					[9]B						[7]B						
					U			[10]R	O				[6]I			[12]O	
					D	[14]W	A	G	E	R		[2]D	N			V	
					G			N	R			I	C			E	
			[15]L	[1]D	E	D	U	C	T	I	O	N	S	O		R	
			[13]C	O	S	T					W	P	M			T	
			A		[3]B	U	Y	I	N	G	P	O	W	E	R	I	
			N								S		[8]T			M	
												[5]B	A	L	A	N	C	E
												B	X				
											[11]S	A	L	A	R	Y	
												[4]F	E	E	S		

124. Skills Mastery Test—Money

1. 61.5 hours
2. $290.00
3. $63.00 – Interest; $963.00 to be repaid; $1,063.00 total cost
4. $72.00 – Interest; $972.00 to be repaid; $1,272.00 total cost
5. $20.86
6. $44.19
7. $1,636.10
8. $0.81
9. $135.05
10. $65.00
11. $1,206.87
12. $27.27
13. $860.63
14. $60.10
15. $87.99
16. $747.20
17. $8,918.70
18. $11.41
19. $103.41
20. $7.27
21. $45.71
22. $101.90
23. $116.91
24. 3 for 49¢
25. 14 @ $7.99 each

SECTION 6   GEOMETRY AND MEASUREMENT—FACTS AND INSIGHTS

125.   Measure Math Match

13	$\frac{1}{4}$ mile or 1,320 feet		19	feet or yards or meters
12	quarts or liters		20	dollars and cents
14	number of students		16	pounds of thrust
14, 2	square feet or square meters		4	cups, teaspoons, tablespoons
7	meters		6, 1	inches or centimeters
10	cubic yards or cubic meters		11	milligrams
15	miles or kilometers		3	decibels
17	horsepower		9	hue
5, 18	milliliter or centiliter		8	pounds or kilograms

126.   Geometry Angles

Name	Size in degrees
Acute	20°
Obtuse	140°
Acute	5°
Acute	35°
Right	90°
Obtuse	120°

Message: The Father of Modern Geometry is EUCLID.

127.   Measuring Triangles

1. 35°	3. 70°	5. 60°	7. 138°	9. 74°	11. 73°
2. 30°	4. 45°	6. 81°	8. 39°	10. 76°	12. 20°

128.   Complementary and Supplementary Angles

1. ∠EFG = 20°; ∠GFH = 17°; Neither

2. ∠ABD = 160°; ∠ABC = 20°; Supplementary

3. ∠ILJ = 60°; ∠JLK = 30°; Complementary

4. ∠MNO = 85°; ∠ONP = 5°; Complementary

5. ∠RTS = 145°; ∠QTS = 35°; Supplementary

129. Measuring Angles

1. ∠ABC = 30°

2. ∠DEF = 105°

3. ∠GHI = 210°

4. ∠JKL = 60°

5. ∠MNO = 155°

130. Metric Measurement

1. 4 mm

2. 8 mm

3. 1 cm 1 mm

4. 4 cm 5 mm

5. 3 cm 2 mm

6. 3 cm 4 mm

7. 4 cm 2 mm

8. 6 cm 1 mm

9. 4 cm 1 mm

10. 3 cm 1 mm

11. 1 cm 9 mm

12. 2 cm 1 mm

13. 7 cm 1 mm

14. 4 cm 5 mm

15. 7 cm 1 mm

16. 3 cm 9 mm

17. 8 cm 7 mm

18. 2 cm 1 mm

19. 5 cm 9 mm

20. 7 cm 9 mm

131. Congruent Line Segments

Order will vary.

1. $\overline{AB} \simeq \overline{XM}$

2. $\overline{CD} \simeq \overline{DV}$

3. $\overline{FH} \simeq \overline{RS}$

4. $\overline{OY} \simeq \overline{PQ}$

5. $\overline{KZ} \simeq \overline{NL}$

6. $\overline{IJ} \simeq \overline{TU}$

7. $\overline{JN} \simeq \overline{PT}$

8. $\overline{AZ} \simeq \overline{CH}$

9. $\overline{KE} \simeq \overline{GW}$

10. $\overline{QS} \simeq \overline{KG}$

132. Congruent Angles

Order will vary.

1. ∠ABC ≅ ∠GHI

2. ∠DEF ≅ ∠JKL

3. ∠QRS ≅ ∠KLM

4. ∠YZA ≅ ∠STU

5. ∠EFG ≅ ∠MNO

6. ∠JPO ≅ ∠HPC

7. ∠JPH ≅ ∠NZP

8. ∠BCD ≅ ∠VWX

9. ∠GKT ≅ ∠AMW

10. ∠PQR ≅ ∠DCE

133. Finding the Perimeter of Figures

1. 27 ft.

2. 10 ft.

3. 12 ft.

4. 18 ft.

5. 12 in.

6. 26.9 in.

7. 72 in.

8. 31 ft.

9. 38 yd.

10. 24 ft.

134. A Serious Perimeter!

2,244 feet

135.   Perimeter Questions About Shane's Hat

   1. 37 in.   2. 39 in.   3. 16 in.   4. 20 in.

136.   Finding Perimeters of Figures or Shapes

Figure Letter	Partial Answer
B	45 ft.
D	108 ft.
G	232 ft.
H	214 ft.
E	252 ft.
C	12 ft.
A	99 ft.
F	316 in.
J	302 yd.
I	132 yd.

137.   The Area of a Triangle

   1. 36 sq. in.   3. 70 sq. ft.   5. 60 sq. ft.   7. 55 sq. ft.

   2. 45 sq. in.   4. 13.5 sq. ft.   6. 20 sq. ft.

138.   The Area of Old MacDonald's Farm

   1. 1,250 sq. ft.   3. 522 sq. ft.   5. 2,094 sq. ft.   7. 2,062 sq. ft.

   2. 432 sq. ft.   4. 3,288 sq. ft.   6. 2,500 sq. ft.   8. 6,127 sq. ft.

   9. 5,492 sq. ft. (Bales, water trough, and corral are not buildings.)

  10. 4,970 sq. ft.

  11. Ei Ei O!

139.   The Circumference of a Circle

   1. 21.98 in.   3. 31.4 in.   5. 43.96 ft.   7. 26.69 yd.   9. 6.4056 yd.

   2. 25.12 ft.   4. 18.84 ft.   6. 47.1 in.   8. 28.574 yd.   10. 34.54 ft.

140. The Area of a Circle

1. 28.26 sq. ft.
2. 153.86 sq. yd.
3. 63.585 sq. ft.
4. 28.26 sq. yd.
5. .2826 sq. in.
6. 52.7834 sq. yd.
7. 176.625 sq. in.
8. 22.8906 sq. in.
9. 379.94 sq. ft.
10. 78.5 sq. miles

141. The Volume of Cubes and Rectangular Prisms

1. 27 cu. in.
2. 9,833,648 cu. miles
3. 216 cu. meters
4. 30,132 cu. mm
5. 2,176 cu. ft.
6. 14,112 cu. yd.
7. 1,404 cu. km.
8. 3,094 cu. meters

142. The Volume of Pyramids and Cones

1. 20 cu. ft.
2. 54 cu. yd.
3. 578 cu. mm
4. 15 cu. in.
5. 144 cu. yd.
6. 225 cu. cm.

143. Map Strategies: Part One

Name of Object	Point Letter	Number Location		Number Location		Point Letter	Name of Object
		N or S	E or W	N or S	E or W		
Basketball	A	5N	2E	7S	4E	G	Soiled top on floor
TV set	H	6S	6E	6N	5W	J	Pile of CDs
Crumpled jeans	F	3S	2E	3N	1W	L	Canadian cat
CD & DVD player	D	7N	7W	2N	7W	I	Bed
Sports equipment	E	7N	7E	1S	5W	C	Serious lint from under bed
Closet	K	7S	6W	7N	2W	B	Computer

144. Map Strategies: Part Two

Point	Latitude	Longitude	Latitude	Longitude	Point
B	60°S	30°W	75°N	30°E	J
H	15°S	60°W	45°N	60°E	N
F	45°S	120°E	75°N	165°W	M
L	45°N	30°W	45°N	105°W	C
I	75°N	45°W	15°N	15°E	G
E	60°N	90°E	60°N	105°W	D
A	45°S	150°W	60°S	150°E	K

145. Definition Puzzle on Geometry and Measurement Terms

1	2	3	4	5	6	7	8	9	10	11	12	13	14	15	16	17	18
								[3]C		[15]M	A	P	[11]S				
								O			[4]D		Q				[8]P
		[10]S	H	A	P	E		N			I		U				E
								G			A		A				R
					[2]C			R			M		R				I
				[1]C	I	R	C	U	M	F	E	R	E	N	C	E	M
[9]M	E	[14]A	S	U	R	E		E			T						E
		N			C			N			E						T
		G			L			T			[5]R	A	D	I	U	S	E
		L			E		[6]R	E	[12]C	T	A	N	G	L	E		R
		E							O								
									N	[7]T	R	I	A	N	G	L	E
							[13]A	R	E	A							

146. Skills Mastery Test—Geometry and Measurement: Part One

1. 18 ft.
3. 41 inches
5. 136 sq. in.
7. 18 sq. ft.
9. 120 sq. yd.

2. 40 ft.
4. 9 sq. ft.
6. 83 sq. ft.
8. 22 sq. in.

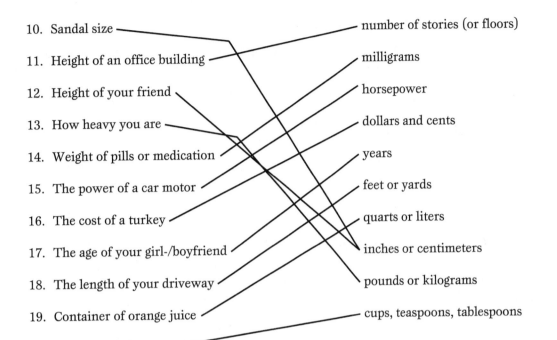

10. Sandal size

11. Height of an office building

12. Height of your friend

13. How heavy you are

14. Weight of pills or medication

15. The power of a car motor

16. The cost of a turkey

17. The age of your girl-/boyfriend

18. The length of your driveway

19. Container of orange juice

20. Recipe ingredients

number of stories (or floors)

milligrams

horsepower

dollars and cents

years

feet or yards

quarts or liters

inches or centimeters

pounds or kilograms

cups, teaspoons, tablespoons

147. Skills Mastery Test—Geometry and Measurement: Part Two

1. 50.24 ft.
8. 38 mm or 3 cm 8 mm
15. 90°

2. 31.4 ft.
9. 43 mm or 4 cm 3 mm
16. 27 cu. ft.

3. 18.84 ft.
10. obtuse
17. 24 cu. ft.

4. 153.86 sq. ft.
11. acute
18. 23.3$\overline{3}$ cu. ft.

5. 254.34 sq. yd.
12. right
19. 9.33 cu. yd.

6. 12.56 sq. yd.
13. 130°
20. 108 cu. cm

7. 28 mm or 2 cm 8 mm
14. 35°

SECTION 7   CHARTS AND GRAPHS
TO STIMULATE AND ENRICH

148.   The Horizontal Bar Graph

1. approx. $20,000
2. approx. $13,000
3. approx. $39,000
4. 3-Window Coupe
5. approx. $20,000

149.   A Cool Bar Graph

1. Diamond Washington
2. 499
3. Yes
4. Candy Barr
5. Billy Bopper
6. 50 points

150.   A Cool Bar Graph (Continued)

1. Candy Barr
2. 400, 500
3. 1,850
4. 357.5
5. 27
6. 350
7. 151
8. 600
9. Molly—700, Candy—650
10. Horizon—240, John Q.—290

151.   The Picture Graph

1. Morgan
2. Each half horse represents 5,000 animals
3. 5,000
4. No
5. 80,000 horses

152.   The Line Graph in Action

1. Baseball
2. Yes, 5 points
3. July and August
4. Fashion & Styles, Video Games, Jobs
5. Fashion & Styles, Jobs
6. Baseball
7. Baseball
8. Yes

153. Constructing a Line Graph

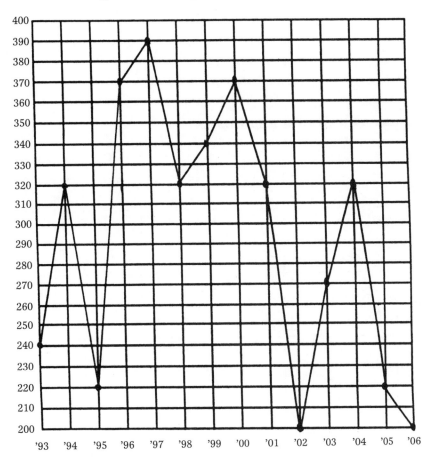

154. Circle Graphs or Pie Charts

Information sheet on "Pies in America" —no answers.

155. Circle Graphs or Pie Charts: Questions

1. 2%

2. 19%

3. 16%

4. 2,420

5. 2.228 lbs. or 2.23 lbs.

6. 222.8 lbs.

7. 2 ounces

8. 3%

9. 57%

10. 1,689.60 pies

156. Circle Graphs or Pie Charts: More Questions

1. 15%

2. 690 lbs.

3. 1,100 pies

4. 4,646.4

5. 3,058

6. 15%

7. 1,980

8. 21,120

9. 44¢ or $.44

10. Answers will vary.

157.   Reading a Chart on Snowboarding

1. 549
2. Candy Barr
3. 65
4. 256
5. 2,308
6. 4
7. 30
8. Bighampton Jones

158.   Definition Puzzle on Graphs and Charts

	[8]P	[3]L	O	T								[11]S	C	A	L	E
		I													
[12]S		N					[2]V							
H		E		[6]O	U	T	C	O	M	E				[13]R
A								R			[14]P	I	E
R				[1]H	O	R	I	Z	O	N	T	A	[7]L			C
E								I		E		[9]D		O
[15]C		[10]S	E	G	M	E	N	T		C		[4]G	R	A	P	H	R
I									A		E		T		D
R								L		N		A
C										D
L		[5]C	O	M	P	A	R	I	S	O	N
E										

159.   Skills Mastery Test—Graphs and Charts

1. Flipper, by $2,500
2. $4,000
3. $3,500
4. $8,500
5. John Q., Molly
6. $3,000 (Molly), $1,500 (Flossie)
7. $1,800
8. $3,000

SECTION 8   HOOKED ON RATIO, PROBABILITY, AND AVERAGE

160.   Probability: Ten Thinking Questions

1. 1 out of 7 or $\frac{1}{7}$

2. 1 out of 4 or $\frac{1}{4}$

3. 1 out of 72 or $\frac{1}{72}$

4. 1 out of 3 or $\frac{1}{3}$

5. 1 out of 1 or 1

6. 2 out of 15 or $\frac{2}{15}$

7. 1 out of 6 or $\frac{1}{6}$

8. 1 out of 13 or $\frac{1}{13}$

9. 1 out of 2 or $\frac{1}{2}$

10. 1 out of 1 or 1

Question: Answers will vary.

161.   Probability: Reading Story Problems

1. 1 out of 5 or $\frac{1}{5}$

2. 1 out of 24 or $\frac{1}{24}$

3. 1 out of 65 or $\frac{1}{65}$

4. 4 out of 7 or $\frac{4}{7}$

5. 3 out of 10 or $\frac{3}{10}$

Question: Answers will vary.

162.   The Application of Average or Mean

Server	S	M	T	W	T	F	S	Totals
Tony	113	141	147	225	68	171	38	903
Kevin	107	182	149	147	42	221	91	939
Karrie	118	191	121	298	191	141	111	1171
Dave	120	228	130	120	247	240	142	1227
Ruth	327	73	328	35	211	362	271	1607
Totals	785	815	875	825	759	1135	653	5847

1. See chart.

2. 227

3. 129

4. 41.14

5. 163

6. 167.29

7. 229.57

8. 167.06

163. Mean, Mode, and Median

1. Mean = 20; Mode = 15; Median = 21
2. Mean = 320; Mode = N/A; Median = 327
3. Mean = 19; Mode = 19; Median = 19
4. Mean = 34; Mode = 35; Median = 35
5. Mean = 17; Mode = 11; Median = 12
6. Mean = 4; Mode = 5; Median = 5

164. Alpha-Numerical Puzzle

Message: THE BEST THINGS IN LIFE ARE FREE.

1. 25	6. 78	11. 9	15. 9	19. 7	23. 44
2. 69	7. 25	12. 75	16. 86	20. 8	24. 40
3. 7	8. 25	13. 78	17. 11	21. 40	25. 7
4. 23	9. 69	14. 11	18. 44	22. 7	26. 7
5. 7	10. 11				

165. Introduction to Ratios

1. 2:7	3. 4:5	5. 4:3	7. 7:5	9. 1:2
2. 5:3	4. 3:7	6. 4:7	8. 2:3	10. 5:2

166. Ratio Word Problems

1. a. 7:10; b. 3:10; c. 3:7
2. a. 9:15; b. 2:5; c. 3:2
3. a. 10:9; b. 9:10; c. 10:19; d. 9:19
4. a. 7:10; b. 10:17; c. 7:19

167. Three-Term Ratios

2. 7:8, 7:4, 2:1
3. 9:11, 1:2, 9:22
4. 1:2, 1:2, 1:4
5. 4:5, 1:4, 1:5
6. A:14, 1:2, A:28
7. B:4, 4:G, B:G
8. 4:7, 7:X, 4:X
9. Y:X, X:2, Y:2
10. A:B, B:C, A:C

Bonus: dropkick, kickoff, dropoff
showman, floorshow, floorman, showfloor

168.   Understanding Forms (Ratio, Fraction, and Written)

Ratio Form	Fraction Form	Written Form	Ratio Form Using "To"
2:5	$\frac{2}{5}$	two-fifths	2 to 5
7:8	$\frac{7}{8}$	seven-eighths	7 to 8
2:3	$\frac{2}{3}$	two-thirds	2 to 3
1:4	$\frac{1}{4}$	one-fourth or one-quarter	1 to 4
5:8	$\frac{5}{8}$	five-eighths	5 to 8
1:7	$\frac{1}{7}$	one-seventh	1 to 7
4:5	$\frac{4}{5}$	four-fifths	4 to 5
4:9	$\frac{4}{9}$	four-ninths	4 to 9
3:7	$\frac{3}{7}$	three-sevenths	3 to 7
7:11	$\frac{7}{11}$	seven-elevenths	7 to 11
3:5	$\frac{3}{5}$	three-fifths	3 to 5
1:10	$\frac{1}{10}$	one-tenth	1 to 10
5:9	$\frac{5}{9}$	five-ninths	5 to 9
4:11	$\frac{4}{11}$	four-elevenths	4 to 11

169.   Proportions Explained (Answers will vary. These are suggestions.)

2. 14:4
    21:6

3. 18:8
    27:12

4. 34:8
    51:12

5. 24:14
    36:21

6. 4:18
    6:27

7. 2:4
    3:6

8. 2:16
    3:24

9. 2:8
    3:12

10. 8:22
    12:33

11. 4:14
    6:21

12. 14:22
    21:33

13. 18:10
    27:15

14. 6:10
    9:15

15. 8:14
    12:21

170. Definition Puzzle on Ratios, Probability, and Average

1	2	3	4	5	6	7	8	9	10	11	12	13	14	15	16	17	18	19	20
							[11]M									[8]P			
			[5]P			[15]P	E	R	C	E	N	T			[14]V	A	L	U	E
[10]A	V	E	R	A	G	E	A									T			
			O				N									T			
			[1]P	R	O	B	A	B	I	L	I	[2]T	Y			E			
			O									E			[4]L	R			
			R				[3]C	O	M	P	A	R	I	S	O	N			
			T									M				S			
			[6]I	N	C	R	E	A	S	E	[7]F	O	R	[12]M	S				
			O											O					
			N	[9]E	Q	U	I	V	A	L	E	N	T	D					
													[13]M	E	D	I	A	N	

171. Skills Mastery Test—Ratio, Probability, and Average

1. 1:2
2. 1:4

3. 1:4
4. 1:3

5. $\frac{2}{5}$
6. $\frac{1}{20}$

7. $\frac{2}{3}$
8. $\frac{3}{4}$

9. 5:1
   1:7
   5:7

10. A:B
    B:Z
    A:Z

11. Answers will vary:
    10:2, 20:4

12. Answers will vary:
    6:14, 9:21

13. Mean = 20
    Mode = 14
    Median = 23

14. Mean = 329
    Mode = N/A
    Median = 350

15. 10 out of 17 or $\frac{10}{17}$

SECTION 9   PRE-ALGEBRA AND EARLY ALGEBRA SKILL BUILDERS

172.   Understanding "N" and "X" in Math

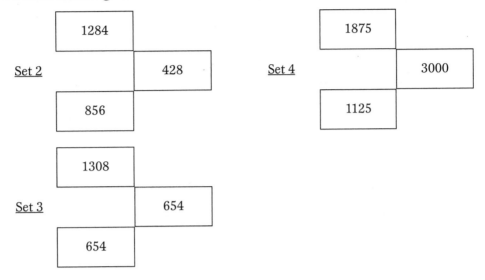

173.   Using the Word "of" in Math

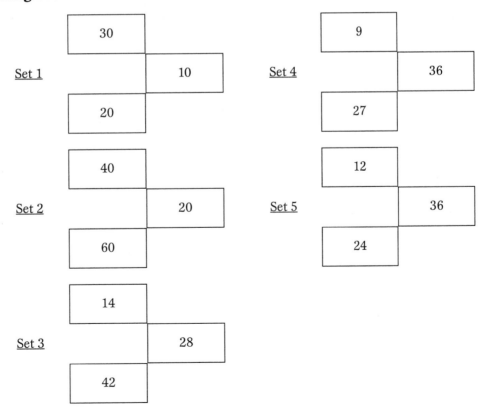

174.   Balance in Algebra

6	(X = 20)	4	(Y = 8)	9	(Y = 35)
8	(Y = 9)	1	(X = 3)	11	(X = 24)
10	(Y = 6)	15	(Y = 29)	7	(X = 17)
12	(X = 2)	5	(X = 11)	2	(X = 10)
13	(X = 12)	3	(X = 5)	14	(X = 44)

175.   The Order of Operations

Set 1

1. 285		6. 398	
2. 17		7. 2	
3. 44		8. 10	
4. 51		9. 31	
5. 83		10. 56	

Set 2

1. 425		6. 1082	
2. 24		7. 18	
3. 66		8. 6	
4. 111		9. 15	
5. 140		10. 350	

176.   A Look at the Language of Algebra

1. $4 + N$	6. $12 - X$	11. $N - 7$	16. $(34)(7X)$
2. $3 - X$	7. $12 + 2(X)$	12. $N - 4$	17. $21 - 6X$
3. $2(X)$	8. $13 - X^2$	13. $(X)(7)$	18. $47 - 2M$
4. $3(X) - 4$	9. $7 - 2N$	14. $(17)(3X)$	19. $20 - 4X + 7^2$
5. $7(X)$	10. $14 - 3X$	15. $17 + 17N$	20. $18 + 2M - 3B$

177.   What Are Exponents?

2. 9	12. 109	22. 4
3. 16	13. 18	23. 47
4. 32	14. 85	24. 35
5. 8	15. 40	25. 18
6. 125	16. 32	26. 4
7. 5	17. 23	27. 5
8. 81	18. 919	28. 46
9. 729	19. 335	29. 32,865
10. 100	20. 119	30. 1

178. Substitution Box Questions in Early Algebra

1. 20	4. 19	7. 21	10. 13	13. 16	16. 0
2. 20	5. 16	8. 7	11. 3	14. 24	17. 80
3. 13	6. 2	9. 2	12. 5	15. 3	18. 130

Message: The life you save may owe you money.

179. Basic Equations: Side Balancing

1. R = 10	5. P = 7	9. F = 1	13. K = 10	17. G = 23
2. A = 11	6. Y = 7	10. N = 37	14. C = 13	18. D = 23
3. U = 22	7. S = 27	11. T = 8	15. E = 64	19. H = 6
4. N = 9	8. L = 6	12. B = 14	16. Y = 3	20. T = 2

Bonus: Reach around and pat yourself on the back because you figured this out.

180. Different Forms of Basic Equations (Number Sentences)

1. Y = 24	7. X = 20	13. T = 3
2. M = 64	8. N = 50	14. X = 8
3. X = 15	9. B = 19	15. M = 1
4. X = 36	10. T = 7	16. M = 14
5. X = 21	11. X = 28	17. X = 44
6. Y = 25	12. X = 6	18. Y = 9

181. Quick Algebra, Right Now

1. 16, 7, 8, 5, 25	3. 13, 14, 9, 11, 24	5. 14, 19, 27, 6, 0
2. 27, 46, 8, 5, 49	4. 11, 6, 22, 9, 15	6. 14, 13, 21, 21

182. Translating from Words to Numbers

1. 39	4. 8	7. 10	10. 4
2. 64	5. 10	8. 55	11. 69
3. 15	6. 12	9. 6	12. 22

183.   Positive and Negative Numbers

A. 3. >   5. <   7. >   9. <   11. >

4. >   6. >   8. <   10. <   12. <

B. 1. 0, +1, +4, +5, +6   6. −91, −37, +91, +94, +97

2. −10, −8, −6, −4, −3, 0   7. −1, 0, +17, +19, +32

3. −5, −3, −2, +4, +6, +7   8. −1000, +14, +9200

4. −7, −5, 0, +3, +8   9. −84, −4, +19, +47, +55

5. −22, −9, −1, +14, +82   10. −17, −14, −11, −4, −2, −1, +19

Bonus Question: −273.16°C or −459.69°F

(according to *Webster's New World College Dictionary*)

184.   Perimeter Expressions

1. 3x   4. 8a   7. m + w + s + b + r   10. 8r + 3

2. 6b   5. 6a + 2b   8. 4p + 8b   11. 9K + 2X

3. 5c   6. 6m + 4y   9. 4M + 2N   12. 4c + 4a

185.   Understanding Integers

Answers will vary.

186.   Locating Integers on a Number Plane (Grid)

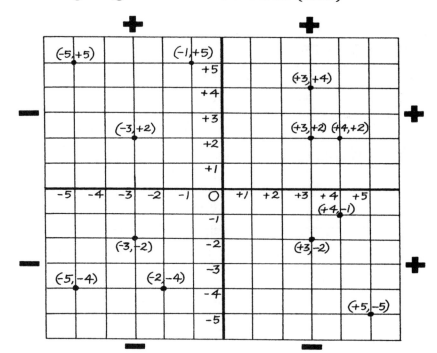

187. Square and Square Root Made Easy

Number or Square Root	Number times itself	Square
1	1×1	1
2	2×2	4
3	3×3	9
4	4×4	16
5	5×5	25
6	6×6	36
7	7×7	49
8	8×8	64
9	9×9	81
10	10×10	100
11	11×11	121
12	12×12	144
13	13×13	169
14	14×14	196
15	15×15	225
16	16×16	256
17	17×17	289
18	18×18	324
19	19×19	361
20	20×20	400

188.   Definition Puzzle on Pre-Algebra and Early Algebra Terms

[13]E	X	P	O	N	E	N	T								
							[2]V						[6]S		
				[1]E	Q	U	A	T	I	[3]O	N		U		[14]B
		[12]V					R			R			B		A
		A					I			D		[15]A	S	[9]B	L
	[4]A	L	G	E	B	R	A	[16]L	E	T	T	E	R	S	A
		U			B		R			O		I		A	N
		E		[7]O		L				N		T		C	C
			[5]D	I	F	F	E	R	E	N	C	E	U	K	E
	[8]S												T	E	
[17]S	I	M	I	L	A	R	I	T	Y	[11]P	O	W	E	R	T
	G													S	
	N		[10]O	P	E	R	A	T	I	O	N				

189.   Skills Mastery Test—Pre-Algebra and Early Algebra: Part One

1. 11	4. 2	7. −16	10. −7 < +8
2. 13	5. +3	8. −2	11. −7 > −8
3. 5	6. +1	9. +7 < +8	12. +7 > −8

13. −7, −3, 0, +2, +8   14. −12, −10, −9, −4, +9, +11

15. 9	18. 30	21. 4 + N	24. 81
16. 5	19. 103	22. 2N + 11	25. 3
17. 4	20. 5	23. 25	

190.   Skills Mastery Test—Pre-Algebra and Early Algebra: Part Two

1. +6	6. 11	11. 12	16. 15	21. 5
2. +11	7. 11	12. 10	17. 25	22. −9
3. +11	8. 2	13. 7	18. 50	23. −2x − 7
4. 12	9. 56	14. 5	19. 3	24. +5y − 9x
5. 36	10. 11	15. 27	20. 1	25. −4y + 2b + 9